D0204738

Hearth and Home

HEARTH AND HOME

Images of Women in the Mass Media

Edited by

GAYE TUCHMAN
ARLENE KAPLAN DANIELS
and
JAMES BENÉT

New York
OXFORD UNIVERSITY PRESS
1978

Printed in the United States of America.

Library of Congress Cataloging in Publication Data
Main entry under title:
Hearth and home.
Includes bibliographical references and index.
1. Women in mass media—United States.
2. Women—United States. I. Tuchman, Gaye, 1943–
II. Daniels, Arlene Kaplan, 1930–
III. Benét, James Walker, 1914–
P96.P6H4 301.41'2'0973 77-17458
ISBN 0-19-502351-X
ISBN 0-19-502352-8 pbk.

Preface

The underlying concern motivating the collection of these readings on the images of women in the media is an interest in the progress we are making toward the full social equality of women in this society. And the media are involved in that progress, just as they are in any other social movement in modern times. That is why thinking about the special part the media play in changing men's and women's lives is of special importance here. While we don't know what actually does change people's minds—why some social movements succeed as others fail—most people believe that media propaganda has an influence. Students of those issues, gathered within the field of collective behavior, have argued about just how strong this media influence is for some time. So far the results of their deliberations are not conclusive.

But the rise of the women's movement offers us another chance to examine the argument as we speculate what the movement's successes and failures have been and will be. This book is an effort to understand more about media impact for many questions of just how the media do construct their messages and why they do it that way (e.g. what is really newsworthy?) are not yet answered.

The questions raised here, and the data collected to answer them, do not pretend to offer a comprehensive array of all the serious issues. But this book is an example and a suggestion to encourage others to study problems and collect information on the interaction between the media and public opinion in the press for equality between the sexes.

The idea for this anthology emerged in 1974 from discussions with Gladys Handy and Kenneth Gayer, then both officers at the National Science Foundation with RANN (Research Applied to National Needs). We talked at length about a West Coast conference on women in the news media. Jim Benét and I developed and submitted for review a plan for a conference which would focus on both the portrayal of women in the media and the place of women in media production. By holding this conference in San Francisco, we hoped to provide regional participation in discussion of an issue usually focused around persons and agencies on the East Coast, the center of news production. We also wished to encourage discussion across interdisciplinary lines by bringing together men and women working in the media, social scientists, and others interested in research and in the formulation of national social policy on these issues. Accordingly, we invited newspaper people, television and radio producers, anchorpersons, directors, and stage managers, as well as feminists interested in the media to join social scientists and foundation and government-agency representatives, in a two-day meeting of East and West. Our format of invited papers and panels included, in addition to the papers you will find in this book, changing the image of women in the mass media, government's role in assuring fair treatment of wmen in the news, the opportunities for women in television and press news, and the influence of specialized women's publications on mass media performance. Unfortunately we could not include this wide array in one volume.

The conference was held in April 1975 under a National Science Foundation grant (ERP74-20802 A10) and the auspices of the Institute for Scientific Analysis. We are particularly indebted to Dr. Dorothy Miller, Director of the Institute, for her support and for the advice she offered throughout the project. We are also grateful to the entire staff of the Institute for managing all the details of the conference. Cassandra B. Curtis and J. Fern Ross earned our special appreciation for their work as rapporteurs and transcribers of the ongoing discussion.

Participants at the conference, in addition to those whose papers are presented here, included social scientists Jessie Bernard, Douglass Cater, Richard Flacks, John Kitsuse, Kurt Lang, Jack Lyle, and Marcia Millman. They also included media representatives Marcia Brandwyne, Valerie Coleman, Carolyn Craven, Beverly Hayon, Carolyn Isber, Mary Ellen Leary, Ruth Miller, Rebecca Mills, Barbara Moran, Pat Palillo, Joan Passalacqua, Irina Posner, Joe Russin, and Peggy Stinnett; community representatives Caroline Charles, James C. Nelson, Jr., and Ellen Newman. Journalism professors Edwin Bayley and Andrew Stern rounded out the array of discussants and panelists.

The interest among participants and those who attended encouraged us to use some of the papers presented and the ideas generated through discussion as the nucleus for this book. When the project reached book stage, the Program on Women at Northwestern University supplied invaluable assistance in completing the manuscript. James Benét and I, codirectors of this NSF project, invited one of our participants, Gaye Tuchman, to become sensior editor. And it was through her efforts that we were able to bring this project to completion.

Maryann Bucek assisted in compiling and checking references. Gerald Barrett typed the manuscript, supplying helpful comments as it developed. Roberta S. Cohen and Lauren Seiler offered needed advice on quantitative practices. Our editor Jim Anderson brought enthusiasm and valued friendship to the project, and Ken Gayer shepherded the book through the necessary approvals at the National Science Foundation. However, any opinions, findings, conclusions, or recommendations herein are those of the authors and do not necessarily reflect the views of the NSF.

Most of all, though, we wish to express our thanks to Gladys Handy, friend and colleague. Former program officer at the National Science Foundation, she offered shrewd advice and warm encouragement from the inception of the project to its eventual transformation into this book.

Evanston, Illinois
October 1977

Arlene Kaplan Daniels

Contents

Hearth and Home

GAYE TUCHMAN

Introduction: The Symbolic Annihilation of Women by the Mass Media

Americans learn basic lessons about social life from the mass media, much as hundreds of years ago illiterate peasants studied the carvings around the apse or the stained glass windows of medieval cathedrals. As Harold Lasswell (1948) pointed out almost thirty years ago, today's mass media have replaced yesterday's cathedrals and parish churches as teachers of the young and of the masses. For our society, like any other society, must pass on its social heritage from one generation to the next. The societal need for continuity and transmission of dominant values may be particularly acute in times of rapid social change, such as our own. Then, individuals may not only need some familiarity with the past, if the society is to survive, but they must also be prepared to meet changing conditions. Nowhere is that need as readily identifiable as in the area of *sex roles*—sex roles are social guidelines for sex-appropriate appearance, interests, skills, behaviors, and self-perceptions.

It is in this area, in the past few decades, where social expectations and social conditions have been changing most rapidly. In 1920, twenty-four percent of the nation's adult women worked for pay outside the home and most of them were unmarried. Fifty years later, in 1976, over half of all American women between the ages of eighteen and sixty-four were in the labor force, most of them married and many of them with children who were of preschool age. One-third of all women with children between the ages of three and five were employed in 1970. Such a transformation not only affects women: it affects their families as members make adjustments in their shared life; and as working men in the factory and office increasingly encounter economically productive women who insist on the abandonment of old prejudices and discriminatory behaviors. In the face of such change, the portrayal of sex roles in the mass media is a topic of great social, political, and economic importance.

This book concerns the depiction of sex roles in the mass media and the effect of that portrayal on American girls and women. In each chapter, social science researchers ask, What are the media telling us about ourselves? How do they say women and men should behave? How women should treat men? How women should view themselves? What do the media view as the best way for a woman to structure her life? What do they tell a little girl to expect or hope for when she becomes a woman?

Based on original research, each of these chapters helps break a new path in communications research. Not surprisingly, little research appeared on these topics until the modern women's movement gained strength in the late 1960s and early 1970s. Until then, psychology, sociology, economics, and history were mainly written by men, about men, and for men. As Jessie Bernard (1973) points out, the interactions of men were viewed as the appropriate subject for social science research, and upwardly mobile male researchers were fascinated with the topics of power and social stratification. No one considered the way women experienced the world. Instead, they were seen as men's silent or unopinionated consorts. (The term "unopinionated" is used, because studies of attitudes by survey researchers frequently neglected to ask women their opinions, concentrating instead upon the attitudes of men. The most well-known exception to this role is a study of influences upon women's consumer habits, funded by a women's magazine in the 1940s [Katz and Lazarsfeld, 1955].)

These generalizations are, unfortunately, equally true of communications researchers. Generations of researchers studied the impact of the media upon political life. In the past, the main topic of concern was male voting behavior. (It was assumed women voted like their husbands; women were swayed by a husband's or father's personal influence [see McCormack, 1975].) More recently, researchers have become fascinated by agenda setting—the way the media structure citizens' priorities and definitions of political issues. Since the women's movement is not a top priority for the news media, little is known about its place in citizens' political agendas. Nobody seemed to care about the effect of the mass media upon the generation and maintenance of sex-role stereotypes. And why should they? Before the advent of the women's movement these stereotypes seemed natural, "given." Few questioned how they developed, how they were reinforced, or how they were maintained. Certainly the media's role in this process was not questioned.

But the importance of stereotyping was not lost on the women's movement; for stereotypes are confining. Sex-role stereotypes are set portrayals of sex-appropriate appearance, interests, skills, behaviors, and self-perceptions. They are more stringent than guidelines in suggesting persons *not* conforming to the specified way of appearing, feeling, and behaving are *inadequate* as males or females. A boy who cries is not masculine and a young woman who forswears makeup is not feminine. Stereotypes present individuals with a more limited range of acceptable appearance, feelings, and behaviors than guidelines do. The former may be said to limit further the human possibilities and potentialities contained within already limited sex roles.

This volume hopes to delineate a national social problem—the mass media's treatment of women. It is a crucial problem, because as Lasswell (1948) points out, the mass media transmit the social heritage from one generation to the next. In a complex society, such as ours, the mass media pass on news from one segment of society, classes, regions, and subcultures to another. Additionally, they enable societal institutions to coordinate activities. Like the Catholic Church in the middle ages—"that great broadcasting center of medieval Europe" (Baumann, 1972, p. 65), the mass media can disseminate the same message to all classes at the same time, with authority and universality of reception, in a decidedly one-directional flow of information. But, if the stereotyped portrayal of sex roles is out-of-date, the media may be preparing youngsters—girls, in particular—for a world that no longer exists.

Suppose for a moment that children's television primarily presents adult women as housewives, nonparticipants in the paid labor force. Also, suppose that girls in the television audience "model" their behavior and expectations on that of "television women." Such a supposition is quite plausible for

> what psychologists call "modeling" occurs simply by watching others, without any direct reinforcement for learning and without any overt practice. The child imitates the model without being induced or compelled to do so. That learning can occur in the absence of direct reinforcement is a radical departure from earlier theories that regarded reward or punishment as indispensable to learning. There now is considerable evidence that children do learn by watching and listening to others even in the absence of reinforcement and overt practice. . . . (Lesser, quoted in Cantor, 1975, p. 5).

And psychologists note that "opportunities for modeling have been vastly increased by television" (Lesser, quoted in Cantor, 1975, p. 5). It is then equally plausible that girls exposed to "television women" may hope to be homemakers when they are adults, but not workers outside the home. Indeed, as adults these girls may resist work outside the home unless necessary for the economic well-being of their families. Encouraging such an attitude in our nation's girls can present a problem in the future: As noted, over forty percent of the labor force was female in 1970, and married women dominate the female labor force. The active participation of women in the labor force is vital to the maintenance of the American economy. In the past decade, the greatest expansion of the economy has been within the sectors that employ women. Mass-media stereotypes of women as housewives may impede the employment of women by limiting their horizons.

The possible impact of the mass media sex-role stereotypes upon national life seems momentous. As the studies collected here demonstrate, this supposition may accurately predict the future. As an illustration of that possibility, the following sections of this introduction examine the media used by an American girl as she completes school, then becomes a worker and, probably, a spouse and mother.[1] Following the format of this book, this introduction starts with an examination of the dominant medium American children and adults watch—television—and then turns to two media especially designed for women—the women's pages of newspapers and women's magazines. But because of the plethora of research about television, we concentrate upon that medium. Finally, we review studies of the impact of the media upon girls and women, again stressing studies of television.

Two related ideas are central to our discussion. These are *the reflection hypothesis* and *symbolic annihilation.* According to the reflection hypothesis, the mass media reflect dominant societal values. In the case of television (see Tuchman, 1974, 1976), the corporate character of the commercial variety causes program planners and station managers to design programs for appeal to the largest audiences. To attract these audiences (whose time and attention are sold to commercial sponsors), the television industry offers programs consonant with American values. The pursuit of this aim is solidified by the fact that so many members of the television industry take those very values for granted: Dominant American ideas and ideals serve as resources for program development, even when the planners are unaware of them, much as we all take for granted the air we breathe. These ideas and ideals are incorporated as *symbolic representations of American society, not as literal portrayals.* Take the typical television family of the 1950s: mother, father, and two children living in an upper middle-class, single-residence suburban home. Such families and homes were not the most commonly found units in the 1950s, but they were the American ideal. Following George Gerbner (1972a, p. 44), we may say that "representation in the fictional world," such as the 1950s ideal family, symbolizes or "signifies social existence"; that is, representation in the mass media announces to audience members that this kind of family (or social characteristic) is valued and approved.

Conversely, we may say that either condemnation, trivialization, or "absence means symbolic annihilation" (Gerbner, p. 44). Consider the symbolic representation of women in the mass media. Relatively few women are portrayed there, although women are fifty-one percent of the population and are well over forty percent of the labor force. Those working women who are portrayed are condemned. Others are trivialized: they are symbolized as child-like adornments who need to be protected or they are dismissed to the protective confines of the home. In sum, they are subject to *symbolic annihilation.*

The mass media deal in symbols and their symbolic representations may not be up-to-date. A time lag may be operating, for nonmaterial conditions, which shape symbols, change more slowly than do material conditions. This notion of a time lag (or a "culture lag," as sociologists term it) may be incorporated into the reflection hypothesis. As values change, we would expect the images of society presented by the media to change. Further, we might expect one medium to change faster than another. (Because of variations in economic organization, each medium has a slightly different relationship to changing material conditions.)

The reflection hypothesis also includes the notion that media planners try to build audiences, and the audiences desired by planners may vary from medium to medium. For instance, television programmers may seek an audience of men and women, without distinguishing between women in the labor force and housewives. But the executives at women's magazines may want to attract women in the labor force in order to garner advertisements designed for those women. (Magazine ads essentially support that medium, since each copy costs much more to produce than it does to purchase.) Accordingly, we might expect the symbolic annihilation of women by television to be more devastating than that of *some* women's magazines.

Without further ado, then, let us turn to images of women in the mass media.

TELEVISION: SYMBOLIC ANNIHILATION OF WOMEN

To say television is the dominant medium in American life is a vast understatement. In the average American household, television sets are turned on more than six hours each winter day. More American homes have television sets than have private bathrooms, according to the 1970 census. Ninety-six percent of all American homes are equipped with television, and most have more than one set. As Sprafkin and Liebert note in Chapter 15, by the time an American child is fifteen years old, she has watched more hours of television than she has spent in the classroom. And since she continues watching as she grows older, the amount of time spent in school can never hope to equal the time invested viewing television.

The use of television by children is encouraged because of parental use. The average adult spends five hours a day with the mass media, almost as much time as she or he spends at work. Of these five hours, four are occupied by the electronic media (radio and television). The other hour is taken up with reading newspapers, magazines, and books. Television consumes forty percent of the leisure time of adult Americans. To be sure, despite increased economic concentration there are still 1,741 daily newspapers in this country. And studies indicate that 63,353,000 papers are sold each day. But the nation's nine hundred-odd television stations reach millions more on a daily basis. In 1976, over seventy-five million people watched one event via television, football's annual Super Bowl spectacular (Hirsch, 1978); and when "All in the Family" first appeared on Saturday night, it had a weekly audience of over 100,000,000, more than half the people in the nation. Each year, Americans spend trillions of hours watching television.

What are the portrayals of women to which Americans are exposed during these long hours? What can the preschool girl and the school girl learn about being and becoming a woman?

From children's shows to commercials to prime-time adventures and situation comedies, television proclaims that women don't count for much. They are underrepresented in television's fictional life—they are "symbolically annihilated." From 1954, the date of the earliest systematic analysis of television's content, through 1975, researchers have found that males dominated the television screen. With the exception of soap operas where men make up a "mere majority" of the fictional population, television has shown and continues to show two men for every woman. Figure 1.1 indicates that proportion has been relatively constant. The little variation that exists, occurs between types of programs. In 1952 sixty-eight percent of the characters in prime-time drama were male. In 1973, seventy-four percent of those characters were male. Women were concentrated in comedies where men make up "only" sixty percent of the fic-

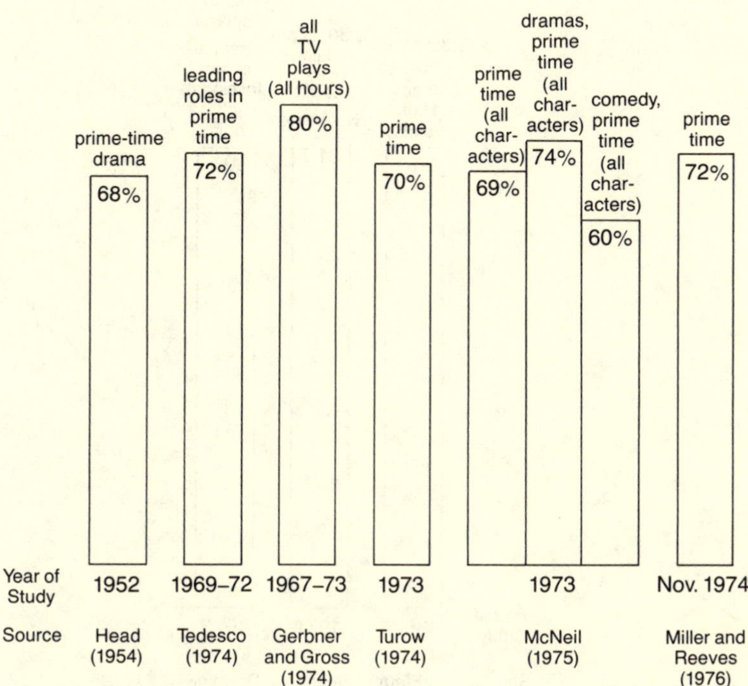

Figure 1.1. Percentage of Males in TV Programs, 1952–1974.

tional world. Children's cartoons include even fewer women or female characters (such as anthropomorphized foxes or pussy-cats) than adult's prime-time programs do. The paucity of women on American television tells viewers that women don't matter much in American society.

That message is reinforced by the treatment of those women who do appear on the television screen. As seen in Figure 1.2, when television shows reveal someone's occupation, the worker is most likely to be male. Someone might object that the pattern

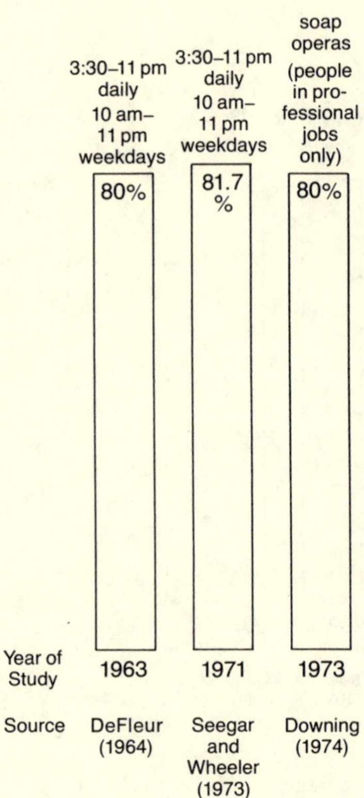

Figure 1.2. Percentage of Males Among Those Portrayed as Employed on TV, 1963–1973.

is inevitable, because men constitute a larger share of the pool of people who can be professionals. But that objection is invalidated by the evidence presented by soap operas, where women are more numerous. But the invariant pattern holds there too, despite the fact that men have been found to be only about fifty percent of the characters on the "soaps" (see Downing, 1974; Katzman, 1972).

Additionally, those few working women included in television plots are symbolically denigrated by being portrayed as incompetent or as inferior to male workers. Pepper, the "Policewoman" on the show of the same name (Angie Dickinson) is continually rescued from dire and deadly situations by her male colleagues. Soap operas provide even more powerful evidence for the portrayal of women as incompetents and inferiors. Although Turow (1974) finds that soap operas present the most favorable image of female workers, there too they are subservient to competent men. On "The Doctors," surgical procedures are performed by male physicians, and although the female M.D.'s are said to be competent at their work, they are primarily shown pulling case histories from file cabinets or filling out forms. On other soap operas, male lawyers try cases and female lawyers research briefs for them. More generally, women do not appear in the same professions as men: men are doctors, women, nurses; men are lawyers, women, secretaries; men work in corporations, women tend boutiques.

The portrayal of incompetence extends from denigration through victimization and trivialization. When television women are involved in violence, unlike males, they are more likely to be victims than aggressors (Gerbner, 1972a). Equally important, the pattern of women's involvement with television violence reveals approval of married women and condemnation of single and working women. As Gerbner (1972a) demonstrates, single women are more likely to be victims of violence than married women, and working women are more likely to be villains than housewives. Conversely, married women who do not work for money outside the home are most likely to escape television's mayhem and to be treated sympathetically. More generally, television most approves those women who are presented in a sexual context or within a romantic or family role (Gerbner, 1972a; cf. Liebert *et al.*, 1973). Two out of three television-women are married, were married, or are engaged to be married. By way of contrast, most television men are single and have always been single. Also, men are seen outside the home and women within it, but even here, one finds trivialization of women's role within the home.

According to sociological analyses of traditional sex roles (such as Parsons, 1949), men are "instrumental" leaders, active workers and decision makers outside the home; women are "affective" or emotional leaders in solving personal problems within the home. But television trivializes women in their traditional role by assigning this task to men too. The nation's soap operas deal with the personal and emotional, yet Turow (1974) finds that on the soap operas, the male sex is so dominant that men also lead the way to the solution of emotional problems. In sum, following the reasoning of the reflection hypothesis, we may tentatively conclude that for commercial reasons (building audiences to sell to advertisers) network television engages in the symbolic annihilation of women.

Two additional tests of this tentative conclusion are possible. One examines noncommercial American television; the other analyzes the portrayal of women in television commercials. If the commercial structure of television is mainly responsible for the symbolic annihilation of women, one would expect to find more women on public than on commercial television. Conversely if the structure of corporate commercial television is mainly responsible for the image of women that is telecast, one would expect to find even more male domination on commercial ads. To an even greater extent than is true of programs, advertising seeks to tap existing values in order to move people to buy a product.

Unfortunately, few systematic studies of public broadcasting are available. The best of these is Caroline Isber's and Muriel Cantor's work (1975), funded by the Corporation for Public Broadcasting, the source of core programming in the Public Broadcasting System. In this volume, in an adaptation of her report for the CPB, Cantor asks, "Where are the women in public television?" Her answer, based on a content analysis of programming is "in front of the television set." Although a higher proportion of adult women appear on children's programming in public television than is true of commercial television, Cantor finds "both commercial and public television disseminate the same message about women, although the two types of television differ in their structure and purpose." Her conclusion indicates that commercialism is not solely responsible for television's symbolic annihilation of women and its portrayal of stereotyped sex roles. Rather, television captures societal ideas even when programming is partially divorced from the profit motive.[2]

Male domination has not been measured as directly for television commercials, the other kind of televised image that may be used to test the reflection hypothesis. Since so many of the advertised products are directed toward women, one could not expect to find women neglected by commercials. Given the sex roles commercials play upon, it would be bad business to show two women discussing the relative merits of power lawn mowers or two men chatting about waxy buildup on a kitchen floor. However, two indirect measures of male dominance are possible: (1) the number of commercials in which only men or only women appear; and (2) the use of males and females in voice-overs. (A "voice-over" is an unseen person speaking about a product while an image is shown on the television screen; an unseen person proclaims "two out of three doctors recommend" or "on sale now at your local. . . .")

On the first indirect measure, all-male or all-female commercials, the findings are unanimous. Schuetz and Sprafkin (in this volume), Silverstein and Silverstein (1974) and Bardwick and Schumann (1967), find a ratio of almost three all-male ads to each all-female ad. The second indirect measure, the use of voice-overs in commercials, presents more compelling evidence for the acceptance of the reflection hypothesis. Echoing the findings of others, Dominick and Rauch (1972) report that of 946 ads with voice-overs, "only six percent used a female voice; a male voice was heard on eighty-seven percent." The remainder use one male and one female voice.

The commercials themselves strongly encourage sex-role stereotypes. Although research findings are not strictly comparable to those on television programs because of the dissimilar "plots," the portrayals of women are even more limited than those presented on television dramas and comedies. Linda Busby (1975) summarized the findings of four major studies of television ads. In one study,

> —37.5% of the ads showed women as men's domestic adjuncts
> —33.9% showed women as dependent on men
> —24.3% showed women as submissive
> —16.7% showed women as sex objects
> —17.1% showed women as unintelligent
> —42.6% showed women as household functionaries.

Busby's summary of Dominick and Rauch's work reveals a similar concentration of women as homemakers rather than as active members of the labor force:

> —Women were seven times more likely to appear in ads for personal hygiene products than not to appear [in those ads]
> —75% of all ads using females were for products found in the kitchen or in the bathroom
> —38% of all females in the television ads were shown inside the home, compared to 14% of the males
> —Men were significantly more likely to be shown outdoors or in business settings than were women
> —Twice as many women were shown with children [than] were men
> —56% of the women in the ads were judged to be [only] housewives
> —43% different occupations were coded for men, 18 for women.

As Busby notes, reviews of the major studies of ads (such as Courtney and Whipple, 1974) emphasize their strong "face validity" (the result of real patterns rather than any bias produced by researchers' methods), although the studies use different coding categories and some of the researchers were avowed feminist activists.

In sum, then, analyses of television commercials support the reflection hypothesis. In voice-overs and one-sex (all male or all female) ads, commercials neglect or rigidly stereotype women. In their portrayal of women, the ads banish females to the role of housewife, mother, homemaker, and sex object, limiting the roles women may play in society.

What can the preschool girl, the school girl, the adolescent female and the woman learn about a woman's role by watching television? The answer is simple. Women are not important in American society, except *perhaps* within the home. And even within the home, men know best, as the dominance of male advice on soap operas and the use of male voice-overs for female products, suggests. To be a woman is to have a limited life divorced from the economic productivity of the labor force.

WOMEN'S MAGAZINES: MARRY, DON'T WORK

As the American girl grows to womanhood, she, like her counterpart elsewhere in industrialized nations, has magazines available designed especially for her use. Some, like *Seventeen,* whose readers tend to be young adolescents, instruct on contemporary fashions and dating styles. Others, like *Cosmopolitan* and *Redbook,* teach about survival as a young woman—whether as a single woman hunting a mate in the city or a young married coping with hearth and home.

This section reviews portrayals of sex roles in women's magazines, seeking to learn how often they too promulgate stereotypes about the role their female readers may take—how much they too engage in the symbolic annihilation of women by limiting and trivializing them. Unfortunately, our analyses of images of women in magazines cannot be as extensive as our discussion of television. Because of researchers' past neglect of women's issues and problems, few published materials are available for review.

Like the television programs just discussed, from the earliest content analyses of magazine fiction (Johns-Heine and Gerth, 1949) to analyses of magazine fiction published in the early 1970s, researchers have found an emphasis on hearth and home and a denigration of the working woman. The ideal woman, according to these magazines, is passive and dependent. Her fate and her happiness rest with a man, not with participation in the labor force. There are two exceptions to this generalization: (1) The female characters in magazines aimed at working-class women are a bit more spirited than their middle-class sisters. (2) In the mid-1970s, middle-class magazines seemed less hostile toward working women. Using the reflection hypothesis, particularly its emphasis upon attracting readers to sell advertisements, we will seek to explain the general rule and these interesting exceptions to it.

Like other media, women's magazines are interested in building their audience or readership. For a magazine, attracting more readers is *indirectly* profitable. Each additional reader does not increase the magazine's profit margin by buying a copy or taking out a subscription, because the cost of publication and distribution per copy far exceeds the price of the individual copy—whether it is purchased on the newsstand, in a supermarket, or through subscription. Instead a magazine realizes its profit by selling advertisements and charging its advertisers a rate adjusted to its known circulation. Appealing to advertisers, the magazine specifies known demographic characteristics of its readership. For instance, a magazine may inform the manufacturer of a product intended for housewives that a vast proportion of its readership are homemakers, while another magazine may appeal to the producer of merchandise for young working women by lauding its readership as members of that target group. Women's magazines differentiate themselves from one another by specifying their intended readers, as well as the size of their mass circulation. Additionally, they all compete with other media to draw advertisers. (For example, *Life* and *Look* folded because their advertisers could reach a larger group of potential buyers at a lower price per person through television commercials.) Both daytime television and women's magazines present potential advertisers with particularly appealing audiences, because women are the primary purchasers of goods intended for the home.

Historically, middle-class women have been less likely to be members of the labor force than lower-class women. At the turn of the century, those married women who worked were invariably from working-class families that required an additional income to assure adequate food, clothing, and shelter (Oppenheimer, 1970). The importance of this economic impetus for working is indicated by the general adherence of working-class families to more traditional definitions of male and female sex roles (Rubin, 1976). Although middle-class families subscribe to a more flexible ideology of sex roles than working-class families, both groups of women tend to insist that the man should be the breadwinner. The fiction in women's magazines reflects this ideology.

Particularly in middle-class magazines, fiction depicts women "as creatures . . . defined by the men in their lives" (Franzwa, 1974a, p. 106; see also Franzwa, 1974b, 1975). Studying a random sample of issues of *Ladies' Home Journal, McCall's,* and *Good Housekeeping* between the years 1940 and 1970, Helen Franzwa found four roles for women: "single and looking for a husband, housewife-mother, spinster, and widowed or divorced—soon to remarry." All the women were defined by the men in their lives, or by their absence. Flora (1971) confirms this finding in her study of middle-class (*Redbook* and *Cosmopolitan*) and working-class (*True Story* and *Modern Romances*) fiction. Female dependence and passivity are lauded; on the rare occasions that male dependence is portrayed, it is seen as undesirable.

As might be expected of characterizations that define women in terms of men, American magazine fiction denigrates the working woman. Franzwa says that work is shown to play "a distinctly secondary part in women's lives. When work is portrayed as important to them, there is a concomitant disintegration of their lives" (1974a, p. 106). Of the 155 major female characters depicted in Franzwa's sample of magazine stories, only 65 or forty-one percent were employed outside the home. Seven of the 65 held high-status positions. Of these seven, only two were married. Three others were "spinsters" whose "failure to marry was of far greater importance to the story-line than their apparent success in their careers" (pp. 106–7). One single woman with a high status career was lauded: She gave up her career to marry.

From 1940 through 1950, Franzwa found, working mothers and working wives were condemned. Instead, the magazines emphasized that husbands should support their spouses. One story summary symbolizes the magazines' viewpoint: "In a 1940 story, a young couple realized that they couldn't live on his salary. She offered to work; he replied, 'I don't think that's so good. I know some fellows whose wives work and they might just as well not be married' " (p. 108). Magazines after 1950 are even less positive about work. In 1955, 1960, 1965, and 1970 not one married woman who worked appeared in the stories Franzwa sampled. (Franzwa selected stories from magazines using five-year intervals to enhance the possibility of finding changes.)

Since middle-class American wives are less likely to be employed than their working-class counterparts, this finding makes sociological sense. Editors and writers may believe that readers of middle-class magazines, who are less likely to be employed, are also more likely to buy magazines approving this life-style. More likely to work and to be in families either economically insecure or facing downward mobility, working-class women might be expected to applaud effective women. For them, female dependence might be an undesirable trait. Their magazines could be expected to cater to such preferences, especially since those preferences flow from the readers' life situations. Such, indeed, are Flora's findings, presented in Table 1.1.

However, this pattern does not mean that the literature for the working-class woman avoids defining women in terms of men. All the women in middle-class magazines dropped from the labor force when they had a man present; only six percent of the women in the working-class fiction continued to work when they had a man and children. And Flora explained that for both groups "The plot of the majority of stories centered upon the female achieving the proper dependent status, either by marrying or manipulating existing dependency relationships to reaffirm the heroine's subordinate position. The male support—monetary, social, and psychological—which the heroine gains was generally seen as well worth any independence or selfhood given up in the process" (1971, p. 441).

Such differences as do exist between working-class and mid-

TABLE 1.1. Female Dependence and Ineffectuality by Class, by Percentage of Stories*

	FEMALE DEPENDENCE			FEMALE INEFFECTUALITY		
	Undesirable	*Desirable*	*Neutral*	*Undesirable*	*Desirable*	*Neutral*
Working Class	22	30	48	38	4	58
Middle Class	18	51	31	18	33	49
Total	20	41	40	28	19	53

* Adapted from Flora (1971).

dle-class magazines remain interesting, though. For they indicate how much more the women's magazines may be responsive to their audience than television can be. Because it is the dominant mass medium, television is designed to appeal to hundreds of millions of people. In 1970, the circulation of *True Story* was "only" 5,347,000, and of *Redbook,* a "mere" 8,173,000. Drawing a smaller audience and by definition, one more specialized, the women's magazines can be more responsive to changes in the position of women in American society. If a magazine believes its audience is changing, it may alter the content to maintain its readership. The contradictions inherent in being women's magazines may free them to respond to change.

A woman's magazine is sex-typed in a way that is not true of men's magazines (Davis, 1976). *Esquire* and *Playboy* are for men, but the content of these magazines, is, broadly speaking, American culture. Both men's magazines feature stories by major American writers, directed toward all sophisticated Americans, not merely to men. Both feature articles on the state of male culture as American culture or of male politics as American politics. Women's magazines are designed in opposition to these "male magazines." For instance, "sports" are women's sports or news of women breaking into "men's sports." A clear distinction is drawn between what is "male" and what is "female."

Paradoxically, though, this very limitation can be turned to an advantage. Addressing women, women's magazines may suppose that some in their audience are concerned about changes in the status of women and the greater participation of women in the labor force. As early as 1966, before the growth of the modern women's movement, women who were graduated from high school or college assumed they would work until the birth of their first child. Clarke and Esposito (1966) found that magazines published in the 1950s and addressed to these women (*Glamour, Mademoiselle,* and *Cosmopolitan*) stressed the joys of achievement and power when describing working roles for women and identifying desirable jobs. Magazines addressed to working women were optimistic about these women's ability to combine work and home, a message that women who felt that they should or must work would be receptive to. Indeed, in 1958 Marya and David Hatch criticized *Mademoiselle, Glamour,* and *Charm* as "unduly optimistic" in their "evaluation of physical and emotional strains upon working women." Combining work and family responsibilities may be very difficult, particularly in working-class homes, since working class husbands refuse to help with housework (Rubin, 1976). But even working-class women prefer work outside the home to housework (Rubin, 1976, Vanek, forthcoming) since it broadens their horizons. Wanting to please and to attract a special audience of working women, magazine editors and writers may be freed to be somewhat responsive to new conditions, even as these same writers and editors feature stereotyped sex roles in other sections of their magazines.

Additional evidence of the albeit limited responsiveness of women's magazines to the changing status of women in the labor force is provided by their treatment of sex-role stereotypes since the advent of the women's movement. The modern women's movement is usually said to begin in the mid-1960s with the founding of the National Organization for Women. The date is of consequence for the study of sex roles in women's magazines because of Betty Friedan's involvement in the National Organization for Women. Her book, *The Feminine Mystique,* published in 1963, provided much of the ideology for the young movement. And, its analysis of sexism ("the problem with no name") was based in part on an analysis of the portrayal of sex roles in women's magazines. In an undated manuscript cited in Busby (1975), Stolz and her colleagues compared the image of women in magazines before and after the advent of the women's movement. Like others, they found no changes between 1940 and 1972. However, a time lag ("culture lag") is probably operating since nonmaterial conditions (ideas and attitudes) change more slowly than do material conditions (such as participation in the labor force).

Several very recent studies affirm that women's magazines may be introducing new conceptions of women's sex roles that are more conducive to supporting the increased participation of women in the labor force. Butler and Paisley* note that at the instigation of an editor of *Redbook,* twenty-eight women's magazines published articles on the arguments for and against the Equal Rights Amendment, a constitutional change prompted by the women's movement and the increased participation of women in the labor force. Franzwa's impression of the women's magazines she had analyzed earlier is that they revealed more sympathy with working women in 1975.* Sheila Silver (1976) indicates that a "gentle support" for the aims of the women's movement and a "quiet concern" for working women may now be found in *McCall's.* By the terms "gentle support" and "quiet concern," she means to indicate that the magazine approves equal pay for equal work and other movement aims, although it does not approve of the women's movement itself. That magazine and others, such as the *Ladies' Home Journal,* continue to concentrate upon helping women as housewives: They still provide advice on hearth and home. The women's magazines continue to assume that every woman will marry, bear children and "make a home." They do not assume that every woman will work some time in her life.

In sum, the image of women in the women's magazines is more responsive to change than is television's symbolic annihilation and rigid typecasting of women. The sex roles presented are less stereotyped, but a woman's role is still limited. A female child is always an eventual mother, not a future productive participant in the labor force.

* Matilda Butler and William Paisley. Personal communication, Fall 1976.

* 1976, personal communication.

NEWSPAPERS AND WOMEN: FOOD, FASHION, AND SOCIETY

Following the argument developed thus far, one might expect the nation's newspapers to be even more responsive than magazines to the changing status of women in American society. With smaller circulations than the magazines and supposedly more responsive to a local population rather than a national one, newspapers might cater to their female readers in order to maintain or even increase the base of their circulation. Such an expectation seems particularly plausible because contemporary newspapers face increased costs and are suffering from the economic competition of the electronic media. But this expectation flies in the face of the actual organization of newswork, for newspapers are *not, strictly speaking, local media.* Rather, local newspapers' dependence upon national news services is sufficiently great for them to be considered *components of a national medium,* designed to appeal to as many Americans as possible. As we have just seen, such a design encourages a rigid treatment of sex roles. An historical review of newspapers' treatment of news about women makes this result clearer.

Unlike the women's magazines, newspapers seek to appeal to an entire family. Historically, they have sought to attract female readers by treating them as a specialized audience, given attention in a segregated women's page, an autonomous or semi-autonomous department whose mandate precludes coverage of the "hard news" of the day. Although women's magazines have been published in the United States since the early nineteenth century, it took the newspaper circulation wars of the 1880s to produce the notion of "women's news." At that time, it appeared that every man who would buy a newspaper was already doing so. To build circulation by robbing each other of readers and attracting new readers, newspapers hired female reporters to write about society and fashion, as well as to expand "news" to include sports and comic strips. Items of potential interest to women were placed near advertisements of goods that women might purchase for their families. The origin of women's news reveals how long newspapers have traditionally defined women's interests as different from men's and how items of concern to women have become non-news, almost oddities. That view continues today. The budget for women's pages rarely provides for updating those pages from edition to edition, as is done for the general news, sports, and financial pages, sections held to be of interest to men. Finally, as is true of other departments as well, women's page budgets are sufficiently restricted to force that department's dependence upon the wire services.

During the nineteenth century's circulation wars, newspapers banded into cooperative services intended to decrease the costs of total coverage for each participating newspaper. A reporter would cover a story for newspapers in different cities, decreasing the need for scattered newspapers to maintain extensive bureaus in a variety of cities, such as Washington and New York. Furthermore, a newspaper in a small out-of-the-way town could be requested to share its story about an important event with newspapers from distant places that would not, under normal circumstances, have a reporter on hand. Aside from playing a limited role in the development of journalistic objectivity (Schudson, 1976), since stories were designed to meet the political-editorial requirements of diverse news organizations, the news services encouraged the expansion of definitions of news. Some provided features, such as comics and crossword puzzles. Others provided sports items, financial stories, and features of concern to women, as well as "hard news." Sometimes the women's items were scandalous revelations of the activities of "Society." More often, they were advice for the homemaker, such as recipes and articles about rearing children. In this century, syndicated and wire-service features include gossip columns about the celebrated and the notorious and advice to the lovelorn, such as that fictionalized in Nathanael West's *Miss Lonelyhearts* or that represented by "Dear Abby."

For women's pages, items like these represent more than an economic investment purchased by a newspaper on behalf of its women's department. They are also an investment of space in the paper. Expected by readers to appear on a Monday, the column inches set aside for advice or gossip cannot be withdrawn for news of the women's movement. Similarly, it may be difficult to turn aside essentially prepaid feature stories about clothing and fashions supplied by the Associated Press or some other news syndicate in order to hire additional women's page staff interested in covering the changing status of women in American society. Commitments like these "nationalize" the local media, because the news syndicate or wire service reaches virtually every daily newspaper in the United States. Because the wire services *as businesses* are necessarily committed to pleasing all (or as many as possible) of their subscribing newspapers, they must shrink from advocating vast social changes. As in the case of television, what goes in New York may not go in Peoria, Illinois or Norman, Oklahoma. National in scope, syndicated and wire-service items for the women's page must seek an American common denominator. For the sex stereotyping of the women's pages to cease, the leadership of the Associated Press and the syndicates would have to be convinced that most of their subscribing papers wanted a different kind of story for their women's pages. Only then, it seems safe to say, would the papers serviced by the syndicates run the kinds of news about changes in the status of women that may be found in the *New York Times* and the *Los Angeles Times,* whose women's pages develop their own stories through independent staffs (see Chapter 11).

For now, a characterization of women's pages provided by Lindsay Van Gelder (1974) seems apt. She speculates thus: Suppose a Martian came to earth and sought to learn about

American culture by reading the women's pages. Bombarded by pictures of wedding dresses, the Martian might suppose that American women marry at least once a week. After all, a Martian might reason that newspapers and their women's pages reflect daily life. That view, we might add, would seem justified by the women's pages' intense involvement with the social life of the upper class (Chapter 9), because upper-class power is a daily aspect of American life. Women's pages feed upon the parties, marriages, engagements, and clothing and food preferences of the wealthy and the celebrated. In this, like newspapers in general (Lazarsfeld and Merton, 1948), the women's pages encourage all citizens to emulate the upper class and to chase after positions of high status and institutionalized importance.

Newspapers' very emphasis upon established institutions and those with institutionalized power may account in part for their denigration of women and the women's movement (Morris, 1974). Most information in the general sections of newspapers concerns people in power, and newspapers justify this emphasis by stressing that such people work in or head societal institutions that regulate social intercourse. But communications researchers view the matter somewhat differently. They argue that newspapers exercise social control: By telling stories about such people, newspapers lend status to approved institutions and chastise lawbreakers. Historically, those few women mentioned in the general news pages belonged to the powerful groups in society. Gladys Engel Lang (Chapter 8) suggests "the most admired woman" list probably reflects the publicity given to specific women. They are mainly wives of the powerful, celebrities and stars, and the few women who are heads of state. But women are mainly seen as the consorts of famous men, not as subjects of political and social concern in their own right.

This situation appears to be changing. Once ignored or ridiculed (Morris, 1974), the women's movement has received increasing coverage as it has passed through the stages characteristic of any social movement. As the women's movement became sufficiently routinized to open offices with normal business hours, some newspapers established a "women's movement beat" that required a reporter to provide at least periodic coverage of new developments (Chapter 11). When increased legitimation brought more volunteers and more funds to wage successful law suits against major corporations and to lobby for the introduction of new laws, newspapers concerned with major institutions were forced to cover those topics (Chapter 12). In turn, these successes increased the movement's legitimation. Legitimation also brought support of sympathizers within other organizations who were not movement members (Carden, 1973). Reporters having those other organizations as their beats are being forced to write about the ideas of the women's movement and women's changing status. For instance, the position of women and minorities in the labor force is becoming a required topic for labor reporters and those who write about changing personnel in the corporate world.

On the whole, though, despite coverage of women forcibly induced by the legitimation of the women's movement, newspapers continue to view women in the news as occasional oddities that must be tolerated. Attention to women is segregated and found on the women's page. As a recent survey of women's pages demonstrates (Guenin, 1975), most women's pages continue to cater to a traditional view of women's interests. They emphasize home and family, only occasionally introducing items about women at work. And those items are more likely to concern methods of coping with home and office tasks than they are with highlighting problems of sex discrimination and what the modern women's movement has done in combatting it. Like the television industry, appealing to a common denominator encourages newspapers to engage in the symbolic annihilation of women by ignoring women at work and trivializing women through banishment to hearth and home.

THE IMPACT OF THE MEDIA

As of this writing, women continue to enter the labor force at a faster rate than in the past—a rate that has far exceeded the predictions of demographers and specialists on the labor force. What are we to make of this discrepancy between the sex-role stereotypes reflected in the media and the employment pattern of women? Does the discrepancy mean that because of culture lag, the mass media reflect attitudes discarded by the population and that the mass media have no effect on the behavior of women? That conclusion seems quite seductive, given the patterns we have described. By entering the labor force at increasing rates, women seem to be ignoring the media's message. But that conclusion flies in the face of *every* existing theory about the mass media. Communications theorists agree that the mass media are the cement of American social life. They are a source of common interest and of conversation. Children and adults may schedule their activities around favorite television programs. And the mass media serve to coordinate the activities of diverse societal institutions. To paraphrase Gerbner and Gross (1976), the mass media in general and television in particular have replaced religion as a source of social control in American life. Like the medieval church that broadcast one message to all social classes, all the mass media disseminate the same theme about women to all social classes: They announce their symbolic annihilation and trivialization.

Equally important, all available evidence about the impact of the media upon sex-role stereotyping indicates that the media encourage their audiences to engage in such stereotyping. They lead girls, in particular, to believe that their social horizons and alternatives are more limited than is actually the case. The evidence about the impact of television is particularly compelling.

Aimee Dorr Leifer points out (1975) that television provides many of the same socialization processes as the family. Like the family, television provides examples of good and bad behavior. The family socializes children through the patterning and power of those examples, and television programming also provides variation in the frequency, consistency, and power of examples. Leifer notes some indications that variations in these factors may have an impact on the child viewer (1975, p. 5). Finally, like the family, television can provide reinforcers (rewards and punishments) for behaviors. However, although the family can tailor reinforcers to the individual child, television cannot.

Most of the documentation regarding the impact of television upon children considers the effect of televised violence, primarily because of the national push for such research after the political assassinations and riots of the 1960s. That research is particularly interesting, for our purposes, because of the unanimity of the findings and because of the diverse methods used to analyze the topic.

Social science researchers frequently squabble about which methods of research are appropriate to explore a problem. All seem ready to admit that the ideal way to explore television's impact would be to perform a controlled experiment in a natural setting. Ideally, one would isolate a group that did not watch television, matching characteristics of individuals in that group with the characteristics of others whose viewing was designed by the researchers. The groups would be studied over a period of some years to see whether the effects of television are cumulative. Unfortunately, such a research design is impossible. Virtually all American homes have at least one television set; and so, one cannot locate children for the "control group"—those not exposed to television. To get around this problem, the violence researchers used both laboratory and field experiments. In the former, children were exposed to carefully selected (and sometimes specially prepared) videotapes, lasting anywhere from ten minutes to an hour. Behavior was analyzed before viewing the tape, while viewing it, and after viewing it. By carefully controlling which children would see what tape (designing "control groups"), the experimenters could comment upon the effect of televised violence on the children. Unfortunately, laboratory studies are artificial. For one thing, both sets of children are already dosed with violence in normal viewing, and both watch television under conditions different from their homes or classrooms. Thus, researchers cannot state in any definitive way how the research findings are related to activities in the real world.

The second approach, field experiments, also has difficulties. Such studies are invariably "correlational." The studies demonstrate that two kinds of behavior are found together, but cannot state whether one behavior causes the other or whether both are caused by a third characteristic of the children studied. For instance, in the violence studies, teams of researchers asked youths and children about their viewing habits (and in one case tried to control those habits) and also measured (in a variety of ways) their antisocial behavior. Although viewing aggression and antisocial behavior were invariably found together, it remains possible that some third factor accounts for the variation.

The fact that different research teams interviewed children of different sexes, ages, social classes, and races from different parts of the country makes it fairly certain that a third factor was not responsible for the association of television viewing and antisocial behavior. And this conclusion is strengthened by the evidence provided by the laboratory studies. Furthermore, since the Surgeon General issued his report in 1973, additional field studies have found "that viewing televised or filmed violence in naturalistic settings increases the incidence of naturally-occurring aggression, that long-term exposure to television may increase one's aggressiveness, and that exposure to televised violence may increase one's tolerance for everyday aggression" (Leifer, 1975).

Although there are not as many studies, researchers have also established that television programming influences racial attitudes. Again, both laboratory and field studies were used. They demonstrate that white children may take their image of blacks from television (Greenberg, 1972), that the longer a white child watches "Sesame Street," the less likely that child will have negative attitudes toward blacks, and that positive portrayals of blacks produce more positive attitudes toward blacks, with negative portrayals producing little attitude changes (Graves, 1975). Aimee Leifer writes of these findings: "Apparently black children increase their [positive] image of their own group by seeing them portrayed on television, while white children are influenced by the portrayal, especially when it is uncomplementary to blacks" (1975, p. 26). The evidence on the impact of the depiction of race is important in assessing television's impact on sex roles because content analyses provide strong documentation that television treats blacks and whites differently. For instance, in this volume Schuetz and Sprafkin's analysis of children's commercials and Lemon's analysis of patterns of domination document differential treatment by race as well as by sex.

Since the documentation on violence is extensive and the documentation on race is strong, it seems more than reasonable to expect that the content of television programs leads children to hold stereotyped images of sex roles. The power of the evidence on race and violence is important, because researchers have just started to ask about the impact of television on societal sex roles. What, then, do we know now?

Suppose, we asked earlier, that television primarily presents adult women as housewives. Also suppose that girls in the television audience "model" their behavior and expectations on that of television women. Such a supposition is quite plausible for psychologists note that "opportunities for modeling have been vastly increased by television" (Lesser, quoted in Cantor, 1975, p. 5). It is then equally plausible that girls exposed to television women may hope to be homemakers when they are adults, but not workers outside the home.

Do girls actually model their attitudes and behavior on the symbolically annihilated and dominated television woman?

This general question may be broken down into several component questions:

1. Do girls pay closer attention to female television characters than to male characters?
2. Do girls value the attributes of female characters or those of male characters?
3. Does television viewing have an impact on the attitudes of young children toward sex roles?
4. Do these attitudes continue as children mature?

As in the studies on violence and race, the available evidence includes laboratory and field studies.

1. *Do girls pay closer attention to female characters than to male characters?* In this volume, Joyce Sprafkin and Robert Liebert report the results of three laboratory experiments designed to see whether (a) boys and girls each prefer television programs featuring actors of their own sex; (b) whether the children pay closer attention when someone of the same sex is on the television screen; and (c) whether the children prefer to watch members of their own sex engaging in sex-typed (playing with a doll or a football) or nonsex-typed (as in reading with one's parents) behavior. To gather information, they enabled the tested children to switch a dial, choosing between an episode of "Nanny and the Professor" and one of the "Brady Bunch." (Children like to watch situation comedies [Lyle and Hoffman, 1972].) For each program, episodes featuring male or female characters were selected with different episodes showing a boy or a girl engaging in sex-typed or nonsex-typed behavior. The findings are clear: In their viewing habits, children prefer sex-

typing. They prefer programs featuring actors of their own sex; they watch members of their own sex more closely; and they also pay more attention when a member of their own sex engages in sex-typed behavior. According to Sprafkin and Liebert (1976), such behavior probably involves learning, for according to psychological theories children prefer to expose themselves to same-sex models as an information-seeking strategy; children are presumed to attend to same-sex peers because they already know that much social reinforcement is sex-typed and must discover the contingencies that apply to their own gender (see also Grusec and Brinker, 1972).

2. *Do girls value the attributes of female characters or of male characters?* The evidence on evaluation is not as clear. A variety of communications researchers, particularly a group working at Michigan State University, have performed a series of laboratory experiments to determine which specific characters boys and girls prefer, and why they do so. They found that invariably boys identify with male characters. Sometimes though (about thirty percent of the time) girls also identify with or prefer male characters (Miller and Reeves, 1976). When girls choose a television character as a model, they are guided by the character's physical attractiveness; boys are guided by strength (Greenberg, Held, Wakshlag, and Reeves, 1976; Miller and Reeves, 1976). Indeed, even when girls select a male character they appear to be guided by his physical attractiveness (Greenberg *et al.,* 1976). Girls who select male characters do *not* state they are basing their choices on the wider opportunities and fun available to men, although the girls who select female characters state that the characters do the same kind of things as they themselves do (Reeves, 1976).

3. *Does television viewing have an impact on the attitudes of young children toward sex roles?* Here the evidence is clearer. Frueh and McGhee (1975) interviewed children in kinder-

garten through sixth grade, asking them about the amount of time they spent watching television and testing the extent and direction of their sex-typing. The children who viewed the most television (twenty-five hours or more each week) were significantly more traditional in their sex-typing than those who viewed the least (ten hours or less per week). Because this study is correlational, one cannot know whether viewing determines sex-typing or *vice versa.* But television does seem to be the culprit, according to laboratory studies on television viewing and occupational preferences.

Miller and Reeves (1976; see also Pingree, 1976) asked children to watch television characters in nontraditional roles and then asked them what kind of jobs boys and girls could do when they grew up. Children exposed to programs about female police officers, for instance, were significantly more likely to state that a woman could be a police officer than were children who watched more traditional fare.

Beuf (1974) reports similar results from sixty-three interviews with boys and girls between the ages of three and six. Some girls had even abandoned their ambitions:

> One of the most interesting aspects of the children's responses lay in their reactions to the question: "What would you want to be when you grew up, if you were a girl (boy?)" Several girls mentioned that this other-sex ambition was their true ambition, but one that could not be realized because of their sex. Doctor and milkman were both cited in this regard. . . . One blond moppet confided that what she really wanted to do when she grew up was fly like a bird. "But, I'll never do it," she sighed, "because I'm not a boy." Further questioning revealed that a TV cartoon character was the cause of this misconception (p. 143).

A boy said, "Oh, if I were a girl, I'd have to grow up to be nothing." Beuf reports, "Children who were moderate viewers appeared to exert a wider range of choice in career selection than heavy viewers. Seventy-six percent of the heavy viewers (compared with fifty percent of the moderate viewers) selected stereotyped careers for themselves (p. 147)."

4. *Do these attitudes continue as children mature?* It is known that sex-typing increases as children mature. Second graders are more insistent in their sex-typing than first graders are. Adolescent boys and girls insist upon discriminating between behavior by sex. But little is known about the impact of television on this process. A longitudinal study presently underway at the University of Pennsylvania's Annenberg School of Communication is the first attempt to answer this question systematically. Chapter 14, which contains a summary of that research, indicates that definitive answers are not yet available. However, analyses based on data from the second year of the study do tentatively indicate an association between television viewing and sexist attitudes. The association is weak, but it does suggest that the more a youngster watches television, the more likely the child will be to hold sexist attitudes.

What can we make of all this? The answer is: The mass media perform two tasks at once. First, with some culture lag, they reflect dominant values and attitudes in the society. Second, they act as agents of socialization, teaching youngsters in particular how to behave. Watching lots of television leads children and adolescents to believe in traditional sex roles: Boys should work; girls should not. The same sex-role stereotypes are found in the media designed especially for women. They teach that women should direct their hearts toward hearth and home.

At a time when over forty percent of the American labor force is female and when women with preschool children are entering the labor force in increasing numbers, the mass media's message has severe national consequences. As demographers (for example, Oppenheimer, 1970) and economists (for example, Bowen and Finegan, 1969) have shown, the maintenance and expansion of the American economy depends upon increasing the rate of female employment. Discouraging women from working presents a national dilemma. Furthermore, it is quite probable that the media's message discourages women from working up to their full capacity in the labor force. And by limiting the *kinds* of jobs held by fictional women, it may encourage the underemployment of women, a severe problem for those working-class families who can barely scrape by with two incomes (Rubin, 1976). And rigid sex-role stereotypes make the burden heavier for all working women who must still shoulder the responsibilities of home and family with limited assistance from their husbands. This problem is particularly acute in blue-collar families (Rubin, 1976). For the nation and for individuals, the message "women belong in the home" is an anachronism we can ill afford.

Throughout this book, in original essays reporting new research, social scientists delve further into the media's symbolic annihilation and trivialization of women. In introductions to each section of this volume, we relate the individual chapters to the themes we have considered here. Finally, in our last chapter we explore the policy implications of all these materials. How can the media be changed? we ask. How can we free women from the tyranny of media messages limiting their lives to hearth and home?

NOTES

[1] Government data indicate that at age twenty, American women are more likely to be members of the labor force than to be married. U.S. Dept. of Labor, 1976.

[2] Sponsors do play a role in public broadcasting. As underwriters of programs, they may refuse to fund controversial materials. Some critics claim the Corporation for Public Broadcasting has avoided controversial topics to maintain corporate grants, and has designed dramatic series to appeal to corporations and foundations. According to informants at WNET, corporate underwriters object when the station delays airing their programs to squeeze in public appeals for contributions to the station.

1

Television

INTRODUCTION

A quick glimpse at contemporary television seems to indicate that times have changed. In the 1950s, Eve Arden as "Our Miss Brooks" and Lucille Ball as Mrs. Ricky Ricardo cavorted across the nation's television screens. Both were dizzy dames. Both alternatively tricked and kowtowed to the men in their respective series—Teacher Brooks to School Principal Conklin, Lucy to her husband.

Eve Arden has been replaced by the competent, although underpaid, Mary Richards of "The Mary Tyler Moore Show" (now in syndication) who is portrayed as an ally of her boss. Mary's friend Rhoda, played by Valerie Harper, has dated, married, separated, and continued to maintain minimal enthusiasm for her work (although she is rarely shown working). Lucy Ricardo gave way to the much-married Ms. Maude Finley, played by Bea Arthur. Where Lucy cried, Maude grows icy and bellows. Where Lucy and friend Ethel (played by Vivian Vance) united to trick their husbands, the united Maude and Vivian (Rue McClanahan) find time for both tricks and squabbles about feminism. (Maude is for feminism; Vivian against.) Additionally, as a glance at *TV Guide* indicates, women now play police officers, private eyes, and candidates for political office.

To be sure, minor details seem to limit television's perfect portrayal of the modern woman: Mary Richards calls her boss "Mr. Grant"; her male colleagues call him "Lou." Edith Bunker does not object when husband Archie tells her to "stifle" herself. Angie Dickinson, the "Policewoman," always needs male help to make an arrest, but Telly Savalas's "Kojak" almost never needs to be rescued from physical danger. Yet, compared with the past, that quick look seems to validate the patronizing words of a cigarette commercial designed to appeal to women: "You've come a long way, baby."

This section of *Hearth and Home* takes a searching look at the portrayal of women on television today. Contrary to our impressionistic glimpse, it finds that the image of women has not improved. Rather, statistical analyses of *patterns* of television content reveal that television continues to engage in the symbolic annihilation of women.

In Chapter 1, George Gerbner suggests that television's treatment of women is more repressive than ever. The same proportion of women appear on television today, as in 1952; today, like then, their depictions are stereotyped. Only thirty-two percent of the people on prime-time television were women in 1952; about thirty percent are women in the 1970s. In the 1950s, only twenty percent of those portrayed as employed were women; that statistic remains the same in the 1970s. Yet, as Gerbner points out in his essay, the condition of women in the United States has changed since the days of "I Love Lucy" and "Our Miss Brooks." Not only are there more women in the labor force (about one-third of all women in 1950; roughly forty-five percent in 1975), but one consequence of the women's movement has been irreversible changes in attitudes toward women as employed workers and as family members. For Gerbner, the disparity between past and present social roles and the similarity between past and present television roles indicates that the reflection hypothesis (suggesting that any medium's content will change as social conditions change, with some time lag accounted for by the economic structure of the medium) is too optimistic. Looking only at television, Gerbner proposes that the constancy of media depictions undermines existing social and economic advances of women and reinforces cultural repression.

Consider only two of the points Gerbner makes. First, examining the symbolic world of violence, Gerbner finds women are in a subordinate position. Whether they have been knocked to the floor by a villain or are helped from the floor by a male colleague, vis-à-vis men, women are still on the floor. Second, when, figuratively speaking, women manage to stand on their own two feet, they are either undercut or isolated in a special world irrelevant to male enterprises. And sometimes, even in that special world, they are undercut by men.

By analyzing dominance patterns in thirty-second interactions, Judith Lemon alerts us to some ways undercutting is achieved by programs either incorporating or eschewing violence. First, consider crime dramas (action/adventure shows) such as "Policewoman" and "Barnaby Jones." In 1975, men dominated women in forty-seven percent of the interactions falling into Lemon's sample; women dominated men in six percent of the interactions; in the remaining forty-seven percent, men and women were portrayed as more or less equal. Male dominance is not as pronounced in situation comedies, the type of program most likely to have women as leading characters. There, men dominate women twenty-three percent of the time; and women dominate men thirteen percent of the time.

Second, in situation comedies, women are mainly shown in the context of the family, while men are mainly shown in work settings. Within the family, men and women are equally dominant. But this may be an artifact of her sample, which includes both shows about black and white families. In all white-family interactions, men are more dominant than women; in all black family interactions, women are more dominant. Ironically, on television's situation comedies, white women are portrayed more favorably outside the family context (for example, Mary Richards or Hot Lips of "M.A.S.H.") than in it (for example, Maude).

Schuetz and Sprafkin's analysis of ads on shows designed for children (in Chapter 3) also reveals different presentations of men and women. Not only are there many more men than women (about two men for every woman), but men are also much more likely to promote products. Indeed, as predicted by the reflection hypothesis discussed in *Hearth and Home*'s Introduction, Schuetz and Sprafkin find that commercials touting products are more stereotyped than commercials propounding ideas. For instance, female characters appear in ads to promote the sale of dolls and miniature household appliances, not toy trucks, toy fire engines, or footballs. And, they note, women are more likely to be seen in ads carried free by networks and television stations—public-service announcements advising rubella shots, using the public library, or promoting interracial harmony.

In Chapter 4, Muriel Cantor details the ways women are stereotyped in public broadcasting. On the public-affairs programs distributed by the Public Broadcasting System, stereotyping means that women discuss topics defined as women's interests, such as education and career planning, art, music and culture, and personalities and biographies. To be sure, women also discuss business, economics, law, and government, but not in the same proportion as men. (Fifty-six percent of the men are concentrated in discussions of those topics; twenty-eight percent of the women.)

Furthermore, as Gerbner predicts in Chapter 1, television isolates women. In 1975, when Cantor did her study, only one public television program, "Woman," considered issues raised by the women's movement. According to the broadcasters whom Cantor interviewed, women's issues are not the most pressing of the day and so do not compare in importance with questions about economic or political affairs. Rather, these spokespersons feel, women's issues are only the concern of a limited number of women identifying themselves as advocates of a special-interest group. That women are forty-seven percent of the labor force—indicating that their problems are linked to economic issues—is ruled irrelevant by the broadcasters.

Taken together, the four chapters in this section indicate that commercial programming, advertisements, and public broadcasting present limited and stereotyped depictions of women and women's concerns. The authors' systematic consideration of television's content belies impressions based upon a quick glimpse at contemporary fare. There have been some changes in the portrayal of women: Maude may have replaced Lucy Ricardo, but her husband Walter, like Lucy's Ricky, still rules the roost.

Chapter 1

GEORGE GERBNER

The Dynamics of Cultural Resistance

Can the image of women in the mass media be changed? My answer is: It depends to a large extent on how one defines change. There are two kinds of change. One kind is a further extension or intensification of the built-in tendencies in the social structure; the other is a change in the structure itself.

My research indicates that the image of women in the mass media is changing within the existing structure, and is changing for the worse, appearances to the contrary notwithstanding. As to the second question, can the structure itself change, the realistic answer is that it cannot change unless and until the structure of social relations no longer works, unless the cost is too high, or unless institutional relationships collapse, none of which has taken place. The structure is still going strong and is entering a phase of counterattacking challenge.

To understand this, one must understand the political dynamics of the cultural management of social movements. It consists of two parts. One is the tactic of resistance and the second is the function of images. By social movements I mean movements that somehow threaten or promise to restructure a particular set of social relations. Once such a movement arises, and this is true for any movement, the dynamics of cultural resistance come into play.

Today television is, for all practical purposes, the common culture. Culture is the system of messages that cultivates the images fitting the established structure of social relations. As such, the main function of culture is to cultivate resistance to change. It functions to make people accept life as good and society as just, no matter how things really are. We have been misled by many of the social scientists and researchers into considering television just another medium. But all other media have been used selectively. That makes a crucial difference because when you can select, you can have a greater variety of uses and gratifications; you can support a greater range of idiosyncratic or family or group cultures. Television is not used selectively. It is used by practically all the people and is used practically all the time. It collects the most heterogeneous public of groups, classes, races, sexes, and nationalities in history into a national audience that has nothing in common except television, or shared messages. Television thereby becomes the common basis for social interaction among a very widely dispersed and diverse national community. As such, it can only be compared, in terms of its functions, not to any other medium but to the preindustrial notion of religion.

Television *is* the new religion. It has to be studied as a new religion, an organic structure of rituals and myths, including the news and documentaries, but primarily serial drama. It is religion in the sense of preindustrial pre-Reformation religion, in the sense of one's having no choice—a cosmic force or a symbolic environment that one was born into, and whose assumptions one accepted without much questioning. If one does question these assumptions one must look at cultural dynamics of resistance to change and the functions of images. There are three main tactics of resistance to change: discrediting, isolating, or undercutting. All have been used by television to resist the changing status of women.

1. *Discrediting.* Suppression does not work under conditions of rapid and omnipresent mass communication. It is more effective to pick up the most bizarre or provocative manifestations of the threatening movement in order to try to discredit it and to mobilize conventional sentiment against it. For instance, when "women's libbers" (as they are pejoratively called) appear on television, they are usually hostile, aggressive, unappreciative of men, and won't listen to reason.

2. *Isolating.* The tactic here is to then pick out a "responsible" (i.e., relatively safe) element of the movement and give it its own limited place—barren though that may be of life's opportunities and choices—such as a reservation, a ghetto, or a kitchen. Once isolated, the media encourage women not to let anyone tamper with their sacred right to rule over "their place." For example, in this volume Muriel Cantor analyzes female participation in programs of the Corporation for Public Broadcasting. There, women are virtually segregated into "Womanhood" kind of programs instead of having their issues considered by all public-affairs programs.

3. *Undercutting.* This is basically the tactic of terror. Terror undercuts the will to break out of the isolation of minority status. In our case this tactic consists of two steps. One is what I call the "institutionalization of rape," which has occurred in the past five years. Television increasingly treats rape as a normal crime, something akin to theft. Rape has even been made a topic of humor, and in one show a woman raped a man. The second step is the acceptance of pornography as a "liberating force" without recognizing its exploitative social content. Pornographic depictions of women exploit them as sex objects; pornography does not identify women as full human beings with hopes and fears and jobs and families. Here sexual liberation may be used as a ploy for sexual exploitation.

The second part of the dynamics of cultural management of social movements concerns the functions of images. An image (sometimes called a stereotype) is a projective device used to make it easy to behave toward people in socially functional ways. You call a group "barbarians" if you want to be brutal toward them. You call people "criminals" if you want to suspend normal laws of decency and behave toward them in what would otherwise be considered a criminal way. You call a group "insane" if you want to suspend the rules of rationality and reason in managing them. That is not to say that there are no real criminals or insane people, but television uses these terms as a projective cultural apparatus to encourage isolating newly identified deviants from "normal people." This has the social function of coping with threats, for its justifies both dismissing and brutalizing these groups.

The image of women has a very particular significance in this regard. It is the major battleground for the development and perfection of cultural instruments of all kinds of domination. It brings the issue of power into every family and every home. The tactics of degrading women that work with women are transportable and exploitable in other areas such as class, race, and minorities. That is why I consider this a seminal issue in the theory and practice of group relations, and probably the most difficult to resolve.

Finally, the imagery of the group that is dominated is likely to exhibit images of victimization. The higher the rate of victimization in the group the more the idea of victimization is felt to be acceptable. Our television studies (e.g., Gerbner and Gross, 1976) include a violence-victim ratio that we found to be an interesting index of social power. We found that women are the victims of violence, not its perpetrators. One can see at a glance the plethora of women as victim images—women lying prostrate in the hands of males who range from noble rescuers to rapists—all showing the same power imbalance.

One of the most interesting double-barrelled cultural tactics—

most visible on television drama—is that when women or other groups that have been denied full access to power are shown as independent, adventurous, or powerful, they are portrayed as *enforcing* rather than challenging the laws that oppress them. They become policewomen, detectives, or soldiers. In other words, they are accepted into the ranks of power provided they act on behalf of the rules designed to protect the interest of the majority groups. And even then they usually need to be rescued by male partners.

What we see in the media is less a reflection of, than a counterattack on, the women's movement as a social force for structural change. Instead of mediating even the actual social change that is taking place, the media appear to be cultivating resistance and preparing for a last-ditch defense. And the gap between actual social reality and what is portrayed in the media is widening. The news that never gets through is that a new breed of women and blacks and Hispanos and old people have appeared like no other that ever lived.

Chapter 2

JUDITH LEMON

Dominant or Dominated? Women on Prime-Time Television[1]

In American society, social power is distributed by class, race, and sex. To explore television's portrayal of women, this article analyzes the depiction of dominance in interactions between two people. The data were selected from situation comedies and crime dramas broadcast in prime time during 1975. Following Sternglanz and Serbin (1974, p. 712; see also Turow, 1974), dominance is defined as "to influence or to control others, to persuade, prohibit, dictate, to lead or direct, to restrain and to organize the behavior of [others]." Situation comedies and crime shows are compared because each genre poses different possibilities for the portrayal of sex roles. Male-dominated crime dramas depict women as peripheral to an action-oriented, usually violent plot. In contrast, situation comedies offer more possibilities for women to participate and dominate, since they include more family situations and plots about interpersonal concerns (see also Turow, 1974). Those possibilities may be enhanced when a woman stars in a show, since television viewers would hardly tune in to watch a bumbling and incompetent star (see also Tedesco, 1974).[2]

This study indicates that whatever the story line, television maintains societal stereotypes in its portrayal of power. Social class, as indicated by the relevant occupations of characters, has more of an impact upon dominance patterns than does sex. Sex, in turn, is more important to the portrayal of dominance than race. Although situation comedies show women more favorably than do crime dramas, they draw on stereotypes of black and white women's relationships to men, particularly on the notion of the black woman as family matriarch.

METHODS

To explore dominance patterns, I listed from several March 1975 *TV Guides* all crime dramas and situation comedies aired during prime time and sorted them into six categories designed to capture sex-role portrayal. These were situation comedies starring women, with female regulars, and without female regulars, and crime shows satisfying the same three conditions. When there were more than four shows in a category, four were randomly selected for analysis.[3] Between March 18 and March 31, 1975, I watched and coded the shows, according to pretested categories. Using a specially prepared timer, I examined the first verbal or nonverbal interaction clearly between two people in thirty seconds of one-minute segments of the programs. I recorded who was dominant, dominated, or equal in each interaction and noted the relevant occupation status, sex, race, and family role of each participant. The scoring scheme was successfully pretested for reliability (judgments were reproducible by an independent coder).[4] Table 2.1 presents the number of observations scored in each program.

I also developed two methods to analyze the raw data. The first, an *intersex measure,* divides two-party interactions between

TABLE 2.1. Number of Observations of Dominance Patterns by Program Type, Female Acting Rank, and Program

		SITUATION COMEDY			
Female Acting Rank					
Star	Maude 17	Rhoda 17	Karen 18	Mary Tyler Moore 18	Total Observations 70
Regular or Co-star	That's My Mama 17	Bob Newhart 17	Hot l Baltimore 18	Good Times 18	70
No regular star	M.A.S.H. 15	Barney Miller 11	Odd Couple 24	Sanford and Son 20	70
				Subtotal for situation comedies	210
		CRIME DRAMA			
Female Acting Rank					
Star	Get Christie Love 35	Policewoman 35			70
Regular or Co-star	Barnaby Jones 35	Mannix 35			70
No regular star	The Rookies 17	Harry O 17	Rockford Files 18	Caribe 18	70
				Subtotal for crime dramas	210
				Total Observations for both genres	420

men and women into those dominated by men, those dominated by women, and those where men and women are portrayed as equals. The second takes into account that television also shows men interacting with men, and women with women. Called the *percentage of total appearances measure,* it contrasts the number of times someone of a particular sex is portrayed as dominant, dominated, or equal with total number of times members of that sex have participated in two-party interactions. Consider a hypothetical example of this measure involving two interactions. In one, a man dominates a woman. In the other, two women are portrayed as equals. The percentage of total appearances indicates that the men had been dominant in all (one hundred percent) of their interactions, and that women had been dominated in one-third of their interactions and had been equal in two-thirds. The percentage of total appearances is thus a more inclusive measure than the intersex statistic.

OCCUPATIONAL STATUS IS MORE IMPORTANT THAN SEX

On television, the social class of men and women, as defined by their relevant occupational status in interactions, is more important than sex in determining patterns of dominance. (I considered occupation relevant only when the subject discussed in the interaction was affected by both interactants' occupations. For instance, if a police officer sought information from a citizen and the citizen's occupational status was irrelevant to the information sought, this interaction was not scored in terms of occupational status. Occupational status was relevant for 358 of the 840 interactants.)

Men are more likely than women to be portrayed as having high occupational status. In the total sample, men had high occupational status in sixty-nine percent of the 274 interactions in which their status was relevant; women, twenty-five percent of the 84 interactions where their occupation mattered.[5] Both men and women were more likely to be portrayed with high occupational status in crime shows than in situation comedies. But, in each genre a greater proportion of men than women have high status (seventy-seven percent of the men and thirty-two percent of the women in crime dramas, and fifty-six percent of the men and twelve percent of the women in situation comedies).

Although men were more likely than women to have high status, ultimately social status is more important than sex in determining dominance in interactions. As shown in Table 2.2, high-status men and women are always proportionately more dominant than low-status men and women; conversely low-status men and women are more dominated. Within categories, the pattern is more complex. High-status males are dominant more often than high-status females. This generalization holds somewhat in situation comedies, but the pattern is dramatic in crime dramas. Low-status women are slightly more dominant than the low-status men in situation comedies, and slightly less dominant in crime dramas. Low-status men are more dominated in both genres. The pattern within categories, although mixed, indicates that relevant occupational status is more important than sex in determining dominance patterns.[6]

GENERALLY, MEN DOMINATE WOMEN

On all programs and in both genres, men dominate women. In part, their dominance may be explained by their greater likelihood of having high occupational status. But this pattern is intensified by men's general domination of women, even when

TABLE 2.2. Patterns of Dominance by Relevant Occupational Status and Sex for All Programs and Types of Programs*

KINDS OF PROGRAMS	KINDS OF DOMINANCE IN NUMBER OF INTERACTIONS AND PERCENTAGE OF TOTAL APPEARANCES			
	Dominant	*Equal*	*Dominated*	*Total*
All Programs				
High Status				
Male	85 (44.7%)	78 (41.0%)	27 (14.2%)	190 (100%)
Female	6 (28.5%)	7 (33.3%)	8 (38.1%)	21 (100%)
Low Status				
Male	6 (7.1%)	37 (44%)	41 (48.8%)	84 (100%)
Female	5 (7.9%)	32 (50.8%)	26 (41.3%)	63 (100%)
Situation Comedy				
High Status				
Male	19 (35.8%)	29 (54.7%)	5 (9.4%)	53 (100%)
Female	1 (33.3%)	2 (66.7%)	0	3 (100%)
Low Status				
Male	1 (2.4%)	28 (68.3%)	12 (29.3%)	41 (100%)
Female	3 (13.0%)	15 (65.2%)	5 (21.7%)	23 (100%)
Crime Drama				
High Status				
Male	66 (48.9%)	49 (36.3%)	20 (14.8%)	135 (100%)
Female	5 (27.8%)	5 (27.8%)	8 (44.4%)	18 (100%)
Low Status				
Male	3 (7.3%)	9 (22.0%)	29 (70.7%)	41 (100%)
Female	2 (5.3%)	17 (44.7%)	19 (50.0%)	38 (100%)

* The Chi Square statistic was not calculated for situation comedies because of empty cells. For all programs, $\chi^2 = 9.7$, $p. < .01$. For crime drama, $\chi^2 = 112.2$, $p. < .001$.

status is irrelevant to an interaction. Ignoring occupational status, men dominated women in twenty-three percent of the situation comedy interactions analyzed by the intersex measure, were dominated by women in thirteen percent of the intersex interactions, and were portrayed as the equals of women in sixty-four percent of those interactions. Men are even more dominant on crime dramas. There, according to the intersex measure, men are dominant in forty-seven percent of the male-female interactions, are dominated by women in six percent of their interactions, and are women's equals in the remaining forty-seven percent of the cases. Women fare better in situation comedies.[7]

The percentage of total-appearances measure presents a similar picture of the portrayal of men and women, as shown in Table 2.3. Again, men are more dominant in both genres. And again, women are portrayed more favorably in situation comedies.[8]

TABLE 2.3. Patterns of Dominance in Total Appearances for Men and Women in Situation Comedies and Crime Dramas*

	KINDS OF DOMINANCE IN NUMBER OF OBSERVATIONS AND PERCENTAGES OF TOTAL APPEARANCES IN INTERACTIONS			
	Dominant	*Both Equal*	*Dominated*	*Total*
		Situation Comedy		
Male	58	194	50	302
	(19%)	(64%)	(16%)	(100%)
Female	16	78	24	118
	(14%)	(66%)	(20%)	(100%)
		Crime Dramas		
Male	110	127	74	311
	(35%)	(41%)	(24%)	(100%)
Female	8	59	42	109
	(7%)	(54%)	(39%)	(100%)

* For situation comedy $\chi^2 = 2.64$ not significant. For crime drama $\chi^2 = 33.01$, $p < .001$.

The dominance of men is so pervasive that it is virtually unaffected by the presence of a female star on a program. Table 2.4 indicates that even in situation comedies and crime shows starring a woman, men are more likely to dominate women than women are to dominate men. However, a woman starring in a crime drama tends to decrease the otherwise overwhelming dominance of men in the crime shows. On crime shows as a group, men are dominant in forty-seven percent of the intersex interactions and are dominated in six percent of them. On crime shows starring women, men are "only" dominant in thirty percent of the intersex interactions and are dominated in eleven

TABLE 2.4. Patterns of Dominance in Intersex Interactions by Type of Program and Female Acting Rank*

	KINDS OF DOMINANCE IN NUMBER OF OBSERVATIONS AND PERCENTAGES OF INTERSEX INTERACTIONS			
	Men Dominate Women	*Both Are Equal*	*Women Dominate Men*	*Total*
Situation Comedy				
Female Acting Rank				
Star	60	26	5	41
	(24%)	(64%)	(12%)	(100%)
Co-star or regular	5	21	4	30
	(17%)	(70%)	(13%)	(100%)
No regulars	3	3	1	7
	(43%)	(43%)	(14%)	(100%)
Crime Drama				
Female Acting Rank				
Star	8	15	3	26
	(30%)	(60%)	(11%)	(100%)†
Co-star or regular	23	14	1	38
	(61%)	(37%)	(1%)	(100%)†
No regulars	10	12	1	23
	(43%)	(52%)	(4%)	(100%)†

* Chi Square was not calculated because of too few cases in some cells.
† Errors due to rounding.

percent of their interactions with women. The importance of top billing is also indicated by the treatment of female co-stars on crime shows. As Table 2.4 indicates, women are treated worse on crime shows with a female co-star than they are in crime shows starring a woman or without female regulars. When a woman was a co-star on a crime show in 1975, she appeared to be treated as a perennial second fiddle. At least, that is the case with "Barnaby Jones" and "Mannix."

WHITE MEN COME FIRST

Sex is a stronger determinant of dominance patterns than race. White men always predominate, as seen in their total number of interactions and in statistics on their dominance patterns. In all of the sampled interactions, there were 471 white men, 140 black men, 192 white women and 37 black women. This same rank ordering occurred in crime dramas (279 white men, 90 white women, 32 black men, 19 black women), but not in situation comedies, where there were more black men than white women (193 white men, 109 black men, 101 white women, 17 black women).[9] By themselves, these rankings do not indicate general male dominance, since black men and white women "switch" their rank order in the two genres. However, the percentage of total-appearances measure, shown in Table 2.5, indicates that men prevail more often than women regardless of race. The black male is markedly more dominant than the white female in both situation comedies (twenty-two percent versus twelve percent) and crime dramas (twenty-two percent versus seven percent), although the percent of dominated appearances is similar for both.

Although as a group women are less dominant than men, limited data suggest that black women are portrayed more force-

TABLE 2.5. Patterns of Dominance in Total Appearances by Program Type, Sex, and Race*

TYPE OF PROGRAM	KINDS OF DOMINANCE IN NUMBER OF OBSERVATIONS AND PERCENTAGE OF TOTAL APPEARANCES IN INTERACTIONS			
	Dominant	*Equal*	*Dominated*	*Total*
Situation Comedy				
White Male	34 (18%)	129 (67%)	30 (16%)	193 (100%)
Black Male	24 (22%)	65 (60%)	20 (18%)	109 (100%)
White Female	12 (12%)	67 (66%)	22 (22%)	101 (100%)
Black Female	4 (24%)	11 (65%)	2 (12%)	17 (100%)
Crime Drama				
White Male	103 (37%)	115 (41%)	61 (22%)	279 (100%)
Black Male	7 (22%)	12 (38%)	13 (41%)	32 (100%)
White Female	6 (7%)	49 (54%)	35 (39%)	90 (100%)
Black Female	2 (11%)	10 (53%)	7 (37%)	19 (100%)

* For situation comedy, $\chi^2 = 24.7$, $p < .001$. For crime drama, $\chi^2 = 44.8$, $p < .001$.

fully than white women are. Table 2.5 also indicates that situation comedies present black women as dominant more frequently than any other group. In that genre, black women are also the least dominated. Similarly, on crime dramas black women are more frequently portrayed as dominant than white women are, although both white and black men are even more dominant. However, black women are primarily shown as dominant within the context of all black interactions, as shown in Table 2.6. That table also demonstrates that relationships between black men and women are shown as more egalitarian

TABLE 2.6. Dominance Patterns for Intersex Interactions for All Programs and Types of Programs by Race and Sex*

	KINDS OF DOMINANCE IN NUMBER OF INTERACTIONS AND PERCENTAGES OF INTERSEX INTERACTIONS			
All Programs	*Men Dominate Women*	*Both Are Equal*	*Women Dominate Men*	*Total*
White Men & White Women	48 (37%)	72 (56%)	9 (7%)	129 (100%)
Black Men & Black Women	2 (10%)	14 (70%)	4 (20%)	20 (100%)
White Men & Black Women	7 (70%)	2 (20%)	1 (10%)	10 (100%)
Black Men & White Women	2 (33%)	3 (50%)	1 (17%)	6 (100%)
Situation Comedies				
White Men & White Women	14 (25%)	37 (65%)	6 (11%)	57 (100%)
Black Men & Black Women	1 (7%)	10 (67%)	4 (27%)	15 (100%)
White Men & Black Women	1 (100%)	0	0	1 (100%)
Black Men & White Women	2 (40%)	3 (60%)	0	5 (100%)
Crime Dramas				
White Men & White Women	34 (47%)	35 (49%)	3 (4%)	72 (100%)
Black Men & Black Women	1 (20%)	4 (80%)	0	5 (100%)
White Men & Black Women	6 (67%)	2 (22%)	1 (11%)	9 (100%)
Black Men & White Women	0	0	1 (100%)	1 (100%)

* Chi Square was not calculated because of too few cases in some cells.

than relationships between either white pairs or black male-white female interactants. Egalitarian treatment for black women, like the possibility of her dominance, is virtually restricted to all black interactions.

That white men invariably dominate the other three groups and that black women are treated differently than white women indicates that race and sex interact with one another in determining dominance patterns on television. However, sex is more important than race.[10]

BLACK AND WHITE WOMEN

In large measure, the more favorable depiction of black women in all black interactions than of white women in all white interactions results from stereotypes of family life. First, that all women are more likely to be shown within the family than outside it indicates an initial stereotypic treatment of women. Although only fifteen percent of the 840 interactants were seen relating to family members, forty-seven percent of those participants were women. By way of contrast, a mere twenty-three percent of those interacting outside the family context were women. Second, women in the family are more favorably portrayed than women interacting with non-family members. Unfortunately, so few women were portrayed as family members in crime dramas that data supporting this generalization (Table 2.7) can only be derived from situation comedies.

A closer examination of interactions in situation comedies reveals now that black and white women are treated differently. For the statement supported by Table 2.7—that women are treated better when interacting with family members—flounders when white and black women are examined separately. (Table 2.7 masks the contribution of race to the generalization.) A different pattern emerges, when one breaks down white-male–white-female and black-male–black-female interactions in situation comedies by the presence or absence of a family context, as in Table 2.8. Then, one learns, situation comedies restrict black

TABLE 2.7. Patterns of Dominance in Total Number of Appearances in Interactions in Situation Comedies by Sex and Family Context*

	KINDS OF DOMINANCE IN NUMBER OF OBSERVATIONS AND PERCENTAGES OF TOTAL APPEARANCES IN INTERACTIONS			
	Dominant	*Both Equal*	*Dominated*	*Total*
Male				
Inside Family	9 (15%)	42 (71%)	8 (14%)	59 (100%)
Outside Family	49 (20%)	152 (63%)	42 (17%)	243 (100%)
Female				
Inside Family	9 (15%)	42 (69%)	10 (16%)	61 (100%)
Outside Family	7 (12%)	36 (63%)	14 (25%)	57 (100%)

* $\chi^2 = 50.2$, $p < .001$.

TABLE 2.8. Patterns of Dominance in All White and All Black Intersex Interactions in Situation Comedies by Family Context*

	KINDS OF DOMINANCE IN NUMBER AND PERCENTAGE OF INTERSEX INTERACTIONS			
	Man Dominates Woman	*Both Are Equal*	*Woman Dominates Man*	*Total*
White Interactants				
Inside Family	4 (27%)	11 (73%)	0	15 (100%)
Outside Family	10 (24%)	26 (62%)	6 (14%)	42 (100%)
Black Interactants				
Inside Family	1 (7%)	9 (64%)	4 (29%)	14 (100%)
Outside Family	0	1 (100%)	0	1 (100%)

* Chi Square was not calculated because of low cell frequency.

women to the family and suggest female dominance in black families. White women are given more latitude in their appearances; they are portrayed outside the family, as well as within it. But, interactions in white families favor male dominance so much that white women are more favorably depicted outside the family than in it.

SUMMARY AND RECOMMENDATIONS

What can we make of all this? Several generalizations are possible:

1. On television, class (as indicated by relevant occupational status) predicts dominance better than sex.
2. However, television generally shows men as more dominant than women.
3. Situation comedies present more favorable depictions of women than crime dramas do, although this tendency is mitigated when a woman stars in a crime drama.
4. Sex is more important to dominance patterns than race, even though sex and race interact in determining dominance patterns.
   - (a) All men, but especially white men, are more frequently dominant than dominated.
   - (b) Black women and white women are treated differently.
     - i. Although confined to a family context, black women are forcefully depicted there.
     - ii. Although they are always more dominated than dominating, white women are depicted more favorably outside the family context.

Television clearly captures societal notions about the importance of social class to the exercise of power, the general domination of men over women, and the greater power of black women within the family.

If we want a society characterized by sexual equality, television's portrayal of women needs to be changed. Although limitations in the data curtail the breadth of recommendations to be made, some suggestions are possible.

First, women should be given roles of higher professional rank and, most important, be shown doing their job on television. As it is, most women for whom occupation outside the home is relevant are in low-status occupations, while most men shown working are of high prestige. When a man and a woman of high occupational status are interacting, care needs to be taken that the woman is not consistently portrayed in the dominated role. Situation comedies outside the family might offer an opportunity here. The medical and legal genres might also produce opportunities for better portrayals of women, since those two professions seem to be the most respected in American society.

Second, the number of shows starring women could certainly be increased. Although television's portrayal of women's professional status has changed somewhat since 1967 (see footnote 2), in 1975 there were still only a few shows starring women. Increasing the number of situation comedies about families is problematic, for the domain of black women needs expansion outside the family, and in situation comedies the family context does not offer an egalitarian portrayal of white women. Additionally, more crime dramas should star women, since their presence decreases male dominance. Also, co-starring or featured parts for women in crime dramas, as they are written for "Mannix" or "Barnaby Jones," must be avoided, since as co-stars, women play second fiddle. We need more than mere numerical change, more than simply increased numbers of women on television, because we hardly want more women systematically portrayed as dominated by men.

Is making such recommendations a naive exercise, ignoring

the economic interests and workings of the television industry? I believe that some of the data, categories, and conclusions of studies like this can be used to understand how the industry chooses television content and may eventually lead to a better understanding of how a concerned and informed public might influence the programmers.

In the television industry, economics is the primary guide for programming decisions. Since production costs are high and losses can be great, decision makers try to make the safest guesses. The new genre is the exception, and copies of last season's successes are the rule, although innovations must inevitably occur to keep the public interested. Successful innovations generate their own sets of copies, as did "All in the Family" and "The Waltons."

We need to understand the process of innovation in the industry. What makes a new programming idea a real innovation? How are its elements unique? And, how must it relate to past success to get on the air? Additionally, how does the industry's acceptance of an innovation differ from the process of accepting a program more directly modeled on a past success? What elements are singled out and replicated? What elements are considered insignificant? Answers to these questions would help the public understand how the content on television changes over time.

There are other things we need to understand in order to change television's portrayal of men and women. What is the relationship between attitudes of industry personnel and television content? Jennings and Walters' report (1977) on Television Station Employment Practices in 1976 shows a slow increase in female employees, although the rate of increase is not as high as it had been in the past. But we need to know whether more women employees will effect change and, if so, where significant female decision makers must be placed. Clear employment data on this question are not yet available.

I hope that the categories raised in studies such as this can be used to investigate the industry's perspective on television content. Perhaps a broader understanding of this issue can lead to more effective consumer action in relation to the portrayal of women on television.

NOTES

[1] I am grateful for the help of Aimee Dorr Leifer, Elli Reshiff, Paul Dimaggio, and Nancy Held in formulating this essay, adapted from my qualifying paper for the Harvard Graduate School of Education.

[2] Very few women star in programs, but what they do occupationally has changed. In the sixties, female stars were occasionally given magical powers so they could do more interesting things; for example, the lead characters in "I Dream of Jeannie" and "Bewitched" were housewives with magical powers; "The Flying Nun" starred a nun with supernatural abilities. In 1975, programs starring women featured a housewife and sometime manager of a real-estate office ("Maude"), a television producer ("Mary Tyler Moore"), the head of a window-dressing business ("Rhoda"), a consumer advocate ("Karen"), a policewoman ("Policewoman"), a police detective ("Get Christie Love"), and a chief of detectives ("Amy Prentiss").

[3] Because this procedure was used, every situation comedy and crime drama did not have an equal chance of being included in the sample. All situation comedies starring women and without a female regular and all crime dramas starring women or featuring a female regular were selected; four of five situation comedies with female regulars and four of ten crime dramas with no female regulars were selected. Since more than one observation was selected from each program, and each of the program's observed interactions were designed by the same writers, directors, and producer, the observations are not really independent of one another. Accordingly, statistical inferences to other populations cannot be made. Nonetheless, significance tests are presented for the reader's information.

[4] After training sessions on four different prime-time shows, the female experimenter and a male colleague viewed and independently coded an hour-long episode of "Manhunter." Defining reliability as percent agreement, the following values were obtained: on whether an interaction occurred, 0.88; on which interaction of a thirty-second segment should be scored, 0.91; on existence of dominance or equality, 0.88; on race, 1.00; on sex, 1.00; on relevant occupational status, 0.87; and on family context, 1.00.

[5] When analyzed with Chi Square, this relationship is statistically significant ($\chi^2 = 50.4$, $p < .001$).

[6] To verify this pattern, partial correlation coefficients were calculated. They also indicated that occupational status is more important than sex in determining patterns of dominance.

[7] $\chi^2 = 11.3$, $p < .001$.

[8] Additionally, the sampled programs rarely showed women relating to women, although they frequently showed men talking to men. Although twentiy-eight percent of all interactants in situation comedies and twenty-six percent in crime dramas were women, women are underrepresented in same-sex interactions. In both genres, fifteen percent of the same-sex interactions are shared by women. (Eight-five percent of them are of men relating to men.)

[9] Arranged in Chi Square tables, only the data on situation comedies are significant ($\chi^2 = 20.0$, $p < .001$). The high number of black men is partly an artifact of the method of program selection.

[10] Additional statistical analysis was performed to gauge the relative contributions of race and sex to dominance patterns. The resulting partial correlation coefficients suggest that race and sex are associated in determining who appears, but sex of interactants influences dominance more than does race.

[11] For all programs, $\chi^2 = 27.2$, $p < .001$. For situation comedies, $\chi^2 = 44.6$, $p < .001$. There is no significant relationship for crime dramas.

Chapter 3

STEPHEN SCHUETZ and JOYCE N. SPRAFKIN

Spot Messages Appearing Within Saturday Morning Television Programs

The overwhelming popularity of television has inspired considerable concern and numerous investigations of the entertainment medium's impact on children's social behavior and attitudes. The result has been an extensive accumulation of knowledge demonstrating that children can learn both aggressive and prosocial behaviors from programs (Leifer, Gordon, and Graves, 1974; Liebert, Neale, and Davidson, 1973). Perhaps more subtle, but no less important, the race, occupational, and sex-role representations and portrayals of groups as they occur on television programs may greatly influence children's attitudes (Frueh and McGhee, 1975; Graves, 1975).

Considerably less attention, however, has focused on commercials—either on their impact on children or on their content. This may seem reasonable in light of a commercial's short duration relative to a program. Nevertheless, one very basic fact highlights the potentially powerful impact of commercials: they are produced specifically to attract and persuade, with every effort made to make them appear credible. In contrast, programs are intended merely to entertain. It is this deliberate goal to change attitudes about the desirability of certain products, services, and behavior, particularly that concerning purchasing and consumption, that points to the importance of knowing what unintended messages, if any, commercials convey, and what effect they have on children. Certainly if programs intended merely to entertain can cause increases in aggressive behavior, then more attention should be focused on high-powered messages designed to have specific effects.

This report describes the preliminary results of a content analysis of spot messages (both for commercial products and public-service announcements) undertaken by Media Action Research Center, Inc. Specifically, it involved an examination of spot messages appearing within all of the programs broadcast by five stations in the New York area between 7:00 a.m. and 1:00 p.m. on one randomly chosen Saturday morning in October 1974. From these stations, which included three affiliates of the major networks (WABC, WCBS, and WNBC), one VHF station (WNEW), and one UHF station (WSNL), forty-two programs were taped off the air and 414 spot messages appeared within them; 372 (about ninety percent) of these messages contained live or animated human characters (the remaining forty-two did not feature recognizable human characters) and there were 2,226 characters in all. It should be emphasized that the spot messages examined were the ones most likely to be seen by children, since only those appearing during programs were included in the analysis; spot messages shown on the hour and half hour were not considered.

We addressed ourselves to one major question in this initial investigation: What is the sex and race of the characters appearing in the spot message?

SEX AND RACE REPRESENTATION

Serious objections have been expressed over the past few years to the biased presentation of sex and racial/ethnic roles on the entertainment medium. Many studies have demonstrated the extent of stereotypic portrayals on television programs and suggested their possible effects. In the present investigation we examined sex and race presentations on spot messages potentially viewed by children.

The major concern with the presentation of stereotypes on television is that the result of such portrayals may be the acquisition of negative attitudes toward certain groups by the audience and the solidification of sexual and racial stereotypes. Evidence that these concerns are justified is now available. Regarding attitudes toward black Americans, for example, Greenberg (1972) reported that forty percent of a large sample of white elementary-school children said they learned most about how blacks look and dress from television. Then, more recently, Graves (1975) demonstrated that negative portrayals of blacks on unedited television programs resulted in the modification of white children's attitudes toward blacks in the negative direction, while positive portrayals of blacks resulted in increased positive attitudes toward blacks by both black and white children. At the same time, Frueh and McGhee (1975) found that children (kindergarten through sixth graders) who were heavy television watchers (twenty-five hours or more per week) maintained more stereotypic sex-role values than a comparable group of light television watchers (ten hours or less per week), a finding that suggests a causal influence.

The process through which television viewers develop attitudes toward social groups has been addressed by Clark (1972), who observed that the psychological legitimization of a group on television involves two steps: recognition and respect. Recognition refers to how often the group appears on television, while respect refers to the formal role status (occupational and social) to which the group is assigned.

The underrepresentation of blacks and females on television is well documented. On children's programming in particular, males outnumber females more than two to one (Sternglanz and Serbin, 1974), and across several studies of adult programs males have been given sixty-six to seventy-five percent of all the possible scripted parts, while whites have filled between seventy and ninety percent of them (Gerbner, 1972a; Head, 1954; Smythe, 1953; Tedesco, 1974; Turow, 1974). The underrepresentation is particularly blatant for females, who make up slightly more than fifty percent of the population. White males are most favorably portrayed, usually highly professional, powerful, and prestigeful (Gerbner, 1972a). In contrast, females are usually portrayed in less respected marital, romantic, and family roles (Gerbner, 1972a), and blacks have been largely presented as entertainers and servants, and more recently as regulators of society (for example, law-enforcement officers) (Clark, 1972; Colle, 1968; Roberts, 1970–71).

There is some information available about the sex and racial portrayals on commercials to which children are exposed. In an unpublished report cited in Sheikh, Prasad, and Rao (1974), Barens (1971) reported that the commercials on Saturday morning programming were underrepresentative of females and minority group members.

Our own work is designed to update the earlier analyses of spot messages and to provide a more detailed analysis than previously available. The information about sex and race representations was obtained by an adult observer who viewed the spot messages and recorded for each the number of male and female characters who were white, black, and nonblack minority members (including Oriental, Hispanic, and American-Indian groups). To ascertain the accuracy of observer's ratings, a second adult observer independently reanalyzed twenty-one randomly selected commercials; very high agreement was obtained between the two raters. (Technically, agreement levels were assessed with a Pearson product-moment correlation, $r = +.95$.)

RECOGNITION OF WOMEN

As Figure 3.1 indicates, out of a total of 2,226 characters, 62.8 percent were male and only 37.2 percent were female. Further, out of all the spot messages containing human characters 37.63 percent had male characters only whereas only 14.52 percent had female characters only (i.e., no male characters).

We are currently examining the representation of males and females in the various types of spot messages. Overall, it appears that the public-service announcements contain a larger proportion of females than do product commercials, the exceptions, of course, are advertisements for female dolls and miniature appliances.

The domination of spot messages by male characters was fairly comparable for the three race categories: 60.5 percent of white characters were male, as were 70.3 percent of all black characters and 69.3 percent of all nonblack minority characters. However, while 69.4 percent of all adult characters were male, only 56.4 percent of the child characters were male. Stated another way, there are significantly more men than women on spot messages, whereas no significant sex difference exists for child characters. What this suggests in Clark's (1972) terms is that television is teaching our children that boys and girls are equally important, but that men are more important than women.

RECOGNITION OF BLACKS AND NONBLACK MINORITY MEMBERS

As Figure 3.2 indicates, of the 2,226 characters, 75.4 percent were white, 19.4 percent were black and 5.2 percent were non-

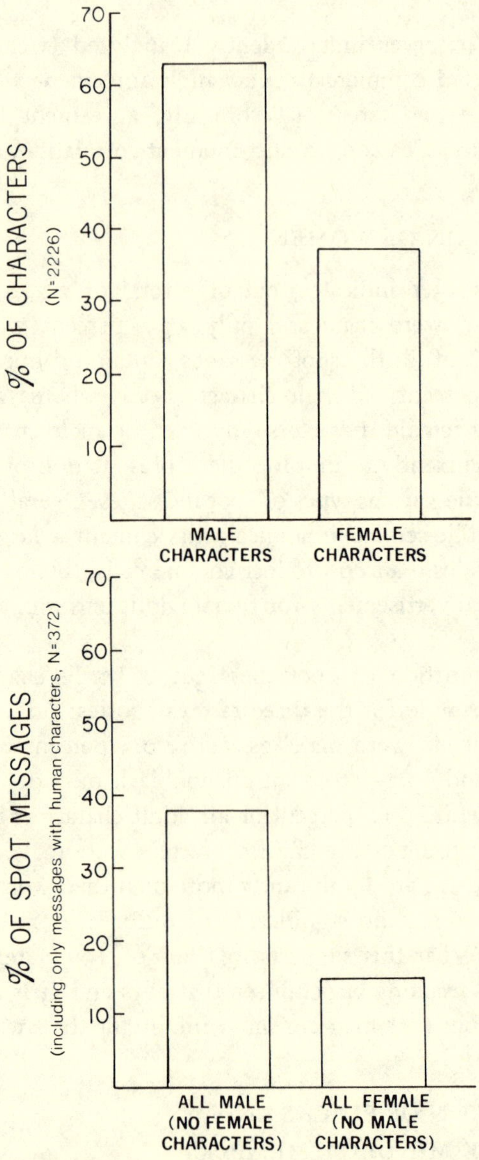

Figure 3.1. Recognition by Sex on Saturday Morning Spot Messages for Five New York Channels (WABC, WCBS, WNBC, WNEW, and WSNL), October 12, 1974.

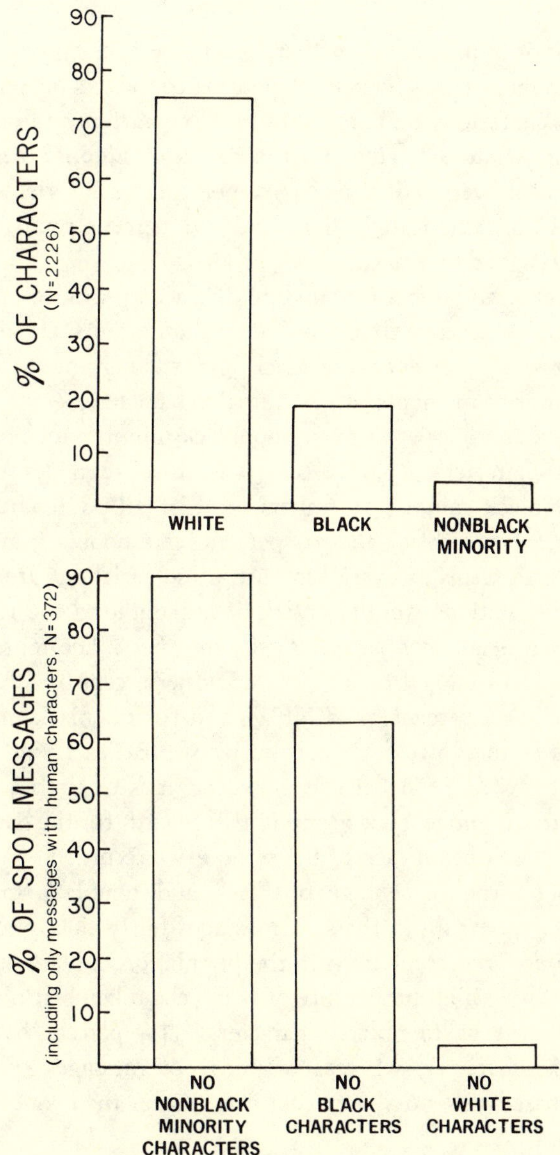

Figure 3.2. Recognition by Race on Saturday Morning Spot Messages for Five New York Channels (WABC, WCBS, WNBC, WNEW, and WSNL), October 12, 1974.

black minority members. Further, of all the spot messages containing human characters, 89.8 percent contained no nonblack minority characters, 62 percent no black characters and only 4.0 percent no white characters. Of the nonblack minority members, 63.7 percent were Hispanic, 19.3 percent were Oriental, 8.1 percent were American Indian, and 8.9 percent could not be reliably assigned to a racial/ethnic group.

The representation of nonwhite characters was comparable for the two sexes as well as for children and adults. Of all male characters 21.7 percent were black and 5.8 percent were nonblack minority members; of all female characters, 15.5 percent were black and 4.4 percent were nonblack minority members; of all child characters, 19.5 percent were black and 3.5 percent were nonblack minority members; and of all adult characters 19.2 percent were black and 7.1 percent were nonblack minority members. In terms of overall impact, these variations are slight.

The five stations were essentially comparable in the recognition of blacks and nonblack minority members. The representations of blacks ranged from a low of 17.3 percent by WCBS to a high of 24.3 percent by WNEW, and for nonblack minority members from a low of 3.3 percent by WNBC to a high of 7.4 percent by WCBS. In balance, however, it is clear that broadcasters are a homogeneous group in this regard, for the basic pattern was the same on each of the stations we recorded.

Although the percentage of black and nonblack minority characters appearing in the spot messages fairly closely matches these groups' representations in the population, a black still has an exceedingly high probability of being the token black. Of the spot messages having black characters, 54.4 percent had only one black character, whereas of the spot messages featuring white characters, 76.5 percent had more than one white character.

As noted earlier, respect is the second component of televised role portrayals that influences attitudes toward certain groups of people. Respect can accrue to a racial or ethnic group via the status of the parts assigned to its members, the kind of behavior they display within these parts, or even the type of products they promote. Our research is now addressing these questions. A few aspects of respect, though, are reflected in the data we have in hand. For example, our findings show that blacks occupy fully forty percent of all human parts in commercials for records while in commercials for box and board games, fewer than six percent of all parts were assigned to black actors. Here, in terms of respect, race bias by product is transparent.

The narrow range of models for females and minorities on spot messages has negative implications for the social role development of child viewers. The youngsters that comprise television's Saturday morning audience are quite sensitive to the portrayals of media characters. Early and middle childhood are critical years for the shaping of attitudes about sex roles and various social groups. While family, teachers, and peers greatly contribute to the development of the child, television's pervasiveness and impact suggest that this medium is yet another determiner of race and sex-role attitudes. Given television's demonstrated effectiveness in influencing children's attitudes and behavior, we hope that character representations will be modified to reflect more accurately gradually changing social roles.

Chapter 4

MURIEL CANTOR

Where Are the Women in Public Broadcasting

INTRODUCTION

This paper compares the visibility of males and females in public television. Under the auspices of the Task Force on Women in Public Broadcasting (see Isber and Cantor, 1975), a content analysis of programs broadcast over the Public Broadcasting Service (PBS) was undertaken in January 1975. The rationale behind this analysis was that the portrayal of women and girls through the media is both a dynamic force influencing attitudes about women and a reflection of the position of women in American society. Because this is the first systematic analysis of the content of public television, it provides comparative information unavailable elsewhere. Until now, no one knew whether public television presented a more diversified picture of women in American society than did commercial television.

Public television was established as an alternative to commercial television so that a "wide variety of programs of excellent quality would be made available to *all* Americans and that Federal commitments would be made to ensure adequate financing of such activities" (italics added) (Lee and Pedone, 1974, p. 1; see also Lyle, 1975). Originally envisioned as both entertainment and instruction, public television was to provide diversity, raise standards and tastes, and offer information leading to greater satisfaction in work and play (Report of the Carnegie Commission on Educational Television, 1967, pp. 14–15). This was a large order. Regarding women, at least, it has not been met.

The first part of this chapter reports on the content analysis done by the Task Force, both its method and findings. A brief analysis comparing how women are presented on public and commercial television follows. Comments then will be made on why women are not presented with more diversity on public television, the functions of public television as an alternative to commercial television, and the position of women as seen by public broadcasters.

THE CONTENT ANALYSIS

METHOD

In order to find out how women and men are portrayed in public broadcasting, one week of television programming distributed through the PBS network (approximately thirty-seven and one half hours) was monitored. Monitoring provides evidence on whether women are seen on the air as frequently as men and how women's roles and activities are portrayed in comparison with men's. Monitoring forms were designed so that characters and participants could be counted; their appearances, timed; their occupation, sex, and race, recorded; and the topic discussed or activity performed, noted.

Fourteen monitors, five men and nine women, were chosen after a trial work period of four hours. Three monitors independently coded the television programs, and the results were checked for reliability. The agreement (reliability) among the coders on the sex, occupation, and topics discussed was perfect.

The week of January 19 to 25, 1975, was selected as representative of ten weeks of transmission schedules studied. All regularly scheduled PBS programs for the 1974–75 season, except for "Soundstage," which was preempted, were transmitted during the week selected. In addition, PBS also transmitted a half hour news conference with then President Ford and a program devoted to the Democratic response to the State of the Union address, broadcast the previous week.

In all, there were thirty-seven television programs, consisting of fifty-eight individual episodes (approximately thirty-seven hours) monitored. For analytical purposes, the programming was divided into five categories:

1. General adult programming (panels, documentaries, news, interviews, public affairs, and general information).
2. Promotions
3. Drama
4. Music
5. Children's programming

The findings on the first four categories will be reported in this paper.

SELECTED FINDINGS

CATEGORY 1—GENERAL ADULT PROGRAMMING

In the adult television programs monitored (Category 1) 200 men (eighty-five percent) and only 36 women (fifteen percent) appeared (see Table 4.1). Of the twenty-eight adult programs listed in this classification, eleven (representing a total of six hours, seventeen minutes out of eighteen hours [thirty-six percent] of the programming) had no women participants.

There were only four black women out of the total 236 participants (see Table 4.2). Officials of the Corporation for Pub-

TABLE 4.1. Sex of Participants on Adult TV Programs (excluding music and drama).*

	No.	%
Males	200	85.0
Females	36	15.0
Total	236	100.0

* Source: Isber and Cantor (1975, p. 84).

lic Broadcasting identified eleven of the twenty-eight programs as public affairs designed for reports and discussions of issues and events of topical importance. Seven of these completely excluded women. In the remaining public-affairs programs, there were eleven women and ninety men. Thus, programming directed to timely issues and events of major importance, such as the economy, government, and foreign-policy issues, almost completely ignored women. Only one program dealt with women's issues and that was "Woman," a weekly series for and about women.

Most individuals on public-television adult programming discuss business, the economy, and law (see Table 4.3). Over one-half of all participants (113) are involved with these topics. A

TABLE 4.2. Race of Individuals on Adult TV Programs (excluding music and drama).*

	MALES		FEMALES	
	No.	%	*No.*	%
White	200	100.0	36	100.0
Black	5	3.0	4	11.0
Unidentified†	10	5.0	4	11.0
Total	185	92.0	28	78.0

* This category denotes backgrounds such as Spanish, Asian, or those who could not be definitely identified.

† These tables are from Isber and Cantor (1975, p. 84).

TABLE 4.3. Topic/Theme Discussed by Participants on Adult TV (excluding music and drama).*

	MALES		FEMALES	
	No.	*%*	*No.*	*%*
Business, Economics, Law, Goverment	113	56.0	10	28.0
Community Action	4	2.0	0	0
Medicine	0	0	1	.3.0
Education, Career Planning	7	3.0	6	16.0
Environmental Sciences	20	10.0	1	3.0
Botany	3	1.5	0	0
Art, Music, Culture	8	4.0	4	11.0
Food, Household	2	1.0	1	3.0
Personalities, Biographies	8	4.0	5	14.0
Human Rights, Sex	1	1.0	1	3.0
Human Rights, Race	1	1.0	0	0
Nonspecific News	7	3.5	1	3.0
General Human Interest	26	13.0	6	16.0
Total	200	100.0	36	100.0

* A variation of this table is found in Isber and Cantor (1975, p. 86).

comparison of men and women show that fifty-six percent of the males, as compared with twenty-eight percent of the females discuss issues of public importance. Because there are so few women, one might challenge the meaningfulness of an analysis of women's participation. After all, the principal finding is that only thirty-six women appeared in eighteen hours of programming. Even so, analysis shows that compared with men, a higher proportion of women are discussing such topics as education, career planning, personalities and biographies, sexual human rights, art, music, nutrition, and household affairs. These topics have been labeled by others as more feminine topics while business, economics, law, and government are considered "masculine" (see Turow, 1974, p. 138).

Analysts of commercial television (Cantor et al., 1972; Gerbner, 1972a; Tedesco, 1974; Turow, 1974; Courtney and Whipple, 1974) claim it stereotypes women and offers rigid definitions of femininity and masculinity. To see if public television does the same, the occupational roles of all participants were noted. On public-television programming, the participants are likely to be experts in their particular field, including journalists, economists, analysts of various kinds, and authors.

Although the total work force is over forty percent female, women are concentrated in female sex-typed occupations such as nursing, elementary school teaching, and secretarial/clerical positions. For this analysis an occupation is defined as female sex-typed if the number of females in the occupation is sixty percent or over (see Sommers, 1974, for details on the number and proportion of women in various occupations in the United States). If an occupation is sixty percent male, this occupation is labelled masculine. Those occupations with between forty to sixty percent males and females are considered neutral, not sex-typed. On the programs analyzed, two of the thirty-six women were housewives. The others were likely to be in relatively high-salaried positions generally considered male dominated or neutral occupations. No men in female sex-typed occupations appeared. Adult public television does not stereotype women as commercial television does. Rather it excludes them from many programs and when they do appear they are a distinct minority (see Table 4.4).

This finding is strengthened when the data on announcers and narrators are examined. Only four percent of the shows had female announcers/narrators; five percent of the programs were moderated by a man and a woman. Ninety-one percent of all shows had male announcers.

CATEGORY 2—PROMOTIONS

Thirty-four promotions (ads for upcoming programs) were transmitted over the PBS network during the week monitored.

TABLE 4.4. Occupational Classification—Adult TV Programs (including drama and music) *

CLASSIFICATION	MALE CHARACTER *No.*	%	FEMALE CHARACTER *No.*	%
Male	163	76.0	20	62.0
Neutral	20	24.0	10	32.0
Female	0	0.0	2	6.0
Total	183	100.0	32	100.0

* This is a variation of Table 9 (Isber and Cantor, 1975, p. 87). Occupations were designated for some participants, which accounts for the lack of agreement with previous tables.

One used both a man and a woman; only one of the remaining thirty-three had a female announcer. In addition to the announcer, promotions often use other characters, by showing a scene from the program. These are also likely to be male, but the proportion of female characters is higher compared with most other programming: Thirty-seven percent of the total characters were female.

CATEGORY 3—DRAMA

Two television dramas were monitored during the sample week: "Theater in America" and "Upstairs, Downstairs." In "Theater in America," eighty percent of the characters were men; twenty percent, women. In "Upstairs, Downstairs," forty percent of the characters were male and fifty-five percent female. These women were cast in female sex-typed occupations.

CATEGORY 4—MUSIC

Musical programs were difficult to analyze because performers in orchestras and choruses cannot be counted accurately. The monitors' impressions were that almost all orchestral musicians were men. At most, two women were members of the orchestra. Featured performers (soloists, duos, and trios) were almost evenly divided between the sexes.

PUBLIC TELEVISION CONTENT VERSUS COMMERCIAL TELEVISION CONTENT

If visitors unfamiliar with American society, culture, and customs were introduced to American life through adult public television, they would get a peculiar picture different from the peculiar picture offered by commercial network programming. Prime-time commercial television (8:00 p.m. to 11:00 p.m.) mostly consists of entertainment (situation comedies and dramas, some variety programs) and sports. Public affairs, and informational or cultural programs are only occasionally shown during those hours. In comparison, adult public television is devoted primarily to public affairs, and cultural and general information. The two kinds of programs cannot be compared on most dimensions. But, on both kinds of television, the content does not reflect the demographic composition of the United States. Visitors watching public television are likely to see one or more males discussing business, the economy, and government. If the visitors were watching commercial television, they might see all male sport teams or a male-dominated dramatic series(see Tedesco, 1974). The occupation of women in starring roles has changed in recent years (see Lemon, in this volume), but the proportion of women to men has remained consistent since Head did the first content analysis in 1954. The work of George Gerbner's group at the Annenberg School of Communication, has involved examining prime-time series since 1969; this work indicates that the commercial networks not only show women as a minority but also present a skewed picture of women's role in society. The studies also show that women are stereotyped in romantic or traditional roles and that masculinity and femininity are narrowly defined (Gerbner, 1972a; Turow, 1974; Tedesco, 1974).

Neither public nor commercial television reflects the heterogeneity of the population as far as sex, race, and social status are concerned. Over one-half of the population and forty percent of the work force are women, many of whom are married with children under the age of five. Also, there is little recognition that at least one-half of all minority persons are women, and that many of them (along with white women) must support themselves and possibly head a family. In March, 1972, there were 6.2 million families headed by women and twenty-five percent of these were black (United States Department of Labor, 1973). The number of female heads of household has increased in the last decade and there is no reason to believe this trend will stop.

Because public television was established as an alternative to commercial television, one might expect its message to be different from that of commercial television. However, the message from both media is clear; women lack power. In commercial television the majority of the characters are male, American, and middle and upper class (Gerbner, 1972a, p. 45; Tedesco, 1974; and Lemon, this volume, chapter 2). On public television eighty-five percent are male and most are part of the intellectual elite. The differences reflect differences in the structure and purpose of each kind of television. Commercial television is primarily an entertainment medium; public television is supposedly both instructional and entertaining. But both kinds of television are similar in their portrayal of women. Minimally integrating women in important programs and relegating them to roles that emphasize their subsidiary status, both kinds of television symbolize women's position in the larger society.

The results of this analysis as well as the analyses of commercial television provide evidence that women are not represented as integral to American life. Not only are they portrayed without power through television's neglect, but they are seen as members of a special category, not as one-half of the population. All television, whether drama, public-affairs programming, the news, or variety programs presents a constructed world. It does not mirror the everyday world, but rather is a prism through which social class, power, and sexual relations are reflected. The dominance of men in all television content and, in particular, in the content of important public-affairs programming is an indicator of the position women occupy in the larger social structure.

In private conversations, I have been told by public-television broadcasters that there are two reasons for the lack of women as commentators and participants in public-affairs broadcasting. First, these broadcasters claim, women in general are not advocating change. Activist women are defined as an interest group; other women (who make up a large part of public-broadcasting audience) supposedly do not care if participants are women. The second reason offered is circular. If women were important in policy-making structures or if activist women were perceived as having more power, more women would be seen on the screen. But this reasoning discourages women from seeking power.

The broadcasters continue: Public television should and does address itself to issues of major public importance, issues relating to the economy, to politics, to important social concerns, and to foreign affairs. Women are primarily in the home, and although their numbers have increased in the work force, they are in positions of relatively little power or importance. Women are not involved in the "important" issues except as consumers, certainly not as active participants. Thus, the broadcasters define the activist women lobbying for change as an interest group similar to Jews, Republicans, and the PTA. Broadcasters believe that women activists do not represent most women but are an elite group and a very small part of the viewing audience. Public television, according to the broadcasters, does devote more time to women's issues than does commercial television. This is difficult to dispute because most analyses have not addressed this question. However, they argue, the collapse of Cambodia and Vietnam, the Middle East crisis, inflation and depression, and the recent political upheavals in this country and elsewhere in the world are more important than equal rights for women or women's changing roles in the home and labor force.

Although public television does provide alternative programming to commercial television, its presentation of women is not more diversified. In fact, it is less so. A few high status, well-educated women appear but they are not representative of women's position in our highly differentiated and complex society. Ultimately, one must conclude, both commercial and public television disseminate the same message about women, although the two types of television differ in their structure and purposes. That message is: Women are not an important part of American society.

NOTE

* Much of the material for this paper comes from the *Task Force Report on Women* (Isber and Cantor, 1975, Section One). Except for the research findings, which the Task Force on Women of the Corporation for Public Broadcasting helped gather and report, I am solely responsible for the conclusions, analysis, and research design of the paper.

APPENDIX A: Adult TV Programs Shown during One Week Monitored*

Category 1: General Adult Programs: Panel, Documentary, News, Interview, Public Affairs, General Information

Lilias Yoga
Romagnoli's Table
Zee Cooking School
NOVA
Consumer Survival Kit
Aviation News and Weather
Firing Line
Wall Street Week
Captioned ABC News
President Ford's News Conference
Washington Straight Talk
Washington Week in Review
Black Perspective on the News
Democratic Responses to the State of the Union Message
Behind the Lines
Assignment America
Book Beat
Bill Moyers' Journal
Gerald Ford's America
Ascent of Man
Eames Celebration
The Romantic Rebellion
America
Black Journal
World Press

Category 2: Promotions

34 Television Promotions

Category 3: Drama

Upstairs, Downstairs
Theater in America

Category 4: Music

Mandolinist, Frank Wakefield
Special of the Week, A Rachmaninoff Festival

* See Isber and Cantor (1975, pp. 20–21) for the complete list of all programs monitored, including children's shows.

2

Women's Magazines

INTRODUCTION

It is difficult to make generalizations about all women; for they vary. They are members of all social classes, all races, and virtually all occupations. They have different interests and attitudes toward work and family depending upon their position in the social world. Working-class women express more traditional attitudes toward women's rights than do their more educated middle-class sisters. Middle-class black women are more likely to work outside the home than middle-class white women. And black women are more likely to favor playing an active role in the labor force than white women are.

As detailed in the Introduction to *Hearth and Home,* women's magazines pick specific target groups for their audience and then design their magazines to attract those readers. Distributed on racks next to the cashier's line in supermarkets, *Redbook* and *Ladies' Home Journal* appeal to middle-class homemakers doing their marketing. Available on newsstands and by subscription, *Ms.* is designed for liberated upper-middle class women. *True Story* tells working-class women that its stories are designed to meet their needs. Yet despite the large variation in women and in women's magazines, the chapters in this section tell us that all women's magazines ultimately project a similar image of women's feminine characteristics. Supportive of others and concerned with emotional well-being, woman supposedly strives to please. When she fails to cater to the concerns of others, she is politely damned.

In Chapter 5, Marjorie Ferguson introduces this ideology of womanhood by analyzing the covers of three traditional British women's magazines. The three weeklies reach eighty percent of British women aged fifteen and older. Ferguson describes how each designs its cover to project a specific image of the magazine with which readers may identify. And, she argues, by identifying with the photographic image on the magazine cover, buyers are encouraged to model themselves after the ideological image the magazine projects.

The magazine covers completely reject women as workers. Instead, they offer models Ferguson describes as "world-of-women women"—women in the isolation of the home, complete and happy with womanly tasks and expectations. Or they show a woman in the work place, acting as supplicant to an attractive man who will sweep her off her feet and carry her to a cozy home removed from the stresses of the supposedly male world of work.

Using content analysis, Ferguson describes how each of the three magazines offers a slightly different image of woman, her mood as indicated by facial expression and her age as indicated by hair style and cosmetics. Additionally, she tells us, each projects the notion that class is irrelevant to definitions of femininity by presenting the world of woman as a middle-class world. The magazines eschew variation by social class. Yet despite these real-life variations, Ferguson insists, the three magazines present a unified picture: All women strive to please.

E. Barbara Phillips (Chapter 6) finds these same elements in the two American women's magazines having little else in common. They are *Family Circle* and *Ms.*, the former designed for the working-class homemaker, the latter for the upper-middle class feminist. By focusing upon the occupations, social class, age, race, and ethnicity of women featured in these magazines' stories, Phillips seeks to learn what images of ideal women these magazines project. Not surprisingly, *Family Circle* purveys images of housewifery and mothercraft; *Ms.* does not. *Ms.* emphasizes women in political life and public service; *Family Circle* does not. And, when both treat the same topic, they do so in very different ways. When dealing with women in business and professional life, *Ms.* highlights women from diverse backgrounds and accomplishments. *Family Circle* features white women said to have paid a price for leaving hearth and home. *Ms.* discusses "serious" arts, painting, and literature. *Family Circle* features women in the popular arts such as movies and television. Although Phillips concludes that *Ms.* is not just another member of the *Family Circle,* she finds it stresses a key element in traditional women's magazines. Creativity and personal growth come from helping others, not from an ambitious (and supposedly male) attempt to satisfy one's own needs.

Carol Lopate continues this theme in Chapter 7. She surveys the treatment of Jackie Kennedy Onassis in twelve magazines designed for very different sorts of women. Among those included in her sample are *McCall's* and the *Ladies' Home Journal* (middle-class), *Woman's Day* and *Lady's Circle,* (working-class), *Movie Mirror* and *TV Radio Talk* (working-class), and *Time* and *Newsweek* (for men and women). She finds that each sort of magazine treats Jackie differently, as though she were a Rorschach inkblot upon which editors and readers could project their aspirations and images of women.

The middle-class women's magazines hint at Jackie's tremendous wealth but stress her inability to control her life. She is a woman formed by men, her father, and her rich husbands; she is personally incapable of banishing sadness from her life. Some working-class magazines stress that Jackie has family problems just as the magazines' readers do. She has difficulties with her teenage children. Her daughter has shown poor judgment in picking friends. The roles of wife and mother conflict. According to Lopate, others stress the passions and conflicts of Jackie's life in terms experienced by any woman in a development or housing project—basic troubles with family, religion, and sex.

Ultimately though, Lopate argues, one theme about women runs through all the images of Jackie. Work outside the home is "negative space," time between the positive moments when women act as wife and mother. It has little or no emotional meaning. When a woman fails as wife and mother, she is to be pitied or condemned. For, according to the magazines, money can't buy happiness, and any woman's happiness is linked to the activities of her man. Like Ferguson and Phillips, Lopate finds woman's role is to serve others selflessly.

Chapter 5

MARJORIE FERGUSON

Imagery and Ideology: The Cover Photographs of Traditional Women's Magazines

The world of women suggested by the covers of traditional women's magazines is one of several sex-segregated worlds our culture presents to females along with others which occur in the educational, occupational, and sporting spheres. Within society, viewed as a heterosexual totality, such women's magazines pursue a policy of purdah both in relation to their editorial content and their social role within a sex-specific market. Through their verbal and visual messages, through their titles—*Woman, Ladies' Home Journal, Elle*—they lay claim to being a gender-genre apart from all other media. Further, their claim of appealing to a world-of-women audience is advanced through an underlying and traditional ideology of femaleness based upon assumptions concerning the characteristics of their audience and its hypothesized responses.

Traditional women's magazines are defined as those magazines whose content and advertising is aimed primarily at a female audience and at female areas of concern and competence, as customarily defined within our culture. Some are directed at selected segments of this world-of-women market, specializing in such consensually agreed areas of female interest as fashion, dressmaking, or beauty; others of a more general editorial persuasion embrace the three C's of traditional role performance—Cooking, Cleaning, and Caring—but wrap them in a package of more widely based information and entertainment. Although social and economic change has produced certain differences in the normative content of the wrapping, many of the packaged goods have remained substantively the same (Ferguson, 1974, and in progress). Within a market orientation aimed at creating and maintaining a female demand-and-supply structure, these media function to transmit cultural prescriptions of female role performance. They also overtly, or by implication, prescribe the male role within society.

As part of a more extensive content analysis, this study classified and evaluated the cover photographs of the three largest circulating British women's magazines, *Woman, Woman's Own,* and *Woman's Weekly,* sampled over twenty-five years (1949 to 1974).[1] Some measure of the exceptional size of this women's weeklies market is necessary in order to understand its potential influence as a media form. Although size is not necessarily related to influence, the audience saturation levels reached by these three weeklies is unique. Notwithstanding declining circulation patterns over the previous decade, in 1974 the total weekly female readership of *Woman, Woman's Own,* and *Woman's Weekly* stood at 17,112,000 of the 21,640,000 British women aged fifteen and over. Four-fifths of these women were classified as housewives.[2]

THE SIGNIFICANCE OF COVERS

To ask "what role does the cover photograph play?" in any exchange of meanings between the magazine producers and their audience is to inquire into two distinct, but related, social processes. First, what do the producers think they are doing in selecting a certain cover image in relation to their understanding of market demographics and audience response? Second, what does the audience bring to that cover in its processes of consumer choice and perception of content?

At its simplest level, the function of the cover is to differentiate—to identify—and to sell a particular magazine. To the publishers and editors, the cover photograph is a uniquely important means of achieving that dual objective.[3] "Identify" here means the cluster of qualities designed to single out one magazine from its competitors, and producers see the cover photograph as a decisive factor in establishing and maintaining a separate brand identity within the women's media market place. To quote one editor, the cover "is like the margarine wrapper, the better it is, the more we sell."[4] (Although words, colors, typefaces and sizes are also employed in this process, their significance is relative to the primacy of the chosen picture and will not be examined here.) It follows that a principal reason for cover photographs to present images of women is to enable female audience members to recognize a "Her" magazine as opposed to a "His" magazine in which photographs of cars, boats, or voluptuaries suggest a segregated male world. In short, the reason most women's magazines feature women on the cover is that they are *about* women and the womanly topics anticipated by their female audience. The cover photograph then, insofar as it represents an editorial stance or identity, also reflects the ideological implications of content that in turn reflect the producers' perceptions of culturally agreed-upon roles, goals, and values.

In addition, producers emphasize cover photographs as potential sources of reader identification, thereby reinforcing the importance attached to their selection and presentation. The editor and art editor collaborate in producing this creative hybrid, which is part way between a billboard advertisement or bookstall poster and a weekly (or monthly) statement of the ideological and ontological status of a particular women's magazine. The impact of a particular cover makes it the object of immediate praise or criticism, covert suggestion, or overt interference, from many quarters within and outside the editorial process. Feedback to the editor on the response provoked by a particular cover can be as terse and vague as "the agents didn't like it" or "black backgrounds don't sell." Or it may be as detailed and sales-oriented as a complaint from a promotions manager that the type size for the words "Free inside" was not large enough.

This importance of the cover for reasons of sales competitiveness, continuing appeal to regular readers, and potential attraction to new readers is well understood by all women's magazine editors. Citing audience "needs" and market imperatives, an editor expressed the acuteness of this understanding as a basis for editorial action:

> "The constant problem is one of trying to find an image for a cover which truly represents an idealistic form of what the readers themselves would like to be, someone they can identify with, on the one hand, and at the same time producing it in a graphic form which will stand out from 200 other titles on newsagent bookstalls. The cover is the personality of the magazine; it is a poster; it is a hook in advertising terms to actually bring the reader into the magazine. This is a problem. I have just come back from New York and one of the reasons I went there was to look for new cover models."[5]

What is a pragmatic problem for editors is also sociologically problematic. Although this statement is representative of editors' consensus on the cover function, none were explicit about the psychosocial mechanisms involved in such hoped-for reader identifications, apart from a general view that cover photographic models should be "someone they [the audience] want to be like."[6] While treating an identification-impulse on the part of the audience as a given, what remains doubtful for them is the nature of the object to be presented. Which definitions of the desirable will be sufficient to induce an identification triggering a purchase? Rarely was conscious recognition of the subjective dimension included in editors' conceptions of this communicative intent. Namely, that a chosen cover model represents one editor's beliefs about what a particular group of readers "want to be like."

In this context, is the significance and ultimate social role of the cover its reflection of a wider cultural reality, the presentation of Identikit* portraits of "femaleness"? Is it a collective kind of mug shot not of a wanted, imperfect Man but of a perfect Woman found? The cover girl projects her possession of, and pleasure in possessing, culturally desirable attributes such as physical beauty and social importance. Her personal importance is stressed by her symbolic dualism in representing both a magazine's identity and its reader idealizations.

The extent to which the model's part in this process is creative or closely directed is a function of her skill and status as well as those of the photographer.[7] The few highly successful international cover girls can choose for whom they will pose. Their uniqueness invests them with the power to give or withhold cooperation in the event of conflict between their self-concept (make up, hair style, their "best side") and that of the editorial stylist attempting to give visible form to a specific magazine's ideology, identity, and understandings of its audience. Overwhelmingly, the majority of women's magazines use professional photographic models as the visual packaging for such complex cover messages, not only in Britain but cross-culturally.[8] For example, 93 percent of *Woman,* 96.5 percent of *Woman's Weekly,* and 87 percent of *Woman's Own* covers in the sample featured professional photographic models.

* British police use this term to refer to sketches of wanted persons composed from witness' descriptions and selections of stock features.—Eds.

THE FUNCTION OF COVER PHOTOGRAPHS

Producers' notions concerning the communicative intent of the cover image raise certain wider questions about the part it plays. These questions may be considered using the psychological and social-psychological concepts of imitative acts and identification (see Freud, 1959, pp. 37–42). Is the magazine's search for a cover identity matched by a corresponding quest for identity on the part of its audience? Do females who seek out a sex-segregated medium do so in a conscious or unconscious search for confirmation of their own femaleness?

At its simplest, the concept of identification suggests that individuals can be seen to respond to other individuals or objects by imitating their behavior symbolically or literally, as in a child's mastery of gender role and learning. Further, the motive for imitative behavior can be ascribed to feelings of threatened self-esteem or anxiety involving threatened self-esteem. In discussing these and other motives for individual responses of this nature, Kagan (1958) has pointed to the importance of the psychosocial model's possession of positive goal-states and the identifier's desire for mastery of the environment. These ideas have received the support of experimental psychology. Bandura, Ross, and Ross (1963), for example, have noted that identification occurs with those who hold or are the source of power and rewards, not with the competitors for power.

Contrast, then, the confident image of the cover girl—the smiling pleaser cast in the mold of perfection—with the cultural composite conjured up by assumptions about housewives as a social group. The traditional low status ascribed to the housewife's role, the classic context for female feelings of low self-esteem, is summed up in the perjorative label "just a housewife" (see Oakley, 1974). In this context, the commercial rationale and editorial ideology that define a woman first and foremost as a housewife or homemaker, offer confirmation that female areas of social control are confined to the domestic sphere and are based on a premise of reduced, contained, and informal power.

THE FORM OF COVERS

Returning to the nature and significance of the cover images themselves: although three-quarters and full-length poses are sometimes used, the dominant visual image is that of the "big head." It resembles the close-up shot of film and television presentations and the head and shoulder studies of portrait photography. Like the latter, it generally presents a decontextualized image emphasizing form rather than content. The only cues given are those of style, age, and social class. Like the family portrait maker, the cover photographer is engaged in *taking* a picture, in *removing* something from a closely directed but essentially passive subject/object, the female photographic model (see Milgram, 1976). What is being taken is considerably more complex than an individual portrait. The model gives form or visual expression to a particular magazine's ontology as this is mediated through editorial selection processes.

The emphasis that the majority of publishers and producers place upon the female face reflects the psychosocial importance society attaches to the human face. This importance is not confined to consumer economies of the industrial West, where a powerful cosmetics industry directs its advertising assaults on female fantasies of an increasingly more perfectly presented (and made-up) visage. In many societies the face is important in terms of status, and the bearer of an important face is doubly important. In Polynesian society, for example, the parts of the body, like the strata of society, were arranged in order of precedence; the head dominated the body because it was literally on top of it (Steiner, 1956, pp. 45–46). Simmel (in Wolff, 1959, pp. 276–81) saw the face as possessing an inner unity and an outer mobility, the latter so conducive to communication that even a limited change in facial expression could project a wide range of emotional moods and social meanings. Argyle (1975, pp. 221–28) discussed the face as a signalling agent for the nonverbal communication of status, identity, emotions, and interpersonal attitudes. It is precisely the compacted communication potential of the human face that predisposes the producers of women's magazines to emphasize its presentation on their covers.

The face of femininity displayed there looks either pleased with itself or determinedly striving to please. In consequence, the message communicated about femaleness is positive: "Not only are we 'world-of-women' women happy with our state, but we strive to ensure that everyone within our orbit, and perhaps particularly the males within it, are pleased that we're pleased." Only rarely is that orbit—the female social world—enlarged to include men. Only rarely is the male admitted to the decontextualized world of the women's magazine cover; when he is it is generally in the guise of the celebrity or the courtier.

The symbolism of the face is also important for another reason. Covers are the face of the women's magazine, as implied by editors' emphases upon wrapping their product with an identifiable image that encourages recognition and reader identification.

It should be noted that *Woman's Weekly* is a partial exception to these generalizations. In the past, that magazine frequently used the three-quarters or full-length pose on its cover. The lower communicative intensity of the nonverbal contact of these three-quarter poses is apparent. There is little of the direct eye appeal and suggestive mouth play so frequently featured on the covers of *Woman* and *Woman's Own*. The head cover photograph does not predominate. In its place are two, three, and sometimes four separate photographs of models, or groups of models, displaying knitting or sewing patterns. Until 1967, when *Woman's Weekly* was transformed from three-color to full four-color process, these covers were typical and a nationally recognized trademark. Reproduced in pink and blue ink, they resembled a patchwork poster, often showing the main knitting or sewing patterns in the foreground with smaller photographs of sweaters for men or babies' layettes in the background. Since 1967 their cover design has gradually changed and moved in the direction of one main photograph frequently featuring a single model. Nevertheless in terms of establishing and maintaining an editorial identity, *Woman's Weekly* has been the most consistent of these three weeklies in presenting a unified image of itself to its audience. It has had its own face.

THE CONTENT OF COVERS

Historically the cover images have changed in their external idealizations of the female face and form. For example, in 1949 *Woman's Own* frequently featured painted rather than photographed cover images. Some of these were the work of (or imitations of) American fiction illustrators, often showing contrived situational portraits. Such covers typically showed a boy-girl situation with the girl smiling in a slightly coy, but smugly secure way. In one example she looks into a filing cabinet while pretending to be unaware of the boy speculatively eyeing "Woman as Object" from the doorway. In another she is shown bending forward from the waist, eyes shut, lips parted expectantly for a kiss while her hand steals around to grasp the jewel box and flowers the male is hiding behind his back. The preeminence of the female figure in these tableaux and the background, supplementary or supplicatory role of the male are clearly established. This was an idealized world of flirtation and courtship, one eternally young and carefree. This was an image of Woman and Man that performed the cultural confidence trick of placing Woman in a position of apparent control within the power structure of male-female relations. The ultimate, if informally based, power adhering to the one who is The Courted rather than the one who is The Courtier confers the right of final choice on the female. This single image communicates the impression that women are superordinate or, at the very least, exercise free will, unfettered by any hint of cultural or biological determinism.[9]

Subsequently, the era of the full-color photograph characteristic of the covers of *Woman* and *Woman's Own,* from the late forties to the present, was made possible largely by the exploitation of photogravure-printing technology, much of it American.[10] With the easing of paper and currency restrictions, the stream of American art work and photography turned to a full flood. Given the extent of this imported technology and expertise (symptomatic of the wider cultural imperialist implications Schiller [1969] has fully examined), it is not surprising that the cover-girl images characterizing the face of *Woman* and *Woman's Own* throughout the fifties reflected American stylizations of womanhood as much or more than British ones during this period. With the advent of specially commissioned cover sessions by American photographers for English women's magazines, trans-Atlantic cultural influence was strong both directly in terms of volume and indirectly when English photographers copied American techniques. From the early sixties, less groomed and glossy, more naturalistic, and more Northern European female models appeared on the covers of the two largest women's weeklies, reflecting perhaps a growing awareness of a national style in the "swinging London scene" as well as a growth of European hegemony. The seventies has seen a trend back to "lip-sticky" curly-haired images, reminiscent of the fifties, less reflective perhaps of broad social and political movements than of the changing facial emphases devised by a sales-conscious cosmetics industry unhappy about the natural or unmade-up look.[11]

Despite this historical variation, each of the three weeklies attempts to specialize in a characteristic look to build readership. Guided by participant observation, interviews, and preliminary visual examination, four descriptive categories were developed to analyze the magazine covers. The labels attached to these categories reflect those used by the participants; their frequency of appearance is given in Table 5.1.[12] The four types are:

1. "Chocolate Box": half or full smile, lips together or slightly parted, teeth barely visible, full or three-quarter face to camera in both the big-head version and the three-quarter body pose. Projected mood: blandly pleasing, warm-bath kind of warmth, where uniformity of features in their smooth perfection are devoid of uniqueness or of individuality.

2. "Invitational": emphasis on the eyes, mouth shut or with only a hint of a smile, head to one side or looking back to camera. Projected mood: suggestive of mischief or mystery, hint of the female interaction potential rather than sexual promise, the cover equivalent of advertising's soft sell.

3. "Super-smiler": full-face, wide-open, toothy smile, head thrust forward or chin thrown back, hair often wind-blown. Projected mood: aggressive, "look-at-me" demanding, the hard-sell, "big come-on" approach.

4. "Romantic or Sexual": a fourth and more general classification devised to include male and female "twosomes"; or the dreamy, heavy-lidded, unsmiling big heads, often with a tinsel or tulle background, particularly favored in the fifties; or the overtly sensual or sexual.

TABLE 5.1. Distribution of Cover Categories By Title, 1949–1974

	PERCENTAGES		
	Woman N = 28	*Woman's Own* N = 24	*Woman's Weekly* N = 28
Chocolate Box	50	21	86
Invitational	22	54	3.5
Super-Smiler	14	8	3.5
Romantic or Sexual	7	4	3.5
Other	7	13	3.5

"Chocolate Box" was the dominant cover image, as Table 5.1 shows. It was preferred by *Woman* fifty percent and *Woman's Weekly* eighty-six percent of the time. *Woman's Own,* more diverse and exploratory in its editorial approach throughout the sampled issues, had only twenty-one percent in this category. The high frequency for *Woman's Weekly* is consistent with the aim expressed by its editors of presenting the reader with a regular weekly meeting with the familiar. "Chocolate Box" represented the familiar visual translation of an editorial ideology defining the female state as both pleasant and unproblematic.

The category of covers described as "Invitational" represents the second most significant group for both *Woman* (22 percent) and *Woman's Own* (54 percent), although it is rare for *Woman's Weekly* (3.5 percent). It is significant that over half of *Woman's Own* covers were in this group.

The category of "Super-smiler" occurred more frequently for *Woman* (14 percent) than for *Woman's Own* (8 percent) and *Woman's Weekly* (3.5 percent). As for the category "Romantic or Sexual," analysis revealed only one instance of the overtly sensual: a cinema actress whose professional repertoire inclines toward that role. Otherwise, the Romantic mood was dominant within this relatively insignificant category. *Woman* had 7 percent, *Woman's Own,* 4 percent, and *Woman's Weekly,* 3.5 percent. In the "Other" category, *Woman* had 7 percent, *Woman's*

Own, 13 percent, and *Woman's Weekly,* 3.5 percent. Examples of covers classified as "Other" were those showing photographs of royalty or a painting of the nativity.

As well as facial stylizations, the implied age of cover models was also examined. The topic of age is important within the demographic structure of a magazine's readership because it has powerful implications both for content and presentation and for individual positioning within an overall market through an appeal to specific advertisers. Patterns of ownership and control within the women's magazine industry are concordant with theories of mass communication stressing the impact of corporate media structures—mass production for mass consumption—on the dissemination of common or hegemonic values (for example, Tuchman, 1974). Integral to this process is the profit motive which aims media content, such as the projected age of the cover model, at definite advertising and readership targets.

The incompleteness of available data does not allow for a meaningful comparison of the readership age structure between the three titles over the entire twenty-five years. Although individual publishers attempted to monitor the characteristics of their audience before 1956, the National Readership Survey did not provide systematic data for all magazines before that year.

As the data in Table 5.2 show, despite an overall downward trend, both *Woman* and *Woman's Own* continue to have a higher proportion of readers in the fifteen (sixteen) to thirty-four-year-old age group than does *Woman's Weekly.* Nonetheless, some sixty percent of the readers of *Woman* and fifty-nine percent of *Woman's Own* readers are over thirty-five; *Woman's Weekly* shows a significantly higher share (seventy-nine percent) of readers in this group.

The three age classifications devised for the analysis of the cover photographs were those of "Teens," "Twenties," and "Any Age." The classificatory criterion was the age the model implied by a combination of physiological features, emotional expression, clothes, and accessories. A "Teens" cover typically

TABLE 5.2. Age Structure of U.K. Women's Weeklies Readership* per week (in thousands)

1957	*16–24*	*25–34*	*35–44*	*45–64*		*65+*	*Total*
Woman	1,600	1,591	1,521	2,574		906	8,192
Woman's Own	1,426	1,356	1,210	2,206		786	6,984
Woman's Weekly	486	570	567	1,019		480	3,122
1967	*16–24*	*25–34*	*35–44*	*45–54*	*55–64*	*65+*	*Total*
Woman	1,920	1,381	1,416	1,473	1,181	1,190	8,561
Woman's Own	1,657	1,253	1,153	1,229	1,069	1,044	7,404
Woman's Weekly	558	520	630	618	632	695	3,652
1974	*15–24*	*25–34*	*35–44*	*45–54*	*55–64*	*65+*	*Total*
Woman	1,365	1,121	881	1,009	879	968	6,223
Woman's Own	1,364	1,167	838	1,026	876	979	6,250
Woman's Weekly	676	660	703	780	791	1,030	4,639

* Source: NRS, IPA, and JICNARS
1957, 1967, 1974. 1957 figures for April to December only.

showed the model's hair tied in one or two bunches, or showed her snuggling up to a kitten or puppy; the expressive range of emotional and cognitive components was confined to two dimensions: young and fun.[13]

Table 5.3 shows that the predominant age group presented by cover models is that of the "Twenties." This emphasis reflects an editorial bid to attract the mid-twenties audience—the buyers of the consumer and household goods promoted by

TABLE 5.3. Age Distribution of Cover Model Images, 1949–74

	PERCENTAGES		
	Teens	*Twenties*	*Any Age*
Woman N = 28	18	68	14
Woman's Own N = 24	17	75	8
Woman's Weekly N = 28	0	50	50

major advertisers in these media. Almost a fifth of *Woman* and *Woman's Own* covers were in this category, as opposed to none of the *Woman's Weekly* sample. The model's facial expression, as well as her hair styling and clothes, was the key to differentiating a "Twenties" from a "Teens" cover. The "Twenties" image is less kittenish, less arch, and less playful. It personifies an altogether more developed and perfected expression of the female state across all four stylizations.

Finally some consideration should be given to the apparently ambiguous category of "Any Age." In editorial ideology terms, "Any Age" quite distinctly means not any age over thirty. The model who communicates her age as late twenties or even thirty is a token symbol in the direction of those females (most women) who have been qualitatively transformed from *young* readers to *just* readers. Although approximately three-fifths of the *Woman* and *Woman's Own* and four-fifths of the *Woman's Weekly* female audience are over thirty-five years old, these magazines stress the desirability of youth and the identification of beauty with youth. *Woman* and *Woman's Own* give token recognition to "Any Age." However, *Woman's Weekly,* the magazine with the oldest readership profile, devotes a full fifty percent of its covers to this group.

In sum, a degree of congruence appears between market orientation and editorial translation; however, a conflict between two types of models for identification also exists. Some covers project a fantasy-like invitation to eternal youth. Others, particularly those of *Woman's Weekly,* take a marginally more realistic approach to demography and admit the existence of a non-youthful (but never old) female population.

Discussing the form and content of traditional magazine covers, reference has been made to the decontextualized presentation of the female face including the general absence of background or situational cues. Cues discussed so far relate to styles of facial expression and implied age. A third and highly significant cue is that of social class. Elsewhere (Ferguson, in progress), I have defined the image of social class presented most frequently by women's magazines as "Consciously Classless" and argued that the customary stratification distinctions of upper, middle, and lower are insufficient in a context of collapsed boundaries and absent categories. By omission rather than inclusion, the general absence of "oppositional categories" (upper and lower class) in women's magazines presents the world of women as a middle-class world. Incorporating ambiguity in stratification, they reflect some of the wider cultural ambiguities about women's social status. Is a woman's status dependent on that of her husband or father? Or does the very fact of dependence mean that women are themselves members of a dependent, but separate, social class, as argued by some feminists?

If we accept this feminist view we must ask how that separate class position influences and is influenced by an ideology of "femaleness." What is the relationship between the generic class "woman" and its specific forms in the media? If we view women's magazines as a contributor to this social and cultural dialectic, through such mechanisms as the cover image and the identification process, then we can analyze the producers' and audiences' shared understandings as an oscillating ideology varying at any moment in the producer-audience interaction. However, the impact of the female ideology created and perpetuated by this dialectic is not confined to women. Men also read women's magazines. For the three weeklies under consideration, men have consistently formed between eighteen and twenty percent of the total readership.[14] Therefore, we must ask about the impact of this ideology of femaleness upon both male and female readers and about the impact of all readers upon one another. A problem as complex as this requires empirical investigation, especially since men play such a significant part in the reciprocal and oscillating process of defining cultural roles for women. They are particularly important in defining the social distribution of resources that bring power and in maintaining the status quo at both the domestic and societal levels.

It is a sociological truism that social control within any society can take many forms. Some of these are brutally direct, some are blatantly obvious, and some are subtly and perversely complex. Any explanation of women's magazine covers and the social processes that build ideology, image, and identity is examination of this kind of complex control. The intricate nature of such relationships reinforces the need for further cross-cultural and interdisciplinary research. Until then, the ideas offered here must be viewed as tentative theoretical formulations. Nonetheless, we may still conclude that the covers of women's magazines present the face of "femaleness" as the face of the traditional woman—the smiling pleaser our culture defines.

NOTES

[1] A note is in order concerning the nature of the study and the structure of the sample. The cover photographs discussed here were the only visual feature analyzed as part of a wider content analysis that concentrated on verbal meanings. The sample consisted of twenty-eight issues of each of the three weeklies, randomly sampled within seven purposively selected years: 1949, 1952, 1957, 1962, 1967, 1972, 1974. Eighty-four issues in all were analyzed. Working from bound volumes, all four covers of *Woman's Own* for 1952 were found to be missing, so its cover sample was reduced from twenty-eight to twenty-four.

[2] For a broader picture of the scope of the British women's magazine market, embracing some forty major titles (monthlies and weeklies) and whose top selling twenty titles had a gross readership of 60,184,000 in 1974, see M. Ferguson (1974). Note: all circulation and readership figures referred to herein may be found in the reports of the Joint Industry Committee for National Readership Surveys (JICNARS), the Institute of Practitioners of Advertising (IPA) and the National Readership Surveys (NRS).

[3] A wider investigation of the editorial processes of women's magazines was carried out in conjunction with the content analysis of the three weeklies, and based upon extensive interviews and previous participant observation. Thirty-four editors of women's weekly and monthly magazines in Britain and the United States were interviewed, as well as 106 other editorial and management personnel. (See Ferguson, in progress, chapters referring to the editorial process and the ideology of editors as an occupational group.) In addition the author

was a previous participant in this work world during the period 1960 to 1968.

[4] Personal interview, British women's magazine editor, 1975.

[5] Personal interview with the late Peter Lawrence, editor of *Woman,* 1974–76.

[6] Personal interview, British women's magazine editor, 1974.

[7] Innovation and diffusion of facial fashion may be seen as part of the wider process of creation and dissemination explored by H. Shrank and D. Gilmore (1973). An example of this process, the role of the individual professional photographic model as a potential "fashion leader," is provided by the case of the late Nicole de Lamarge, much used by *Elle* and imported to Britain by *Woman* for cover photography in 1962. Without direction she created a series of cosmetic and hair styles which simultaneously anticipated and legitimized the emphasized eyes, minimal lipstick, and straight hair characteristic of Britain facial fashions for a decade.

[8] One may speculate on the extent of segmented and fragmentary audience imitation of the model's repertoire in order to feel like the model or express her style. Is a stronger or weaker version of identification involved when an individual identifies with an anonymous model representing a desired goal such as physical perfection, or with a less perfect, but more famous female face? Do women identify with Queen Elizabeth or Jackie Onassis more readily or more completely than with an unknown cover girl? Any answer might be in part a function of how much fantasy is involved in such imitative behavior and then how far a woman might envisage herself replicating aspects of the cultural blueprints of perfection or social power presented to her.

[9] In its visual form this observation raises the question central to my wider study of this medium: to what extent do the contents of these magazines reflect the social reality of a given historical period? Or have the cover images of the British women's weeklies consciously located themselves in an idealized, ahistorical realm where the producer's aim of audience-identification is sought on a predominantly fantasy level (Ferguson, in progress)? In this case, is that fantasy pure or partial, unlimited or contained within the limits of perceived social reality?

[10] As, for example, the Dulchen process and Goss presses used during this period by Odhams, Watford, Ltd., printers of *Woman* magazine.

[11] The shifting of cover emphasis between the two erotic areas of the female face, the eyes and the mouth, is primarily a reflection of trends created and promoted by the cosmetic industry. The current movement away from the natural look of the late sixties towards a more fully made-up face with special emphasis on the lips may be related to the recent appearance of oral sex as a subject worthy of comment by these women's magazines.

[12] Both "Chocolate Box" and "Invitational" were specifically labelled by the late George Watts, Art Editor of *Woman,* 1937 to 1966. The former referred to the sugar-sweet images of femininity once used to decorate boxes of candy in Britain; the latter to a captured quality of "je ne sais quoi" attributed to certain exemplars of female charm.

[13] The "Teen" face was short-lived on the covers of *Woman* and *Woman's Own.* Largely confined to the fifties, it reflected an editorial and advertising awareness of growing teenage spending power which culminated in the creation and exploitation of a separate "young woman's" magazine market launched by *Honey* in 1961.

[14] Between 1957 and 1974 male readership has declined slightly. It varied from twenty-three and twenty percent of total readership to between twenty-one and eighteen percent. The fluctuation may be due in part to changes in sampling techniques. (See Joint Industry Committee for National Readership Surveys, 1975).

Chapter 6

E. BARBARA PHILLIPS

Magazines' Heroines: Is Ms. *Just Another Member of the* Family Circle?

Less than a decade ago John Mack Carter, editor of the *Ladies' Home Journal,* gazed out his New York office to the nearby headquarters of *Look* and *Life.* He didn't question "the importance of what they're doing." But, he wondered, "Does anyone really care? Do people need those magazines?" Then he looked down at a copy of his successful *Journal,* patting it with affection. "Our readers need this," Mack said. "I know it" (quoted in Welles, 1972, p. 27).

Apparently editor Mack put his finger on the formula for magazine success in the television age—reader need. Many mass magazines of general interest, like *Look* and *Life,* have since become extinct. Others have quietly retrenched, decreasing their circulation numbers while upgrading the kinds of readers they attract (preferably the relatively young, urban, and consumption-prone segment of the population). Meanwhile, Mack's *Journal* and other mass periodicals appealing to specialized audiences have done well. As a former business editor of *Life* pointed out, "The most financially successful magazines of the past ten years have designed to appeal to highly particularized intellectual, vocational, and avocational interests and are run by editors who know precisely what they are saying and to whom they are saying it" (Welles, 1972, p. 31).

Women in America have been considered a specialized audience since at least 1837 when Sarah Josepha Hale started editing *Godey's Lady's Book.* (Incidentally, *Godey's,* the first American magazine published for women, became the nation's first popular, mass magazine.) Yet, women have long been viewed as a much more homogeneous market for magazines than men. That is, their interests were—or were assumed to be—less fragmented, and this is reflected at the newsstand. Magazines edited primarily for men run the gamut of leisure-time and work interests, from *Sports Illustrated, Motor Trend, Gun World, Popular Mechanics, Fortune, Playboy,* and *Esquire* to "adult" publications such as *Stag.* But women's magazines remain largely in the narrow fashion-food-home mold. They serve as family gatekeeper, controlling the flow of salad dressings and soapsuds into the home; and women have traditionally represented an easy-to-reach mass market. Accordingly, large-circulation magazines edited for women (and their advertisements) have featured women as homemakers or, in the case of Helen Gurley Brown's *Cosmopolitan,* women who can catch a man and become homemakers.

Family Circle, billed as "The World's Largest-Selling Woman's Magazine," exemplifies the most traditional homemaker fare. Nearly eight million people pay thirty-five cents for it monthly as they check out at the supermarket counter. Its table of contents reveals its orientation at a glance: regular sections on fashion/decorating, food/nutrition, beauty, health, and money management. Published since 1932, its readers know what to expect—family and consumer advice, not information on how to swap husbands, or why consumption should be curbed for ecological well-being, or what emotional rewards accompany singlehood.

This traditional house-and-garden variety of women's magazines still dominates the market, but the narrow spectrum has expanded somewhat since the early 1970s. For the social forces that gave rise to what is loosely termed "the women's movement" and the movement itself have left their mark on the magazine world, as literary newcomers *WomenSports* and *Ms.* demonstrate. Buttressed by the movement, *Ms.*, for instance, was born in 1971 when a group of women met in New York City to put together a national monthly—by women, for women. Within weeks of the first issue in 1972, over 20,000 letters from readers supporting "our" magazine poured in. With awe, *Ms.* announced that it had "tapped an emerging and deep cultural change that was happening to us, and happening to our sisters." This change perceived by *Ms.* became translated into articles about world issues, national problems, and women's achievements outside the home: Third World political prisoners, the UN, unknown artists, and women's studies programs. By 1975, the abbreviation "Ms." had become an accepted form of address and the magazine claimed a circulation of 380,000.

Both *Ms.* and *Family Circle,* like other media products appealing to specialized audiences, compete in the marketplace by creating a distinct identity and by making themselves "needed." One way to capture reader loyalty is to tailor nonfiction features about women to the specific audience, hoping that readers will identify with the heroines portrayed. This is sound business too; advertisers believe that reader loyalty will carry over to their products, thus spurring sales.

Aside from a prescription for financial health, this editorial-advertising formula for success—reader identification and specificity—provides an opportunity to compare the kinds of women portrayed in the homemaker-oriented and feminist-oriented periodicals. Taking *Family Circle* and *Ms.* as representatives of these two ideal types, this chapter will explore the range of female role models presented by each type.

One caveat should be noted at the outset. Media analysts debate whether any mass-media product creates or reflects "needs" and "wants." In other words, do people get what they want or want what they get? But, either way, it can be assumed that women featured in magazines become "important vehicles of social values" (Johns-Heine and Gerth, 1949, p. 105). For women's magazines can act as silent persuaders, conveying and reinforcing norms and values. Further, clues to changing norms and values in American society may be revealed via a comparison of the current crop of nonfiction heroines with magazine heroes and heroines of a past era.

CONTENT ANALYSIS OF CONTEMPORARY HEROINES

To establish the range of female role models available in homemaker-oriented and feminist-oriented women's magazines, this analysis will focus on one dimension—occupation. It will pose one simple question: What do the women chosen by *Ms.* and *Family Circle* as subjects of feature stories or biographies do? Secondarily, it will examine the social backgrounds of the heroines—their race, ethnic identity, age, class origins, and nationality. Finally, it will investigate the attitudes toward the heroines, as conveyed by the writers' word choices; the excerpts used in the analysis are suggestive, indicating the tone of the nonfiction portrayals.

Using a random selection of *Ms.* and *Family Circle* issues between 1974 and 1976 one learns that the two magazines differ in terms of the attention they give to individual women as well as the role models they present.[1] To begin with, *Ms.* spotlighted 120 specific women in eight issues while *Family Circle* featured only 18 women in twice as many issues.[2]

Not unexpectedly, given the differences in readership and presumed "needs," the distribution of occupations is most dis-

TABLE 6.1. Distribution of Biographies and Features about Women According to Occupation in *Ms.* and *Family Circle* between 1974–76

	Ms. (8 sample issues)		*Family Circle* (16 sample issues)	
	No.	%	No.	%
Political life and public service	58	48	0	0
Business and professional	19	16	5	28
Entertainment				
"Serious arts"*	23	19	0	0
Popular arts and sport†	9	8	1	6
Housewifery, mothercraft‡	0	0	11	61
All other§	11	9	1	6
Total	120	100	18	101§§

* This subcategory includes literature, fine arts, dance, theater.

† This subcategory includes cartoon art, pop music, and television.

‡ This category includes women whose fame or status derives from their husband's fame or fortune (e.g., Betty Ford) and those whose claim to fame rests on domestic service to the rich or powerful (e.g., Ethel Kennedy's housesitter).

§ This category includes such varied persons as Kathryn Kuhlmann, the evangelist; women who have attained notoriety for their feminist stands or sexual identity (e.g., Jan Morris), and a young girl who exemplified personal courage in the face of physical disability.

§§ Error due to rounding.

similar. Table 6.1, which summarizes the occupational data, shows that *Family Circle*'s norm is the homebody: the wife or mother. "Back-to-home movement," for example, depicts five professionals who gave up full-time jobs to become full-time mothers. The question that these five white, middle- or upper-middle class housewives asked themselves was succinctly put by one of them: "Do you owe more to yourself than to your children?" All five, the author writes, "felt a subtle, unspoken pressure to give up their jobs, settle down, and be home for their husbands and children." Other articles, focusing on political wives of the famous, such as Betty Ford, emphasize intimate details of their private life, turning readers into inside dopesters. Readers are told, for instance, that Cornelia Wallace "wears little makeup" and "engages in facile conversation."

In stark contrast, not a single *Ms.* heroine is primarily a homemaker. While *Ms.* heroines may indeed be wives and mothers as well as writers, politicos, or professionals, this side of their lives is downplayed, if mentioned at all. Instead of asking, "Do you owe more to yourself than to your children?", *Ms.* implies a very different question: "What do you owe to the larger society?"

In the *Ms.* sample, the largest percentage of heroines come from political life and public service. This group includes a cross section of women, including a teenage African freedom fighter; a Puerto Rican union organizer; Vietnamese prisoners of conscience; a Chinese-American assemblywoman from California; and a middle-aged, high-echelon bureaucrat in France. Many of these personalities are extolled for their personal courage and their dedication to causes above self, for which they fought and sometimes died. Emily Wilding Davison, a British suffragette and an exemplar of selflessness, "sacrified her life by throwing herself under the King's horse during the [English] Derby as a protest against the treatment of women everywhere."

While *Ms.* heroines vie for political office, fight wars of liberation, and struggle against injustice, *Family Circle* ignores the political realm altogether. In the sample of sixteen issues, there were no personalities in political life or public service, except those who married into it, like Betty Ford. This pattern is reminiscent of the editorial instructions of editor Hale of *Godey's Lady's Book* in the nineteenth century; she refused to publish "disquisitions on politics or theory because we think other subjects are more important to our sex, and more proper for our sphere." Times haven't changed that much, at least in the pages of *Family Circle*.

However, both magazines reflect the increasing number of

women in business and professional spheres. *Ms.* introduces its readers to a varied group, from *Newsweek*'s Katharine Graham, "the most powerful woman in America," to the chairperson of Puerto Rican Studies at a New Jersey college. Again, as in the case of its political personalities, *Ms.* tends to highlight the relatively unsung heroine—a Kashmiri doctor who fought Muslim tradition; a Boston newspaperwoman who spoke out against anti-Semitism in the 1940s; and a housing specialist in Massachusetts who helped organize community action. And *Ms.* does not concentrate all its attention on white, middle- or upper-middle class women. Instead, there are black surgeons, Hong Kong factory workers, and Indian educators. This array may reflect a conscious effort by *Ms.* editors to break down class, race, and national barriers historically serving as obstacles to feminist consciousness. The founder of a direct mail firm and her employees are praised, for instance, because the business "transcended age, socioeconomic class, and everything else that could possibly separate women from each other." This attentiveness to women of varying backgrounds may also be rooted in a political vision, a liberal vision that emphasizes interpersonal equality and social responsibility to provide equal opportunity for all.

Again, the business-professional heroines in the *Family Circle* sample differ greatly from those in *Ms.* First, the author's attitude toward the subject is shown in that the "price" of leaving hearth and home is often noted. In television newscaster Barbara Walters' case, readers learn that reaching the top of the professional heap "may have cost Barbara some of the softness and femininity other women would not be willing to sacrifice." Second, the heroines are—to a woman—lily-white Americans. Further, they tend to be well-born, famous, and long-dead, such as Jane Addams. This neglect of women from minority group and lower-class backgrounds may reflect the editors' perceptions of audience wants, rather than their own notions of who counts in society. Differences in magazine content, after all, do reflect differences in the composition of the readership. Perhaps editors assume that housewives yearn vicariously to share the excitement of the famous and well-to-do. Thus, they provide gossip for the masses, adding reminders at the same time of the emotional joys of being an anonymous housewife. In any case, the formula works, as the circulation figures indicate, and there is little correspondence between the generally high status of *Family Circle* heroines and the generally lower status of the homemakers who read about them. Conversely, *Ms.*, the higher-priced periodical, selling for $1.00 at the newsstand and advertising products and services appealing to the relatively educated and affluent (for example, openings in the Department of State, and subscriptions to *Psychology Today* and the Literary Book Guild), seems to bend over backwards to introduce its readers to lower-status heroines.

Another notable difference between the traditional and feminist-oriented ideal types concerns the type of entertainer-heroine portrayed. *Ms.* emphasizes what was once called "high" or "serious" art—theater, fine arts, literature, and dance.[3] Poets, writer-intellectuals, composers, and painters predominate. Even popular or mass-culture personalities, such as television comedienne Lily Tomlin and singer Helen Morgan, become "serious" artists in the authors' hands. Pop singer-composer Laura Nyro, for example, "is first of all a poet [who] writes her own gospel, the metaphors mixed with a secret metaphysic in mind." On the other hand, *Family Circle*'s sole heroine from the entertainment field, Valerie Harper, is portrayed as neither serious nor self-propelled; the "real" Rhoda of the television sitcom series needed a nudge from "her husband who virtually kicked her out of the kitchen and back onto the nearest stage."

In sum, then, the new *Ms.* is far from just another member of the *Family Circle*. While the majority of *Family Circle* women remain tied to homespun activities and a narrow world of self-centered and family concerns, *Ms.*'s women think about Great Issues and participate in Social Welfare. *Ms.* sends out its message loud and clear: The New Woman is independent, serious, and productive. Heroines of the New Order are culturally important, politically engaged, economically productive, and socially active.

With less than five percent of *Family Circle*'s readership, *Ms.* represents a minority view of female role models and expected behavior patterns, a view that is in tune with emerging models of women in American society. Further, *Ms.* itself reflects a minority cultural view, that of the upper middle class. The values it transmits and its content (for example, numerous biographies of individual achievement, the women's liberation movement, and the possibilities open to women) are part of what Herbert Gans (1974) has called "the taste culture" of the upper middle class, that is, a set of values and cultural forms specific to well-educated "professionals, executives and managers and their wives who have attended the 'better' colleges and universities" (1974, p. 81).

Family Circle, conversely, reflects the dominant culture in America today, that of the middle and lower middle class. According to Gans (1974, pp. 85–86), the users or public of lower-middle culture seem "to be less interested in how society works than in reassurance that it continues to abide by the moral values important in lower-middle-class culture. . . . Its heroes are ordinary people, or extraordinary ones who turn out to be ordinary in that they accept the validity of traditional virtues." Following Gans's line of thought, it can be inferred that homemaker-oriented magazines, like *Family Circle,* systematically glorify traditional values and female role models at a time when women's public roles are undergoing change; praise for the good wife and mother acts to reassure readers, to reaffirm their own moral values in the face of competing definitions of "reality."

BABY, HAVE YOU REALLY COME A LONG WAY?: HEROIC FIGURES, PAST AND PRESENT

In a satirical sketch, typical of the era, Washington Irving wrote that his "Aunt Charity Cockloft" was a "great beauty, and an heiress withal, [but] never got married . . . she declined all attention of the gentlemen and contented herself with watching over the welfare of her fellow creatures" (1808; rpt. 1962, p. 5). The comedy of the portrait of this lady, published in an 1808 issue of *Salmagundi* magazine, lay in its role reversal, its total departure from the norm of female behavior. Women were expected to be dependent, unproductive, and unliberated from household cares.

Just about a century later, college student and future anthropologist Ruth Benedict told her diary, "We turn in our sleep and groan because we are parasites—we women—because we produce nothing, say nothing" (in Filene, 1974, p. 23). Benedict's feeling that men alone were socially productive agents was mirrored in mass magazines of the general period. During the early part of this century, women were rarely featured as subjects of magazine biographies; their life stories were not considered models for emulation. Fictional heroines played the role of happy homemaker and later, in the 1920s and 30s, also the successful career woman who suffers emotionally for her achievement (see Johns-Heine and Gerth, 1949). Given that norms of female behavior had largely remained intact since Washington Irving's day, this magazine treatment of women is not surprising.

What may be surprising, however, is how much pre-World War I magazine heroes resemble *Ms.* heroines of today. Both sets of heroic figures are, in large proportion, what Leo Lowenthal (1944) calls "idols of production." That is, they are rooted in the socially productive life—politics, business, the professions. In a content analysis of the *Saturday Evening Post* and *Collier's,* two carriers of common American success themes, Lowenthal found that prewar magazine biographies focused on political figures, just as *Ms.* does now. Further, as Table 6.2 shows, over three-quarters of the entertainers spotlighted by the *Post* and *Collier's* in the 1901–1914 era came from the realm of "serious" art or, like Charlie Chaplin, represented a "serious" attitude toward their art. Again, the parallel to *Ms.* heroines is striking; seventy-two percent of its entertainers are "serious" artists, and even those classified as pop culture figures are often portrayed as having a serious attitude toward their art, like Laura Nyro.

Between 1901 and 1914 and between 1940 and 1941, there was a sea change in the pattern of heroic figures portrayed in *Post* and *Collier's* biographies. Table 6.2 outlines this big switch from idols of production to "idols of consumption" (Lowenthal, 1944, rpt. 1961). By World War II, almost every magazine

TABLE 6.2. Proportion of Biographies of Men and Women in Differing Occupations in *SEP/Collier's* in Selected Years and Proportion of Female Biographies and Features in *Ms.*, 1974–76

	Saturday Evening Post/Collier's				*Ms.*
	1901–14	1922–30	1930–34	1940–41	1974–76
Political life	46%	28%	31%	25%	48%
Business & professional	28	18	14	20	16
Entertainment	26	54	55	55	27
Serious art	77	38	29	9	72
	100%	100%	100%	100%	91%*

Data on *Saturday Evening Post* and *Collier's* comes from Leo Lowenthal (1944; rpt. 1961), Tables 4-1 and 4-2, pp. 111–12.
* Nine percent of *Ms.* heroines were classified as "other." See Table 6.1.

hero in some way "related to the sphere of leisure time: either he does not belong to vocations which serve society's basic needs (e.g., the heroes of the world of entertainment and sport), or he amounts, more or less, to a caricature of a socially productive agent" (1961, p. 115).

With its idols of production rather than consumption, *Ms.* appears to be out of synch with the times. At first glance, the feminist-oriented magazine appears to be replicating the themes and values of a bygone era. Viewed from this angle, it might be inferred that *Ms.* heroines are staging a dramatic role reversal. That is, in this century magazines heroines (and American women in general) have been tied to the sphere of consumption. In the 1970s, with new opportunities, they can—for the first time—become idols of production. In this view, women are merely catching up to where men were sixty or seventy years ago.

Yet *Ms.* heroines are hardly female look-alikes for earlier male idols of production. Biographies of the 1901–1914 period were characterized by themes of upward social mobility, personal success, and rags-to-riches fortune. The classic success story featured the "self-made man"—Horatio Alger-like figures, captains of industry, and the rich and the powerful. These personalities reflected an optimistic era, an era of rugged individualism and social Darwinism. Generally, there was a belief in the American dream that the rungs of its social ladder could be climbed by anyone.

Ms.'s idols of production, by contrast, are rarely described as "self-made women" who have climbed the ladder of success and status; instead, most often they are exemplars of people who improved the lot of others, who struggled for social (not personal) goals. This emphasis may reflect a larger shift in American values away from an exaltation of the business hero to praise for more democratic values, including group instead of self-betterment; it may also signal the closing of the frontier of vast opportunity (or disbelief in the myth that promoted the

"American dream"). It is noteworthy that female dedication to social causes is rewarded neither by upward mobility, prestige, nor love. Instead, "virtue is its own reward." For *Ms.* heroines, self-actualization comes from helping others, from producing beautiful music, from making a notable contribution to society. It is vaguely ironic that virtues long considered "feminine" (for example, selflessness or dedication to causes above self, traditionally those of the family rather than the larger society) fuse with elements long considered "masculine" (for example, independence and autonomy) to produce the *Ms.* heroine: the New Woman for the New Order.

Just how new is this New Woman and New Order? *Ms.* heroines, blending the traditionally masculine roles of achievers and traditionally feminine feelings, appear to affirm the hotly debated view that "anatomy is destiny." For *Ms.*, like much of the mainstream of the women's movement, implies not only that women are somehow *different*—and better—but that the world will be more humane when women hold important positions. Ironically, at the personal level this view locks women into so-called "feminine consciousness" and at the political level, into conserving the existing social order, albeit with a gentle touch. Ultimately, *Ms.* heroines are liberal, but not liberated. Such a vision of the New Woman precludes the possibility both for radical psychic and social evolution that Carl Jung had in mind when he said, "The modern woman stands before a great cultural task, which means perhaps, the beginning of a new era" (quoted in White, 1972, p. 57). And, such a vision precludes the possibility of an alternative social order from which a New Person might possibly emerge.

NOTES

[1] A New York based free-lance writer notes that some authors contribute to both of these women's magazines (personal communication, summer 1977). Since *Family Circle* offers better pay than *Ms.* and also

provides an expense account, these authors take some of their ideas for feminist articles to *Family Circle.* Although the size of the overlap between *Ms.* and *Family Circle* authors remains unknown, its existence suggests that differences in these magazines' portrayal of women result from editorial policies.

[2] Readers of women's homemaking magazines, such as *Family Circle,* probably consume fewer nonfiction articles (except for "how-to-do-it" and "fix-it" features) than readers of feminist-oriented magazines like *Ms.* (See Gans, 1974, pp. 86–87 for speculation on the different tastes of magazine publics.) Accordingly, to maximize the possible range of role models in traditional magazines, twice the number of *Family Circle* issues were used in this analysis.

[3] Sociologist Herbert Gans, for one, argues that the difference between popular or mass culture and high culture has been exaggerated and that furthermore they are "equal in value" to the extent that each reflects the particular standards and characteristics of their publics (1974). However, the dichotomy will be maintained here for purposes of comparisons that follow.

Chapter 7

CAROL LOPATE

Jackie!

For years, Jackie Kennedy Onassis has been a heroine for women's magazine readers. Any month of the year one can find her on the cover of half-a-dozen women's magazines. In early 1975, I surveyed twelve women's magazines in order to take a new look at "the Feminine Mystique." In contrast to Betty Friedan (1963), who had coined the term partly after looking at magazine fiction, my focus was solely on Jackie—Jackie as a popular heroine. Her second husband, Aristotle Onassis, died during the spring, and thus the turmoil surrounding his death and Jackie's inheritance filled the pages of the women's magazines, as well as the weekly news magazines, for a large part of the year.

While Betty Friedan had reviewed only those magazines serving middle-class women, I looked at both middle- and working-class magazines. Friedan had made the image of women seem uniform. But reading a wide range of magazines showed how, in fact, the images vary with the class of readers the magazines are trying to reach.

Magazines gear themselves toward women with a specific

amount of money to spend and who have a certain parameter of social possibilities and aspirations. Those magazines aimed at middle- or upper-middle-class readers play down the role of mothering and stress the importance of consuming: shopping, decorating, and attending cultural events, for example. Those magazines intending to reach working- and lower-class women, on the other hand, minimize these costly activities and focus instead on the activity that all women are biologically capable of—being a mother. Advertisements, which lie face to face with almost every page of copy, help to delineate these differences. What may look like a "liberated" or feminist point of view in one magazine, can therefore be seen instead as economic privilege that allows the readers with more money to purchase large-scale items—automobiles, life insurance, air travel—and to create more autonomous life styles.

McCall's and the *Ladies' Home Journal* contained several articles on Jackie during the winter and spring of 1975, all of which detailed "daily life" in society in such a way as to indicate her vulnerability and so draw out the tragedies that can occur to the rich. The *Ladies' Home Journal* piece was an excerpt from a teenage diary written and illustrated jointly by Jacqueline and Lee Bouvier twenty-three years earlier. The passage described the girls' experiences during an evening of chamber music among Parisian society. Its human interest lay in the girls' snobbishness and enchantment with royalty and wealth, as well as in their fears of doing something wrong and embarrassing themselves.

The daily life of the rich also supplied much of the interest in three *McCall's* articles, although here what softened the portrait of lavish wealth was the poignancy of loss and sorrow, rather than the nervousness of little girls. The earliest, a memoir written by Jackie's interior decorator in the period after Jack Kennedy's assassination, described several visits in which the widow requested rapid redecorating of one home after another, including, finally, the Skorpios estate. But the flamboyance and waste of wealth was merely a luxurious setting for the decorator's "intimate moments" with the widow. Although periodically surprising the man with rushed phone calls from homes that needed decorating, Jackie appeared as the lonely tragic housewife and mother. Her concerns were with her home and her children.

The second article, a portrait of Onassis, and indirectly of Jackie, published shortly after the Greek merchant's death, contained the same themes of high life and its vulnerability. Jackie and Onassis were pictured as lonely and misunderstood by their friends and acquaintances as well as each other.

The third *McCall's* article made its theme the tragedy of Jackie's wealth. Published in early summer, the article was advertised as "a penetrating new look at a legendary woman who has always seemed to have 'everything'—but never enough." Personal entanglements surrounding Onassis's death and Jackie's inheritance possibilities were detailed. But most of the space was devoted to drawing a psychological portrait of Jackie, on the one hand, and of the *McCall's* readers who are assumed to be so involved with her, on the other.

For the author, the tragedy of Jackie's wealth was twofold: both her obsession with it, and our unrealistic expectations of her in relationship to it, given her handicapped past. For those who looked on: "Jacqueline Kennedy and money always seemed to go together, and that certainly was part of our fascination with her. All through the years during which the world admired her most, her lifestyle, which was firmly grounded in money—pots of money—was what we gaped at, looked up to, and let's face it, enjoyed." Yet, according to the author, when Jackie let the "workaday underpinnings" of her glamorous life show, she was both less than she might ideally be and a great disappointment to her watchers. When we learned about "unpaid bills, wild extravagances and spats about money with two husbands, and it appears that Jacqueline really *cares* about money, bickers about it like a mere mortal, and really likes most to spend it on herself, we are first disillusioned and then increasingly cynical about her and finally feel somewhat betrayed." The ethic of *McCall's* thus differentiates between what is disillusioning in a man and in a woman. Onassis may wheel and deal for his empire, but Jackie should have money and spend "pots of it," without being conscious of it or touched by it. She sould remain untainted by the hard world of cash flow.

Having criticized her heroine for allowing us to see below the fairy princess surface to the greed and maneuverings, however, the author created a psychological profile to clear Jackie of her soiled reputation. It was not that Jackie was bad. Rather, she has been formed by men who have made life difficult for her. "She is one of those women who is entirely the creation of men—Jack Bouvier's daughter, Jack Kennedy's wife, and Aristotle Onassis's wife." Everything has gone wrong for her, "*everything,* she had a dreadful childhood. And two rotten marriages." Thus, although we may not be able to admire her any more, we will have to "sympathize with her enormously and believe that a woman who had from childhood on known sadness cannot be called upon to bear the burden of *our* fantasies and expectations."

In sum, the article defended Jackie by asserting that she is not responsible for her actions. Most important for the readers, there is the implication that a bad marriage, like a bad childhood, has nothing to do with the person involved. It is outside her power. Women lose their identity in the men to whom they are married (just as they presumably lost it to their fathers first). In merging, they become what they have passed through, without ever having made their own lives themselves. Since Jackie has lived in the shadow of gods—two financial titans and a political hero—her passive stance toward her life takes on the quality of tragedy. She is a character who cannot do differently because of the monumentality of the men who have formed her.

The *McCall's* and *Ladies' Home Journal* articles assumed a strong identification among the readers with the niceties of wealth. Like most mainstream magazines, these articles rest on the presupposition that the wealthy have the right to their money, including the right to spend it as lavishly as their pleasure leads them. Neither politics nor Puritanism are assumed to interfere with the readers' vicarious enjoyment of the world of wealth—as long as it can be seen to have its human vulnerabilities.

In the working-class magazines, from *Woman's Day, Family Circle* and *Lady's Circle* to the television/movie and gossip/confession magazines, one finds a dramatic shift in the image of Jackie. No longer is she a society lady involved in spending money; now she is a wife and mother, caring (or not caring) for her husband and children. Jackie, and in fact all the Kennedys, are popular topics in these magazines. But in all of them, the details of finances and high life-style are either omitted or asserted to be irrelevant in order to make "ordinary" people out of the characters.

The July 1975 issue of *Lady's Circle,* for example, focused on Jacqueline Onassis's role as mother. According to the article, "it wouldn't matter if Jacqueline Onassis had a billion or a trillion dollars . . . she is in exactly the same boat as you are when it comes to raising teenagers." The article documented Jackie's motherly concern about whom her daughter was dating by quoting a report that when Caroline recently went out with a rock drummer, "Jackie put her foot down." But while the article included the information that the rock group was unemployed and that, " 'Caroline is said to feel that she is a victim of her mother's old-fashioned and out-dated class consciousness,' " it made nothing of the probability that the sons of most *Lady's Circle* readers would be in exactly that social class that Jackie was trying to keep her daughter away from. Rather, the question was made to be the universal one of how to keep teenagers away from trouble or the wrong people.

The article also presented Jackie as having been caught in the conflict between the role of wife and the role of mother; moreover, it explained her choosing the latter as her husband's advice, or even command. Jackie's intercontinental travels before Onassis's death were merely an attempt to be both at her husband's side and with her children as much as possible, according to the article. They were the result of the terrible problem of having one's family in two places at once. "Ari, reportedly, told her to return to the United States to be with her children and see the documentary on television that Caroline had had a part in working on in Tennessee." Not only did Ari understand her role as mother in this instance, but, "No doubt, he wanted to spare her sitting with another dying husband." Thus Ari was also thinking of Jackie's tragic past; he was putting her welfare before himself. And Jacqueline was taking her orders from Ari; she would be responsible for neither staying nor going.

While the article asserted that Jackie's new widowhood would free her to "devote herself" to her children, it warned that they had been left without a "father figure." The author reminded the readers, "These are not going to be easy days for the still young widow trying to raise two lively teenagers without a man around the house." The implication was, of course, that Ari had "been around the house." Finally, putting the case even more strongly than the *McCall's* piece, the *Lady's Circle* article asserted that, "Jackie's no woman's liberationist—for her, men have always held the answers in life."

Thus the article converted what rich and powerful men have given Jackie into a more palatable form which *all* women theoretically can get from men, that is, strength and emotional support, as well as advice and orders. But it also concluded with the important message: Women cannot be alone, and men both take care of women and bear responsibility for women's lives.

In the television/movie and gossip/confession magazines, a third Jackie emerges: one who is caught in a web of family, sex, and sin. But the world of these magazines is also one of allusions and false leads, for the reader is constantly given a scent or insinuation, only to have it pulled back, to be told, in effect, that she had something more shocking or dirty on her mind than what was really happening. This is the world of false promises, hearsay, and deception that surrounds millions of women—made into an art form that titillates with, at the same time as it mirrors, the dead-ended maze of this kind of existence.

The July *TV Radio Talk* and the August *Movie Mirror* contained Jackie stories. The latter led with the headline:

JACKIE RETURNS TO THE CHURCH!
REVEALED: THE SHOCKING SIN
SHE MUST PAY FOR

instantly calling up visions of sexual and other transgressions. But the article itself was about Onassis's death, framed in terms of Jackie's conversion to Eastern Orthodoxy upon her marriage to him, and the hope and prayer of the Kennedys that she would return to Catholicism and to their fold now that her husband was dead. In this case, the "sin" was that Jackie was away from Onassis when he died—perhaps not even taking care of her children. "While her husband was in the American Hospital in Paris, Jackie was shopping at Ungaro's, visiting the Louvre three times, dining with friends in famous restaurants and cafes, going to the hairdresser and even seeing *The Towering Inferno."* Thus Jackie's sin, in the article's own words, was a "sin against decorum." Apparently a wife need not love her husband or feel sorrow at his death, but she ought to look as if she does, and Jackie may well have been having fun.

As for the payment for Jackie's "sin": "There are reports that while she was away, and Christina hovered around his bedside, Ari changed his will!" Jackie paid for her carelessness by losing part of her potential inheritance. After making calculations as to Jackie's financial condition, the article ended on a quasi-religious note: "Certainly no one can deny that Jackie is any less in need of God's love and forgiveness than the rest of us. And Jackie still has many friends. Like Rose and Caroline Kennedy, they must be praying for her now, praying that God will extend to

Jackie the same forgiveness that all people pray for, and that for her all the tragedy and loss are now in the past." Although the article provided the reader with enough hints to condemn, it was ultimately forgiving. Paralleling the message about responsibility these articles give readers, the authors themselves do not want responsibility for their descriptions. If they pass judgment, it is behind their own backs.

The *TV Radio Talk* article took the "bad Jackie" image a step further, resulting in the theme of familial eroticism. On the cover of the magazine were photographs of Jackie and Edward Kennedy, separated by the title:

JACKIE MAKES TEDDY FATHER AGAIN!
THE TRUTH ABOUT THE BABY SHE HID FROM THE WORLD

Do we all have dirty minds, or do these articles make us have them? Inside were pictures of Jackie and Ted, interspersed with photos of other Kennedys, as well as of Jackie and Onassis. Only by reading deep into the article could one discover the truth about the title. "Jackie makes Teddy father again" meant that, since Jackie had no husband, Ted would probably play the role of father for her children. "The truth about the baby she hid from the world" referred to a child Jackie had while still married to Jack Kennedy—a child who lived only a few days and whom, in fact, most people who read newspapers did know about at the time.

However, the intimacy between Jackie and Ted implied in the title was carried through with further intimations inside the article: "Teddy and Jackie have shared both joy and heartbreak. When Ted's father, Joseph Kennedy, was dying, Jackie spent all night alone with Ted in his father's bedroom—to help him bear the burden of that loss." Or again: "Today, Ted is still the man Jackie turns to when she needs someone to lean on. But few people realize the extent of their friendship."

What is important in the *Lady's Circle* article, and even more so in the *TV Radio Talk* and *Movie Mirror* pieces, is that Jackie's life has been reduced to those passions and conflicts available to any woman in a housing development, a housing project, or a trailer park. Although Jackie is more glamorous and she has more freedom than any of the readers, this aspect of her life only filters through and gives glitter to her more basic struggles of family, sex, childrearing, and religion. These are the kinds of social boundaries available to women without any money to maneuver with, women whose lives in all these areas are often equally stormy, or at least have that potential.

Both *Time* and *Newsweek* ran articles on Jackie during the early months of 1975; but the theme was the question of the Onassis estate. Although both news magazines included a good deal of the same information as the women's magazines, this formed the padding that rounded out the news and was not the core—at least apparently—of the articles. For these magazines, details of romantic involvements, shopping, and children are the stuff of "gossip," not news.

The distinction between news and gossip symbolizes and reflects both the hierarchy between men and women and the general difference between women's and men's relationship to real political and economic power. This distinction exists between the sexes within the same class. Much of what the middle-class women's magazines discuss is considered gossip by the hard news standards of the general news magazines, which are aimed at the same, or an even lower, class of men.

But among the women's magazines, class differences in the readers can also be related to different attitudes toward news and gossip. The proportion of news to gossip declines as one moves down the socioeconomic scale. The middle-class magazines such as *McCall's* and the *Ladies' Home Journal* are written in a style that de-emphasizes news, even when it is included, and focuses instead on human interest and the psychological world—on the details of family and social life. Thus even when women may be discovering the same "facts" as men are, they are at the same time being told that these facts do not hold the same priority in their world.

The working-class reader of *Lady's Circle* or the gossip magazines, by contrast, is excluded from much of even the background "facts." For her, the world has been reduced to hearsay, inferences, false leads, and insinuations about the private lives of the rich, successful, or aristocratic. The very writing style, laden with the language of gossip ("a friend said," "there is evidence that"), belies the distance between these women and what is really going on. Symbolic and symptomatic of this distance, even the commodities that are advertised in these magazines can only be purchased through mail order. They cannot be seen, touched, judged, or witnessed in advance.

Yet these women's magazines are not separate from politics. Without ever conveying any of the real issues of the political and economic relationships of the country, these magazines are important in forming public opinion in the political arena. The portrayal of Jackie in all the magazines inevitably ties in with the fate of the Kennedy family in politics.

The women's magazines are also integrated into politics at another, more structural level. The way in which they present the world disguises true differences in wealth and power in America and softens the anger working-class people potentially have toward the rich. Thus, middle-class women are allowed to glean some images of Jackie's incredible wealth, but little information is given on the political and economic empire behind the $30,000 a month clothing allowance or the variously decorated homes and apartments. Working-class women, on the other hand, are spared most of even these details, and are instead assured that in essence Jackie's life is exactly as theirs. Obviously, no analysis tries to connect the life-style of Onassis or the Kennedys with the amount of money and power available to working people and their families. Rather, a complex ethical configuration emerges that protects the way things are. Ordinary people should not lust after money. If it comes through luck or men's hard work, that is one thing. But insofar as it is lacking, one can always reassure oneself that money doesn't buy happiness.

Finally, the women's magazines are integrated into the political and economic world in the very way in which they present women and women's needs. Work outside the home, whether it be creative and fame producing, or routinized and mundane, can only be the negative space between the moments when women define themselves as women through their roles as wife and mother. With this definition, women remain the group that can be pushed in or pulled out of the labor force, depending on the economy's needs. And that is really the essence of the feminine mystique.

3

Newspapers and Their Women's Pages

INTRODUCTION

Abbie Hoffman once bitterly juxtaposed two news items: "The headline of the Daily News today reads BRUNETTE STABBED TO DEATH. Underneath in lower case letters: '6,000 Killed in Iranian Earthquake.' . . . I wonder what color hair they had" (1968, p. 182). Hoffman meant to suggest that news presentations slight humanity and important events, while sensationalizing a comparatively minor occurrence. In this section, some authors take the opposite tack, arguing that newspapers and their women's pages slight significant items about women, degrading women and their achievements as they do so.

Gladys Engel Lang opens this section with a discussion of the "Most Admired Woman." Noting that the news media are "both potential agents of change and captives of their own assumptions," she asks about the characteristics of those making the pollster's list of the ten women most admired by the American public. Theoretically, Lang reasons, such a list should indicate the characteristics of those spotlighted by the news media, an assumption shared by the pollsters who have since discontinued the most-admired woman survey. (The pollsters decided the list was an artifact of media publicity and thus was of dubious value as an assessment of independent public feeling.) Generally, Lang finds, the most admired women are satellites of men with high status. Through their husband's resources, these women have some control over the image they project. Nonetheless, these women are shown with the full array of traditional sex-role stereotyping, as are women of independent achievement. Lang associates this stereotyping with the treatment of women in the press corps. Isolated from the pooled information of their male colleagues, sometimes mocked when they ask questions at news conferences, the women of the press have difficulty eradicating the sexist assumptions of the media. Lang suggests that one antidote to this kind of discrimination is the success of the few female reporters who break into the elite news corps: By their counterexample, they can help break down the stereotypes nurtured by their male colleagues.

In Chapter 9, G. William Domhoff addresses treatment of women on the women's page. Domhoff's frame of references is quite different from Lang's. Lang uses the focus provided by the media themselves to explore changes in the popular imagery of women. Domhoff uses the media to examine the loss of power in society and how women's activities support it. Domhoff argues that women's pages provide a key to understanding the exercise of power in America because they emphasize women as satellites of the powerful.

Through their emphasis upon satellites, Domhoff and Lang echo Carol Lopate's analysis of Jackie Kennedy Onassis (Chapter 7). For, Lopate argued, Jackie serves as more than a Rorschach test of the attitudes toward women of magazines serving different social classes. Treatment given her also reveals how the media help to keep women of diverse social classes from obtaining an understanding of the significance of wealth as a source of power. Lang and Domhoff indicate that readers of newspapers and of women's pages in particular are taught to admire and supposedly to emulate the wives and daughters of the wealthy.

Harvey L. Molotch continues this theme of news as the maintenance of the status quo in his examination of newspapers. Rather than explicitly dealing with social class (as do Domhoff and Lopate), he views newspapers as revelatory of the power of men over women and as part of a social process in which men speak to men. When issues of women's liberation are treated, they are viewed from the vantage of men. This perspective was particularly clear in the early days of the movement, when the news media emphasized bra burning and ignored inequality of pay. Bra burning is a concern of men, Molotch tells us. "It is men who worry about women losing their femininity. It is for men that women exist as sex objects and frail nurturant/succorants." And, it is men who own and edit papers and dominate the press corps. On those rare occasions when women appear by name on the general pages of the newspaper, it is from a perspective embedded in "locker-room talk." Otherwise, newspapers reduce women to that nameless brunette "stabbed to death" (Hoffman, 1968).

In Chapter 11, Tuchman explores questions posed by Lang's and Molotch's essays. Can women reporters successfully challenge the news media's sex-role stereotyping? Can they alter coverage of the women's liberation movement? Tuchman suggests that reporters who are feminists (as opposed to women reporters who are not feminists) may use the women's page as an enclave for telling news about women to women. But they can only accomplish this presentation under certain conditions. First, their ability depends upon an adequately funded staff responsible for covering stories for the women's pages (as opposed to editing copy designed for them by syndicates and wire services). Second, they must depend upon organized social movements. In some stages of the women's movement, discussion of issues in newspapers could be accomplished more readily than in others. Third, feminist reporters must adopt high standards of professionalism, while resisting the sexism occasionally implicit in those standards. Those professional practices necessarily mean that radical views will be defused and made more amenable to the maintenance of the status quo.

Cynthia Fuchs Epstein rebuts Tuchman in Chapter 12. Epstein argues that news of the women's movement does not belong on the women's page. Just by appearing there, the stories maintain the status quo, for they tell both women and men that news of the women's movement is not of general concern. This story placement creates the impression that the women's movement and women's position in society is irrelevant to men's lives, and so it impedes the liberation movement. Furthermore, relegation of the women's movement to the ghetto of the women's pages means that movement news will receive the same treatment as society news. For the *New York Times* (the primary source of Tuchman's data), that treatment means mocking participants, much as society women were gently satirized under Charlotte Curtis's editorship of the women's page. Tuchman's analysis may also be generous to the *Times,* because topics of traditional concern, such as food, fashions, furnishing, and family each appear much more frequently than does news of the women's movement (see also Guenin, 1975).

Taken together, these five chapters suggest, news of women has not changed very much at all in the past decade. Still a sex object to men and the satellites of a man, women are not considered independently to be "real news." Adjuncts to the world of men, they remain wives, mothers, daughters, and nameless blondes and brunettes.

Chapter 8

GLADYS ENGEL LANG

The Most Admired Woman: Image-Making in the News

The news media can focus attention on an issue long ignored, but this is not the same as remedying it. Paradoxically, the heightened sensitivity of the press, if it confuses symbolic change with change in the real world, can actually highlight the discrepancy.

What the press actually disseminates is always subject to some constraint. The news media are both potential agents of change and captives of their own assumptions. Knowing the perversity of reality, we shall examine the imagery of women disseminated by the press: the most admired women as a product of the news media; the treatment given First Ladies as representatives of womanhood; the coverage of women in politics; and, finally, some long-term implications of the new visibility of women *in* the media.

THE MOST ADMIRED WOMAN

From 1948 until fairly recently, the Gallup Poll has been asking a national sample of men as well as women, "What woman whom you have heard or read about living today in any part of the world do you admire most?" No list of names is provided. Respondents are free to nominate whomever they wish—a procedure that tends to favor women prominent in the news. The top ten names of the list therefore tell us something about the media coverage of women and of the images of "womanhood" it conveys.

Heading a recent list (December, 1974) of "most admired" was Golda Meir. She was followed by Betty Ford, Patricia Nixon, Rose Kennedy, and Happy Rockefeller. Also on the list were three other First Ladies (Lady Bird Johnson, Jacqueline Kennedy Onassis, and Mamie Eisenhower) as well as Shirley Chisholm, Coretta King, and Indira Gandhi.[1] Two newcomers—Ford and Rockefeller—were replacements for 1973's Queen Elizabeth II and Ethel Kennedy.

While some of the admiration expressed was undoubtedly for stoicism in the face of personal tragedy, most seem to have won their places through their satellite position vis-à-vis a "worthy" man whose fame puts them in the limelight. The American woman becomes newsworthy when she has mothered, married, or been sired by a man of achievement. The few foreigners are far more likely to make the list in their own right.

We can pursue this impression more systematically by applying three categories of feminine status. Women who are adjuncts or appendages to men of prestige and power are accorded *satellite status.* In the devilishly appropriate phrase of Veblen, their "vicarious recognition" contributes to the glory of the men behind them. *Autonomous status* and recognition conferred on a woman for personal achievement is the opposite, but there is also an in-between category: the woman who first gains attention by her relationship to a prominent man, but then earns her own way, has *sponsored status.*

Certain trends are apparent over the years:

1. The number on any year's list by virtue of their satellite status has progressively increased;

2. The number with sponsored status has gradually dwindled, so that since 1965 not more than one has made the list;
3. The number with autonomous status has remained just about constant;
4. Turnover was greatest for "women of achievement" whose status was autonomous; they form something like a rotating lower half. Except for such world figures as Prime Minister Gandhi and Golda Meir they seldom get close to the top; and
5. There are a total of eight women who made it "on their own" three or more times during this twenty-seven-year period.[2] This group includes Kate Smith, Helen Keller, Marian Anderson, Sister Kenny, and Pearl Buck—all either in the healing professions or the arts, typically in those careers that, because of their succoring and expressive components, are considered "feminine" and suitable for women. Save for the three women in "masculine" professions who also made the most admired list three or more times—Senator Margaret Chase Smith, Oveta Culp Hobby of the Eisenhower cabinet and Representative Shirley Chisholm—there is little to contradict the long-standard stereotypes about women of distinction.

If the most admired list reflects the female stereotype, what can be said about the role of the news media? There are two sides to the question. On one side, a part of the press has collaborated with the fashion industry to create jet-set celebrities, the "beautiful people." These superconsumers can be used to promote every kind of conspicuous consumption. How artificially created glamor gives rise to a new kind of feminine mystique can be illustrated by Princess Grace Kelly, the only one on the list whose career reverses the sequence of sponsored status. She first achieved autonomous renown as a movie star and then acquired the status of satellite.

Princess Grace has been among the ten most admired six times—her debut came in 1956 just after her marriage that

Spring. Marilyn Bender, *New York Times* fashion reporter, wrote of that marriage: "Almost all of the American press was manic over that event. Miss Kelly had everything—a snooty kind of beauty, chic, money and a second generation Irish-American aristocracy which Americans were soon to be nourished on via the Kennedys. She was also a movie star who had won a prince, albeit of a kingdom the size of Central Park" (Bender, 1967, p. 80).

More than anywhere else, this kind of idolatry was promoted on women's pages and in women's magazines. But "votes" on the most admired women come from both sexes. And so we must look at the regular news sections and programs to see how the image of women's accomplishments is also sustained by certain time-honored, taken-for-granted, journalistic news values.

Women with satellite status are in a better position than autonomous women to control (together with those male luminaries whose status they reflect) the stream of publicity about themselves. Much as some may complain about press incursions on their privacy, the information provided the public may have only the loosest resemblance to reality and, in fact, reflect only what public relations feed to a press corps thirsting for inside information. The news treatment of the satellite female, the one who dominates the most admired list, can be shown by considering the publicity concerning the First Ladies of the land.

FIRST LADIES IN THE NEWS

Brit Hume, now an ABC reporter, makes a useful distinction between two kinds of public figures: those who take on this role voluntarily and those who, so to speak, have it forced upon them (Hume, 1975). Prominent among the latter are the wives of the men who wield political power. For whatever reason, the press provides a constant flow of news about these women. Curiosity about the president's wife has always been considerable, and this curiosity, if unsatisfied, has often caused rumor to flourish (Miller, 1973). A good many of the rumors cast the wives in the role of passive martyrs, determined to hold their husbands in spite of bad treatment from them and ready to bow to their fate.[3]

One significant exception to this portrayal of First Ladies was Eleanor Roosevelt. Given the revelations that have recently reached the public about the estrangement between her and FDR, one can not help but wonder why, in view of all the flurries of rumors about her, none pictured her as the "martyred wife." The target of much criticism (some of it malicious), she was always depicted as very much a person in her own right, an image she had earned and which could only be strengthened by reports of her unladylike public appearance in riding pants and other evidence of inattention to her dress and personal appearance. Her rise to prominence by virtue of satellite status did not keep her from using her position as a springboard for campaigns to improve the status of minority groups, including women. Her position as one of the most admired was finally established. Not once, until her death in 1962, did she fail to make the list.

In the years since the Roosevelts occupied the White House, press coverage of the president and his family has increased considerably without Eleanor Roosevelt ever becoming the model. The First Ladies have usually projected an image of femininity, passivity, and non-assertiveness that may have had little basis in fact. Bess Truman, for example, worked closely with her husband while he was a senator. As the wife of the president, she was rarely heard in public. Nothing prominently reported ever contradicted the picture of the passive, small-town housewife, completely dedicated to the well-being of her husband. In the judgment of someone who had observed her closely over the White House years, the privacy was a mask for "the role she played in public life. She probably had more influence on political decisions than Mrs. Roosevelt had on social issues . . . a keenly, intelligent, well-educated, politically experienced person . . . she acted as [the president's] editor. . . . Her mind was one of his greatest assets" (West, 1973, p. 27). But this image did not fit the stereotype. Whether the press knew better or not, much was printed about her as a "good wife" and almost nothing about her political role.

Mamie Eisenhower, who reigned in the heyday of the feminine mystique, was great copy for the women's page and appeared to enjoy promoting the image that she had, as she put it, "only one career and its name is Ike." Everyone was in love with Mamie, who regularly patronized Elizabeth Arden's lush beauty resort and did all the other things that beauty and fashion editors love to fill their columns with. However, according to J. B. West, the White House chief usher, she was perhaps not quite so lovable. "The public saw a friendly, outgoing lady, rather like Mrs. Average American, the member of the garden club, the congenial suburban housewife. . . . Though many identified with her, she's never even been a suburban housewife. . . . [Within the White House] she ruled as if she were Queen" (West, 1973, p. 77).

By the time the Johnsons moved into the White House, there were eighty-five reporters (all of them women) explicitly assigned to the distaff side. Image management had become complex, but what added to Lady Bird Johnson's difficulties was the press treatment afforded her predecessor. Jacqueline Kennedy, superconsumer of fashion and star of television who became a tragic heroine, was an editor's delight. Liz Carpenter, an experienced newspaperwoman, was hired as press secretary for Mrs. Johnson. Liz Carpenter's strategy went beyond putting the First Lady into new clothes. If Mrs. Johnson was to be allowed to do something "on her own" and still project a feminine image, news about her had to be controlled. Accordingly when there was no news, Ms. Carpenter kept the press busy writing stories "we could live with"—rather than leaving them the time to "write the ones we couldn't" (Carpenter, 1970). Special activities were planned so that Mrs. Johnson could make news on her own. Going on trips was one way to move news about the First Lady off the women's pages; editors assigned their top women reporters for these occasions.

In terms of how image management reenforces feminine stereotypes, Pat Nixon's career surely offers material for a classic study of "The Making of a First Lady." She had long ago made her first major debut before a national television audience when, during the famous Checkers speech, she appeared as the "constant wife." For years afterward, there was relatively little about her in the press. Nevertheless, her image seems to have been carefully cultivated—as was her husband's—by appearing to be available to the press while not being available, to appear active while not being active. Toward the close of Nixon's first term as president her image was altered to be more in line with what the president believed the public expected of a First Lady. As the women's movement surfaced, Mrs. Nixon became a person on her own, an Ambassadress of Good Will (Radcliffe, 1974).

The attention that the press continually accords the wives of powerful men suggests that this intensive coverage may create the public interest the press insists it must cater to. But, because so much of that coverage is replete with sex-role stereotypes, the construction of images that serve as conduits for press releases does nothing for the self-esteem of millions of women. Rather, the reverse may hold true: A satellite image may discourage women news readers from grasping control of their own lives. This tendency is changing though. With the liberation of women everywhere, the wives of the men in public life will come to see their own role in much the same way as other liberated women see theirs and not shun—so as to conform to some imagined popular expectation—an active role. Publicity given to Betty Ford in promoting the Equal Rights Amendment is perhaps a reflection of changing expectations. More "satellites" may seek "sponsored status."

WOMEN OF ACHIEVEMENT: POLITICAL NEWS

There is today greater acceptance of women in public life than ever before. Susan and Martin Tolchin (1975, p. 235) discern a surge of electoral support for women as a response to Watergate. If "women candidates are now finding their sex an advantage in politics and its drawbacks substantially reduced in comparison with the past," they write, this is because they are generally viewed as more "honest" than men. The corruption issue that was part of Watergate thus rebounded to their advantage partly—if the Tolchins are correct in their assessment—because of the traditional stereotype that one sex is somehow both more pure and more fair than the other.

Such a connection, if it exists, gives no cause for comfort. Because the "corruption in government" issue is cyclical, it provides no firm base to build upon. To be successful in politics, women have to be viewed not only as superior in honesty, but also as equal to men in competence. There is no other way for the activities of political woman to become as taken for granted as those of political man.

In the past, news media have enveloped the women in politics with a curtain of silence. And on those occasions when they did not ignore them it was, for the most part, because the press was hostile. In this it did no more than reflect the prevailing public sentiment. The media did not, after all, create images of women in political roles (Lane, 1959, p. 212). Women were welcome to participate in community activities, to help out in schools, charity drives and to do volunteer work, especially as these were not considered rough-and-tumble political activities. Moreover, political reporters themselves probably "are genuinely as discriminatory as the politicians they cover" (Tolchin and Tolchin, 1975, p. 121). Male reporters on the campaign trail with a woman candidate have on occasion used all their journalistic skills to report selectively all those personal foibles and idiosyncrasies, those little touches, that take on meaning and bear out the still-prevailing negative stereotypes of women. The 1974 campaign of Congresswoman Bella Abzug offers graphic evidence that only those women in politics, such as Margaret Chase Smith, who act "feminine" and do nothing to appear "aggressive" are apt to get a good press—or at least not a bad press. The success Abzug enjoyed in attracting media coverage only confirmed for other politicians that there was something unfeminine about her behavior. Of course, there is also the opposite offense. What women do is discounted as "too feminine and emotional" all too often and for no apparent reason other than reporters' prejudice. These were precisely the words leveled at the newly elected Lieutenant Governor of New York, Mary Anne Krupsak, when shortly after her term began she publicly criticized the governor for his appointment policies involving discriminatory behavior against competent women. It lies in the nature of their profession that journalists rely on vivid stereotypes, such as "the emotional woman."

Prejudiced or not, what counts about today's newsmen (and they are still mainly men) is what they write and what gets edited in and out. Here is where the new rise in awareness begins to be felt. The deliberate avoidance of sex stereotyping in straight reporting has its counterpart in the political woman's downplaying of "femininity." One technique for neutralizing the public's response, based on sexist views, to a woman candidate was "wearing a gray flannel suit at every appearance . . . to blend into the gray sky and into the equally gray male political arena, so that the voters would be forced unconsciously to identify her with the issues, and forget about the fact that she was a woman." Another woman candidate never allowed herself to be photographed flanked by her family. Both devices are protective and are done to avoid being typed rather than any effort by these women to negate their sexuality or to play the "career woman," a role that enjoys no high repute. A low-key style is necessary because charges of irrationality and emotionality, of erratic behavior are all too frequent (Tolchin and Tolchin, 1975, pp. 14–17).

INTRODUCING CHANGES

Instances of blatant sexism reported in the news media will in all likelihood lead to remedial action. In 1970 Dr. Edgar Berman, a member of the Committee on National Priorities of the Democratic Party, was reported to have argued against women in the policy-making bodies of the party on the most extraordinary ground that "raging hormonal influences subject women to curious mental aberrations." "Suppose," he asked, "that we had a menopausal woman President who had to make the decision on the Bay of Pigs?" The publicity given demands by feminist groups for his resignation soon forced him out (Tolchin and Tolchin, 1975, p. 92f).[4]

With respect to other important political events in which women received heavy play from the media for their part—especially in events that were televised—the ultimate consequence of heavy news coverage is not nearly so unambiguous. Given the unprecedented number of women delegates at the 1972 Democratic nomination convention and their high visibility, enthusiasts were convinced this convention had laid to rest, once and for all, the stereotyped notion that women are good for political scut work but should leave the strategy to men. But others have raised questions about how faithfully the media portrayed this new role of women. Observers for the annual Dupont-Columbia Survey of Broadcast Journalism, an examination of news and public-affairs programs, thought that women had been given short shrift by television, even though not all networks were equally unfair to female delegates. One third of the interviews on CBS were with women but only a quarter of those on NBC—and forty percent of the delegates were female (Barrett, 1973, pp. 140–51).

Be this as it may, it is also possible that the media carried the picture all too clearly. What had seemed powerful and positive to some was no doubt perceived as a clear and present threat by others. Even George McGovern has been quoted as having "thought the convention was great, but what came across on television, apparently to many of these guys [blue-collar workers in South Milwaukee] was *they saw a lot of aggressive women* . . . I think it offended a lot of them" (Thompson, 1973, p. 470). In this respect the effort by some reporters to give full play to the "new" Democratic constituency and the successes women delegates had in getting on the air may actually have backfired, at least, in the short run.

A far more positive impact on sex-role stereotyping can be attributed to two other live spectacles. In each of them women conducted themselves with a competence, coolness, strength, and ability ordinarily considered the preserve of men. I refer, first, to the performances of Representatives Barbara Jordan and Elizabeth Holtzman during the House Judiciary Committee hearings on presidential impeachment and, second, to the ballyhooed but exciting tennis Battle-of-the-Sexes between Billie Jean King and Bobby Riggs, which, while not strictly a political event, was certainly big news. Both events can have had—judging by press reports, letters to the editors, and surveys available[5]—nothing but a positive impact on the image of women. Given the buildup, the sense of drama, and the element of suspense on both occasions, audiences were spectacularly large, and even those prejudiced had to give grudging admiration (Phillips, 1974). Like the activities of women with "satellite" and "sponsored" status, these dramas are part and parcel of the media's construction of images. And they both create and respond to public interest. Coupled with increased hiring of women by the news media, more dramas may promote increased respect for the autonomous woman. But a battle against discrimination must continue to be waged.

Discrimination against women working in the media persists despite the fact that, throughout the years, so many first-rate women journalists earned the full respect of the men for whom and with whom they worked and of the public who came to know them. Women in the media must still struggle not only against discrimination in hiring and promotion, but also against the prejudices that continue to prevail among the public. It may be symptomatic that political reporters are still called "the Boys on the Bus," the name of Timothy Crouse's fascinating (at least to an outsider) 1973 book. Going through the volume, I counted at least ten woman among the "boys."

Crouse himself writes of the grudging respect paid the competence of these women by men on the press plane who were "not necessarily friends of the feminist movement." The status of women as "outsiders" had something to do with first-rate reporting done by people like Mary McGrory of the *Washington Star,* Helen Thomas of UPI, Catherine Mackin of NBC ("one of the few TV reporters print men on the bus admired"), and Marilyn Berger then of the *Washington Post* and now of NBC. "Forbidden to join in the cozy, clubby world of the men, these women had developed an uncompromising detachment and a bold independence of thought which often put the men to shame" (Crouse, p. 210).

Particularly revealing is Crouse's description of Sarah McClendon, who struggled on her own against adversity to become a Washington reporter for the North American Newspaper Alliance and a handful of Texas newspapers and radio stations: "No matter what she asked [at press conferences] all the male reporters laughed. Sarah McClendon was vulnerable because she was a woman in a male chauvinist profession and *she did not work for a large paper.*" Nevertheless, she wrote some of the most hard-hitting pieces on the 1972 campaign. She was, Crouse writes, tough: "a . . . thousand bullying and petty cruelties had not daunted her" (Crouse, pp. 209–10).

What gives women a special stake in breaking through the barriers that keep them off the air and off camera is the visibility afforded those who do get through. No other occupation provides a daily example to many millions of women—and men—of women working as equals in a male domain.

Women had been kept off radio news in the past because audiences were thought to prefer a male voice. This, too, has changed. At least the assumption has recently been put into question by a study at the University of Wisconsin. Prejudice against women newscasters on television was less deeply ingrained than news directors believed (Stone, 1973–74). But what resistance there was to women as television reporters was still mainly related to the preference for the male voice, because this was what people were used to. The study infers that as more newswomen get on camera and hearing a woman's voice becomes more common, people will cease to care about the difference. When this happens, we will have come a long way in breaking down some sex-role stereotypes.

Meanwhile some hurdles remain to be jumped. As Marya Mannes (1970) has argued, it is not enough to put a pretty young woman on the air to report on the weather or on what a White House daughter likes to eat or to send her on the road for a human-interest story. There have to be women speaking in their own right, as commentators, as voices of authority. Barbara Walters' assumption of the position of ABC's co-news reader (or "co-anchorman," to use an antiquated term) is not enough. But the flurry of news releases accompanying her new employment opens a possibility for the future: The drama of promoting women in the media—the theatrical quality of competent women versus traditional stereotyping—may help to break down public resistance to women with autonomous status.

NOTES

[1] A tie brought the list to eleven.

[2] Not including 1975 and 1950 (for which I found no poll).

[3] During the Kennedy campaign for president, a widely circulated rumor (which turned up in a class project I ran on rumor at Queens College) had Jacqueline Kennedy being bribed by Joseph Kennedy to maintain the marriage until after election. Similar rumors involved a "long-suffering" Lady Bird Johnson, tired of indulging her husband's amours, and Mamie Eisenhower, driven to drink, while Joseph Kennedy (again!) paid off the general's wartime consort to go back to England until after the election. No such rumors flourished about Pat Nixon possibly because her husband "didn't like women," as the late Martha Mitchell put it in a *Newsday* magazine interview.

[4] The story is taken by the Tolchins from other sources.

[5] A survey Kurt Lang and I conducted on Long Island after the resignation found both Jordan and Holtzman high on the list of persons who impressed the audience. A study of responses in a conservative Missouri town to the hearings also indicated this.

Chapter 9

G. WILLIAM DOMHOFF[1]

The Women's Page as a Window on the Ruling Class

Whatever feminists may think of the women's page, and I know their opinions vary, it is one of the most valuable pages in the newspaper when it comes to understanding power in America. It is one of the few parts of the paper—perhaps the only part of the paper—that reveals to us how fully and deeply our rulers meld together and form an authentic ruling class. In short, the women's page is a window on the ruling class, and hence the title of this essay, which is adapted from James Benét's "The California Regents: Window on the Ruling Class" (Benét, 1972).

I regularly read the women's page—now "people's page" in this new age—of the *San Francisco Chronicle.* And I also clip articles from it. If I had more time, I'd read *Women's Wear Daily, Town and Country,* and the women's pages of the *New York Times* and *Washington Post,* but I have to settle for the most interesting feature articles and tidbits from those sources that are reprinted in the *Chronicle.*

In social-science jargon, the society news, gossip, and other alleged "trivia" appearing on the women's page are useful for dealing with the problem of whether or not we have a "cohesive" ruling class in the United States, or whether we have just a collection of experts and bureaucrats and hired executives sitting atop various institutional hierarchies, sharing only a few common values, barely knowing each other, struggling like hell just to keep total chaos from erupting, and certainly not in any way connected with or interested in all those jet setters and socialites who are tripping through the women's pages. Most American social scientists believe the theory that features clever experts and struggling bureaucrats, probably because they don't read the women's page, just the serious "news" and "opinions" that the ruling-class publishers and their carefully socialized hired hands give them on the front page and the editorial page (Breed, 1973; Molotch and Lester, 1974).

In denying the existence of a cohesive culture that binds the wealthy into a ruling class, social scientists are in effect ignoring the fact that there are women in the ruling class. They are overlooking the important roles women have played in maintaining the institutions and attitudes that keep wealthy people involved in the intimate relationships that are an important dimension in defining a social class (Domhoff, 1970). They are accepting the relegation of women to a separate and "unimportant" page in the newspaper, and thereby missing the opportunity to develop impressive evidence for the "cohesiveness" of the ruling class. Let me give a few examples.

Preparatory to this paper, we did some research on the *Chronicle*'s coverage of the International Industrial Conference, a meeting of major industrialists and top managers from all over the world that takes place in San Francisco every four years. It is a very big affair indeed, lasting over a week, with lots of discussions and speeches and heavy pronouncements. What we did was to re-read the *Chronicle* for the week or so in which the conference was being covered—for the years 1957, 1961, 1965, 1969, and 1973. From the regular news pages we learned that the Americans at the conference were concerned about foreign trade, balance of payments, the Third World, inflation, and other such familiar topics, but from the women's pages we learned that these men were part of an American ruling class and an emerging *international* ruling class; that they brought their families with them; that there were special parties for their youngsters where they played with children from the Bay Area; that luncheons were held at all the "right" social clubs and "in" eating places in San Francisco; that post-debs seated the delegates at Henry Luce's luncheon in honor of Vice President Richard M. Nixon in 1957; that leading ruling-class families in the Bay Area gave innumerable dinners and parties for the visiting industrialists and their wives; that special performances were put on by the San Francisco Opera House. Perhaps three paragraphs from the *Chronicle* describing one party during the 1973 conference will give the flavor:

> Between the International Industrial Conference, which has brought fat-cat industrialists from all over the world to the City, and other assorted visitors from England, there has been no lack of partying this week.
>
> The Christian de Guignes III gave a dinner Tuesday evening for a very tony group that included the Henry Fords. Cristina doesn't really need a summery red organza print with bare back to turn heads—but it was a smashing dress.
>
> Others at the party were the Henry Fowlers (he's a former treasury secretary and is now a partner in Goldman, Sachs and Co. in New York), the Johan Andresens (he's a chairman of a tobacco factory in Norway) and the Konrad Henkels. Not only is Mr. Henkel a leading German chemist and industrialist, but his wife, Gabriele, maintains what comes closest to being a salon at their Dusseldorf home—she entertains artists and intellectuals at some of Germany's most prestigious parties (September 21, 1973, p. 26).

Evidence for the cohesive culture of the big rich and top managers in the United States also appears on the women's page of the *Chronicle* each year when it is Grove time, that is, when the rich and powerful from all over the country trek up to the Bohemian Club's 2,700-acre encampment on the Russian River, seventy-five miles north of San Francisco, there to drink, party, be entertained, whore, talk shop, and burn the body of "Dull Care" in a fantastic cremation ceremony in front of their huge Owl Statue. (There's no "culture" here, of course, just a little drunken "R & R" for a bunch of overgrown boy scouts.) During the last two weeks of July, when the rulers gather at the Grove, the women's page abounds with evidence of the familial and social connections of the San Francisco branch of the ruling class with the branches in New York, Philadelphia, Los Angeles, and just about every other city you'd care to name.

This even includes cities in Texas, and I want to use a Texas example because so many people are uncritically accepting the poetically tempting but empirically unfounded thesis that the ruling class is split into nice, patrician, restrained, moderate "Yankees," on the one hand, and gross, boot-stomping, uncultured "cowboys," on the other. Here is an example that leads into a network analysis showing that the Houston branch of the ruling class has all the kinds of ties and interminglings with the rich of other major cities that justifies talking about these people as part of a national ruling class:

> Mrs. (William H.) Crocker III (of Washington, D.C.) was one of the guests last night at a dinner party given by Mr. and Mrs. Andrew Jackson Wray of Houston, who come out each year while Mr. Wray goes up to the Grove. The Wrays, who are staying at the St. Francis, invited guests from all age groups, including the Beauregard girls, Mrs. N. R. Tucker, the Douglas Carvers, Donna and Lyman Casey, the Richard K. Millers, Mr. and Mrs. Joseph Cochran III and the Robert Fords. Among the family members at the bash in the Admiral's Cabin at Trader Vic's were the Wrays' daughter and son-in-law, Mr. and Mrs. Anderson Todd of Houston . . . (July 18, 1975, p. 15).

Although the focus of this chapter is Houston, we should begin by establishing the bona fides of the San Francisco contingent. Mrs. Tucker, still going strong in her 80's, is one of the grandes dames of San Francisco society. The daughter of the founding publisher of the *Chronicle,* she is listed in the San Francisco *Social Register,* sits on innumerable charitable and welfare boards, and is a member of exclusive women's clubs in San Francisco, New York, and Paris. As for the Carvers, Caseys, Cochrans, Crockers, Fords, and Millers, they too are in the *Social Register,* with membership in either or both of the two most exclusive male clubs in San Francisco, the Pacific Union and the Bohemian. (The Beauregard "girls" mentioned in the story are the daughters of Mrs. Crocker.)

Turning to the Wrays and Andersons of Houston, we find that Mr. Wray is the chairman of Marsh and McLennon of Texas, a branch of the nationwide company of the same name. He is an Episcopalian (which is the thing to be in the higher circles), a trustee of the United Fund, a listee in the Houston *Social Register,* and a member of the most exclusive clubs in his home city—the Allegro, the Houston Country, the Bayou, the Ramada, and the Eagle Lake Rod and Gun Club. As for his son-in-law, Anderson Todd, also listed in the city's *Social Register,* he is a professor of architecture at Rice University and the senior partner in his own architectural and planning and consultant firm. As befits his professional skills, he is chairman of the building committee of the Houston Museum of Fine Arts.

Mr. Todd lists no private school or social clubs in his brief biography in *Who's Who in America,* but that is not the end of the matter, for an examination of alumni lists and club membership lists shows that he is a graduate of an exclusive Eastern prep school, St. George's School, and a member of the same hunting club as his father-in-law, the Eagle Lake Rod and Gun Club. (We have found that non-reporting such as Todd's is quite frequent in upper-class circles. This creates a problem because many club and alumni lists are not available to researchers, as shown by Baltzell, 1958, p. 439n.)

Wray's membership in the Bohemian Club and Todd's attendance at St. George's led us to look into the possibility that other members of the Houston social elite have outside connections. Checking available alumni and club lists that have geographical information, we quickly learned that a great many men who live in Houston, and Texas generally, are members of such clubs as the Links in New York (16 men), the Duquesne in Pittsburgh (18), and the Bohemian in San Francisco (10), and have graduated from exclusive eastern schools such as Lawrenceville in New Jersey (223), The Hill School in Pennsylvania (168), and St. Paul's in New Hampshire (55). Table 9.1 provides the specifics for all schools and clubs we were able to

TABLE 9.1. Texans in Non-Texas Ruling-Class Organizations

Clubs	*No. of Texans*	*No. of Houstonians*	*Houstonians in the Social Register*
1. Boston Club (New Orleans)	34	21	16
2. Duquesne (Pittsburgh)	18	7	0
3. Links (New York)	16	10	8
4. Bohemian (San Francisco)	10	7	4
5. Chicago (Chicago)	10	4	2
6. Piedmont Driving (Atlanta)	7	4	2
7. Rancheros (Santa Barbara)	5	2	0
8. Century Association (New York)	3	1	0
Schools			
1. Lawrenceville (New Jersey)	223	87	40
2. The Hill School (Pennsylvania)	168	60	33
3. Woodberry Forest (Virginia)	114	37	13
4. Episcopal High (Virginia)	112	54	25
5. Deerfield (Massachusetts)	91	31	11
6. Hotchkiss (Connecticut)	59	21	10
7. St. Paul's (New Hampshire)	55	27	12
8. Kent (Connecticut)	51	12	3
9. Cranbrooke (Michigan)	28	8	0
10. St. George's (Rhode Island)	16	4	4
11. Portsmouth Abbey (Rhode Island)	12	5	0
12. Milton (Massachusetts)	9	2	1
13. St. Mark's (Massachusetts)	9	3	1
14. Thacher (California)	7	1	0

check, and includes the number of Houstonians among them who are in that city's *Social Register*.

But not all members of the Houston branch of the ruling class go away to prep school. Some stay right in town and attend the well-endowed St. John's School, which has ten Social Registerites and two Eagle Lake members among its fourteen trustees. Perhaps the rich who go to this school are the "cowboys" who differ from their eastern brethren. Aside from the fact that St. John's is modeled after eastern schools, a check of where its graduates went to college between 1951 and 1973 casts doubt on that possibility, for as many went to Harvard, Stanford, Yale, Princeton, and Williams (128), as went to the University of Texas (124), and as many went to Duke, Vanderbilt, Tulane, and Washington and Lee (113) as went to Rice, Southern Methodist, and Texas Tech (113). The top thirteen university choices for St. John's graduates are listed in Table 9.2.

The Houston well-to-do also are represented in important policy-planning organizations of the national ruling class. In fact, their most prominent leaders are part of that dreaded arm of the "Eastern Establishment," the Council on Foreign Relations. The CFR has sixty-five members in its Houston committee, with seventy percent of them listed in the Houston *Social Register*. (Twelve of the seventy-six Eagle Lake Rod and Gun Club members are in the local CFR committee, but Andrew Jackson Wray and Anderson Todd are not among them.) An

TABLE 9.2 Colleges and Universities Most Frequently Attended by St. John's Graduates

University of Texas	124	Vanderbilt	28
Rice	68	Stanford	27
Occidental	33	Yale	24
Tulane	32	Duke	24
Harvard	31	Princeton	24
Southern Methodist	30	Williams	22
Washington & Lee	29		

even more exclusive group is the Business Council, a private policy-making association composed of corporate leaders which holds several off-the-record meetings with government officials each year, we find 4 leading Houstonians among the 197 members as of the late 1960s. At least as far as Houston is concerned, then, the ruling class is intertwined far more than the Yankee-cowboy thesis can support, with its emphasis on the social and policy isolation of the two groups from one another (see also Sloan, 1973).

In 1967, women's page editors commented on the upper class at my request. At that time I was involved in research that was essential to further work on the upper class, namely, a project to develop a set of indicators that would tell us who is and is not a member of the ruling class. Since the individual and his or her relationships are the starting point in power-structure research, it is important to know if the individuals you are tracing into corporations, policy groups, and government agencies are in fact part of the class you are studying.

When I first undertook such studies, there was one good indicator of upper (ruling) class standing, the *Social Register,* which had been uncovered in the systematic work of E. Digby Baltzell, a sociologist who also happened to be a member of the upper class and knew where to start (Baltzell, 1958). However, there was the suggestion in Baltzell's work that other blue books, as well as certain club membership lists and private school alumni lists, might be useful indicators. So, to extend the indicators from the *Social Register,* we undertook two very different studies.

One study involved a rigorous statistical analysis of the private schools and clubs listed by a sample of 3,000 people appearing in *Who's Who in America.* With a technique known as "contingency analysis," and the help of a computer, we were able to find out which clubs and schools appeared together, and there was a conjunction with the aforementioned *Social Register* more often than could be explained by chance (Domhoff, 1970, pp. 11–14). But no one method is perfect, even an objective and statistical one, so we also went completely in the other direction and developed subjective and qualitative data on the problem.

To do this, we wrote a questionnaire type of letter to the women's page editors for all newspapers in cities that had a chapter of the Junior League, the Junior League being a nationwide service organization of young, upper-class women and aspiring middle-class women that can be taken as a lower benchmark, a starting point, in the quest for exclusive social organizations. In the letter we asked the editors to tell us the names of the most exclusive clubs, schools, and blue books in their cities. The response of the editors was extremely gratifying—128 of the 317 responded—and we had usable information on every major city in the country. The schools and clubs they mentioned were the same ones we had discovered by our contingency analysis (Domhoff, 1970, pp. 14–17). According to social-science methodology, this was the best of all possible worlds—we had "triangulated" in on our target, finding the same results by means of two methods with very different sources of "irrelevant error," and hence had increased the believability of our findings (Webb *et al.*, 1966, p. 3).

But the story does not end there. For at the bottom of the one-page questionnaire-letter, we wrote that "if you have another minute or so, perhaps you could turn over and comment on the question of whether or not rising corporation executives are assimilated into 'High Society,' " High Society being the socially acceptable euphemism for ruling class. In other words, we asked them for information on the question social scientists continue to raise, whether or not corporate executives, and rising corporate executives at that, are part of the cultural and social life of the very rich who are the ruling class.

The responses to the brief questions on the second side of the questionnaire, which I have not reported hitherto, were quite consistent. Of course the rising executives are taken into ruling-class social organizations, and especially those organizations having to do with charities and the arts, which are almost universally volunteered by women's page editors to be the "proving grounds" and socializing agents for new recruits to the inner circles. And of course a great many of them, especially in the larger cities, send their children to private schools, another important avenue through which the upper class infuses new blood into its ranks. Of the eighty editors answering the question about how many rising executives send their children to private schools, thirty-one percent said "many" or "most," eighteen percent said "half and half," twenty-three percent said "some," and twenty-eight percent (mostly from smaller cities in the Midwest and Southwest) said "very few."

The editors made it clear, however, that not just any corporate executive is assimilated into the upper class. A lot depends on his "personality" or "manner," and on the style or manner of his wife. Here are some representative comments that give us a feeling for the process by which a cohesive culture is maintained by the ruling class:

> There is no doubt about it, top executives and their wives, if attractive, are welcomed into society, especially if the men and women work for charity or community causes. I could cite a dozen examples.
>
> (*Los Angeles*)

> As for young corporation executives and high society, they can make it if they try, if their wives play the committee game, work hard at charity things and make a good impression. Entry to society can come with business deals, if the climbers are attractive, but if they are impossible, personally, that is, and never learn to fit in with the rest of the social set, business deals may wind up only with a men's luncheon, not an invitation to a private dinner.
>
> (*San Francisco*)

> It is possible for personable men with acceptable wives to become "high society" quite rapidly—though the route to take is

> support of certain charities. . . . Savoir-faire, a little culture, and discretion are required.
>
> (*Portland, Oregon*)

But I don't want to give the impression that the results were all of a piece. They were consistent in one direction, but not monolithic. A few editors did say that it was very hard, or even impossible, for rising executives to crack "high society" in their cities. A woman in Boston said:

> Boston Society generally begins at birth and many of the most successful executives never make the *Social Register*. Family is the prerequisite and you marry into—or out of—it.

An editor in Charleston, South Carolina:

> Charleston's is a peculiar—perhaps unique—society. You're either accepted, or you aren't, and position in the business world and salary don't have a damned thing to do with it.

From Hartford, Connecticut, came these words:

> The four hundred of Hartford stay aloof mainly. They lend their names to community projects and affairs. One or two tables show up at a function—just enough to give impetus for the newcomers in the social strata to feel that they are "in." But they really aren't.

Women's page editors not only earned my gratitude for answering my questions, but for what they wrote over and beyond the questions. Their comments and insights were often quite useful—or amusing. For example:

> We widows wish that more single corporation executives would be assimilated into society. . . .
>
> (*A large city in California*)

> I trust this information will remain confidential. I need my $85 a week to live on.
>
> (*A small city in the Northeast*)

> The criteria are money and who you know. If you apply yourself, you can get to know anybody.
>
> (*City in upstate New York*)

From the information I've reported so far in this paper, you might gain the mistaken impression that social scientists have done considerable work utilizing the women's page. Actually, the opposite is the case—the material on the women's page remains in the area of the potential. About the only exception to this statement lies in the area of intermarriages, for there have been two studies on that topic. In the first, reported in 1947, the authors studied 413 marriage announcements that appeared in the *New York Times* on Sundays in June for the decade 1932–42. They found a considerable amount of intermarriage among listees in the New York *Social Register*. Of 188 marriages where at least one partner was in the *Social Register,* forty percent had both partners listed. The authors interpreted their findings in terms of upper-class endogamy, a basic indicator of group or class cohesion (Hatch and Hatch, 1947).

The second research report on intermarriage returns to the *New York Times* for Sundays in June for 1962–72 and improves on the 1947 study by Hatch and Hatch. This study concludes that upper-class marriage patterns and in-class marriages remain surprisingly constant despite all the changes in the United States over the past thirty to forty years. Using *Social Registers* for twelve major cities, these authors found that forty-four percent of listees were marrying within the *Social Register* in the early seventies, down from sixty percent in the early sixties (Blumberg and Paul, 1975).[2] They also note that eighty-four percent of the brides and seventy percent of the grooms went to private secondary schools such as those reported by our women's page editors. Socially registered brides and grooms were more likely to attend the most exclusive of private schools and the most prestigious colleges and universities; brides listed in the *Social Register* were more likely to report a previous debutante party—sixty-nine percent versus forty-five percent for non-*Social Register* women.

Thus far I've been talking as though the women's page is only useful in studying ruling-class connections. But I would be remiss in my overall task if I did not do justice to the usefulness of the women's page on a related topic—the life-style of the ruling class and the mentality they share. For this purpose, my favorite columns appear on Sunday in the other daily San Francisco newspaper, the *Examiner.* They present portraits of little-publicized leading lights in the Bay Area by people's page columnist Albert Morch. Reading back through several dozen of these portraits gives one the distinct flavor of ruling-class life, with its parties and travel and gracious living, its tastefulness, its regard for culture. Perhaps my most favorite, because it captures so much of the whole package, appeared on December 9, 1973, and featured William Kent III, a Republican member of a prominent family that also boasts leading northern California Democrats. We learn that Mr. Kent went to Town School, Thacher, and Yale, and that he is a member of the Bohemian Club and the Pacific Union Club. Beyond that, we find that he has a considerable involvement in the arts as a member of the California Arts Commission, a director of the San Francisco Symphony, and founding president of the Spring Opera Theater. For fun, he is an amateur gourmet who makes his own wine (forty cases a year). He also does fireworks displays including "flashes and puffs of smoke" for the Bohemian Club. According to Morch, Kent is quite often open in his admiration of private clubs and debutante balls, and he confirms his elitist mentality in the process of denying it (Freudians call it affirmation by denial): "I'm not an elitist, but there is something to be said for exposing your kids to good manners, culture and the company of their peers. Going out on your own is tough enough these days."

A more recent portrait (April 27, 1975) chronicles the life of a thirty-four-year-old member of the ruling class, Bradford Walker, from a mainline Philadelphia family. Walker came to San Francisco in 1970 when he took a position as a vice president of Continental Pacific Mortgage Company, and soon became involved with the cultural life of the area, working with the University Art Museum and the American Conservatory Theater. In addition to a home in the exclusive Pacific Heights area of San Francisco, he and his wife have a little farm in the nearby countryside where they like to spend weekends.

The Morch portraits are especially useful because they don't feature the most famous or richest members of the ruling class, but just your everyday ruling-class person. You see them as rather ordinary people going about their conventional interests—the arts, wine making, and tending a small farm on the side, which are admittedly a little unconventional by most standards. You see that the ruling class is not made up of inhuman monsters, or only of the super-rich like the Rockefellers, but of relatively mundane people doing lots of relatively little things that add up to something very big. This helps people to realize that it is the cumulative impact of the ruling class that is the problem with America, that the problem is "structural" and not a matter of "bad" people.

In Walker's case, for example, he'd like to think of more ways to "make art really fun for people." He may even become a museum administrator or curator someday. And when he was back East he "went to so many debuts and truly overwhelming opulent parties that I've had enough to last a lifetime"—a statement we can take at face value even while we learn much from it about the "culture" of the ruling class. But for all Walker's decency and good will, we should not overlook the fact that many generations of his family have lived the good life and ruled America, and that his children likely will do so too, while other people are systematically excluded from such opportunities by the nature of the socioeconomic system. So the Morch columns, with their wealth of personal information, lend credence to our view that there is a ruling class while at the same time forcing us to realize once again that the ruling class must be thought of in impersonal terms as a structural feature of our society.

In closing this panegyric to the women's page, I hope I have shown that it contains a good deal of important and useful sociological information, perhaps even more than what is found on the other pages of the newspaper.[3] It is on the women's page we learn that our business, cultural, and government leaders, for all their public differences on specific issues, share in a deeper social community that keeps them as one on essential questions concerning the distribution of wealth and the system of property, questions that seldom become issues, questions that rarely receive attention on the straight news pages. Only on the women's page does the newspaper tell us each and every day that there is a ruling class in America. It is truly a window into what the United States is really all about when it comes to social structure.

NOTES

[1] The author wishes to thank Deborah Samuels-Robinson and Susan Kay Sloan, his research assistants, for the empirical work they did in connection with this project.

[2] For a non-newspaper study, which found only thirty-one percent of marriages by Philadelphia listees for 1941 within the Social Register and an even lower twenty-one percent for 1961, see Lawrence Rosen and Robert R. Bell, 1966.

When we reanalyzed the Rosen-Bell data using all the upper-class indicators revealed by contingency analysis and women's page editors, the in-class marriages rose to forty percent for both years combined. If we include other exclusive schools and clubs, and especially those in the Philadelphia area, the figure rises to fifty percent. Further studies are needed on intermarriage patterns, and the strategy used by Rosen and Bell, which begins with marriages listed in the *Social Register,* is a very good starting point.

[3] A possible exception is the obituary page, which is often quite revealing. This is especially the case with the *New York Times,* for its reporters actually interview important people before their deaths about what should be in their obituaries. For a study that makes a start in utilizing obituary page information, see Herman Akhminov, 1961.

Chapter 10

HARVEY L. MOLOTCH

The News of Women and the Work of Men

News is a social process; it is an artfully executed maneuver by those who possess the extraordinary ability, common among human beings, to know the social location of another and to use every current moment to construct every future moment. That is, people have the ability to see the world from the standpoint of the other and hence have the ability to plan. They do this constantly, even when not aware of it.

These abilities make interaction possible, whether in news making or any other social activity. In this chapter I want to describe some ways in which these abilities function in the process of doing news, with particular reference to doing news about women. It is helpful to begin at a very basic level. I meet a friend on the street who says, "What's new?"

He is asking me to say something; he is asking for news. What specifically he is asking for is not clear: Does he want information about me personally, my friends, the place I live, my marriage, my work? Does he want to know what happened yesterday, last week, a minute ago? Does he want to know what happened in the physical space we now share, in the house I live in, the university where I teach, the tennis court I play on? Topic, time, and space are all unspecified. News differs in this way from other forms of information. I take this to be a defining attribute: News is about any and all such topics, relevant to any and all such spaces, and even relevant to any particular time frame of the past. News thus differs in its open character from other kinds of information such as washing-machine instructions or a college textbook.

This open quality of news provides a very special kind of challenge to the person asked to provide it. If instead of asking for news, my friend had asked instead for the time of day, my work routine in generating an answer would have been clear-cut. But when asked for news, difficulty is sometimes experienced—a moment of indecision, sometimes quite difficult to endure. This moment is symptomatic of the challenge provided by the inherently ambiguous nature of the question and the exceedingly complex work which must be undertaken to provide an answer. When in a nonthreatening and familiar area, giving news is a pleasure, but when the questioner is not known well, when there is reason to be suspicious of his or her intentions, when we ourselves are not sure of our own identities in the scene at hand, there can be pain in giving news. Even when the scene is familiar, the work of answering the question "What's new?" is creative and artful, but so routine as to render the artfulness invisible.

When I get home from work, my wife and I often ask one another, "What's new?" I have an infinite array of possible answers. One might be: "Three traffic lights in a row were green on my way home and the fourth was red." This configuration of lights was unique and happened to me very recently. But it is not news. The test of its not-newsness is contained in my wife's rejection of it as interesting. She might reply, "Come on, I asked you the news." My answer did not work and that makes it not-news. Neither uniqueness nor recency makes an occurrence news. Only if it works is it news.

A response that would provide more evidence of the fact that I am a competent human being would be something like: "I went to a department meeting. That son-of-a-bitch, Bob Jones, gave me more of his crap."

By providing this information, which is hardly the report of a unique occurrence (Bob Jones always gives me crap at department meetings), my wife accepts my remark as news. With this answer, I trade on my wife's enmity for Bob Jones and her anticipated solidarity with me on the issue. I know something about her place in the social world and what kinds of information are potentially gratifying to her. I also gain some sympathy for having had this experience, a cost I paid which perhaps my wife escaped during the course of her day. As part of the news, delivered at that moment or later, I might say: "I've got a real headache from it all; I've got to lie down."

Through a series of steps, always contingent from moment to moment on further concurrent events, I have built a structure that develops pleasant solidarity with my wife, that earns me the right to (plausibly) lie down, and absolves me of my normal responsibilities of housework or childrearing for part of the evening. I have managed to dovetail my own interests in certain events (event needs) into the life-space of my wife; I have coordinated my event needs with hers. I have "done" news.

It follows that what is or is not news on any occasion depends upon who is talking to whom. There are event needs of the talker-writer which, if they are to be fulfilled, must be done in a manner consistent (in various degrees) with the news needs of the hearer-reader. No two persons have identical news needs. When the news needs of the talker-writer are different from those of the hearer-reader, the challenge to the more active participant is all the greater. But when the power relationship between the two parties is asymmetrical, much of the problem is solved.

In the doing of news, as in most other realms of social life, women are in an inferior position relative to men, in several respects. For example, in those familiar scenes where providing news is nonthreatening and thus a resource for pleasure and self-affirmation, men tend to give the news, the women to receive it. Pam Fishman (1975) has done research on everyday talk among couples by placing tape recorders in their homes. She finds a tendency for women to ask most of the questions, including, "What's new?" and the men to give the answers. Women tend to punctuate life with these questions—invitations for conversation which then are male-dominated. She calls this role of women in everyday talk one aspect of "conversational shitwork."

Men's talk in these situations is contingent upon women's news needs only to a very limited degree. Being asymmetrically dependent upon the man for interaction/confirmation, she must take pretty much what he gives and find interest in it. Should she not participate in this way, the man will find her to be less than fascinating, or pleasant to be with, and so forth. Ordinarily, what can be said to women and still be interesting enough to work as news is rather broad. This makes women easier to be with than men—easier in the sense that less creative work is needed to provide news. Hence, men find women less threatening and less competitive. It also means they don't have to be taken into account quite so much.

The mass news media—television, radio, newspapers and magazines—are institutionalized means of answering people's collective question, "What's new?" In providing such news, some attention must be paid to the news needs of the listener-reader. But not at the expense of the news needs of the more active party, the generator of the news. As in everyday talk, there are asymmetrical relationships in the mass-media news process. Some people are the perpetual askers, others the perpetual tellers. Publishers are the key tellers in the newspaper business and they are not by any means a random sample of the American population. Their news needs are not random at all. Publishers are joined in the telling process by others who are influential: advertisers, editors, and reporters (in decreasing order of significance). They are also joined in this process by those to whom they provide routine media access—national politicians, corporate executives, lobbyists, protesters (equated with kooks by many newsworkers), and random members of the general public (again, in roughly decreasing order of significance). Marilyn Lester and I (Molotch and Lester, 1974) have endeavored to argue that mass media represent the powerful talking to the less powerful. We have stressed (as have others) that the primary news need of those who control mass media is to perpetuate the general status quo of the United States social and economic structure. This goal is achieved not through conspiracy or coercion (at least not typically), but rather through powerful people inexorably giving shape to news-generating institutions such that news is produced that merely interests them—that is, which is of use to them.

More specifically relevant to the present topic, the formal news business is not only the powerful talking to the less powerful. It is essentially men talking to men. The women's pages are a deliberate exception: Here it is the case that women who work for men talk to women. But in terms of the important information, the news pages, women are not ordinarily present. Women are not present either as news producers or as persons for whom news is intended. Those who publish news perceive women as being in the kitchen, just as they have traditionally been whenever men have important things to discuss with one another. News is a man's world.

Those who actively do news count among their members a minority of people who are women, some of whom have achieved prominence in the profession (for example, Georgie Anne Geyer and Helen Thomas). But the significance of the presence of such women journalists should not be exaggerated. Not only are a minority of journalists women (especially in the elite press), but, more importantly, the news business is controlled by men.

The editors, publishers, and wire service executives are men, Ms. Graham notwithstanding. News supervisors have means to institutionalize their preferences, and given the inherent ambiguity faced by the on-line worker, conformity is rather easily generated through models of expertise and efficiency, without recourse to discipline or even explicit guidance.

What then are the news needs of men, as distinct from those of women? Do they have a collective nose for news, a common sense of relevance, a common sense of what is "interesting"? I believe they do; it follows from their different and commonly held situation in the social world. The topics of their discourse bear the marks of man-to-man talk. The newspapers do not cover events of daily life with which women traditionally have had to deal. Omitted from the news pages is the world of immediate experience, the *processes* of life and death involving diapers and suffering, vomit and dirt, serious intimacies and personal horrors. Descriptions and consideration of such topics are placed elsewhere—the women's page, if anywhere at all. As Dorothy Smith (1973) has pointed out, these are the topics of life as lived by women—the women who cover for the men who think the social world rests exclusively in those bloodless, remote-from-life decisions made at business lunches, meetings, and reported at press conferences. But I would argue that the news needs of women who raise children and do housework (often in addition to "outside" work) create a need for information about such so-called "trivia." A solution to a problem such as that posed by the routines of a woman's real life can provide an extra hour of leisure, a bit of peace of mind, a less-debilitating day, even a spark of liberation. But the definition of such concerns as trivia rules the media and, hence, news regarding them is relegated, *separately and unequally,* to the women's pages.

Men have no need of information that may cause women to wish to abandon their traditional social roles altogether. Serious treatment of women's liberation has been difficult to come by in the media because of this lack of interest to men. (Just as people do news, they also do non-news, and the process is equally subtle in the negative case.) Thus, the coverage of women's liberation in the early years seems to have centered on the supposed burning of bras and the fear that women might, by abandoning cosmetics and delicate costuming, lose their femininity, i.e., their sexual and companionship utility for men. For whom would such concerns be paramount? It is men, I think, who gain a bit of a lascivious quiver with just the talk of bras (it was one of the words I looked up in the dictionary as an adolescent in desperate search for pornography in those dry years, the late fifties). And it is men who worry about women losing their femininity. It is for men that women exist as sex objects and frail nurturants/succorers.

But the other issues of women's liberation were less prominent: the extent and implications of women's lower pay scales; the chronic and clear-cut (to women) discrimination in education, job, and credit access; the stereotyping by the media of women as trivial-minded, unreliable, and mercurial; and the invidious administration (or non administration) of rape laws. My point is only to show through illustration that the media report women's issues selectively and, apparently, through a man's sense of the world.

This early coverage of the women's movement is symptomatic of the kind of attention women's activities generally receive in the media. But the first point to make is that women receive very little attention in the media, one way or another (see Bogart, 1973). Not envisioned as an important audience (man reads papers while woman tries to get his attention—a thousand cartoons and sitcoms tell us women are actually *anti-news*), women are also (and for some of the same reasons) not very worthy of coverage. All powerless people in this society lack ready access to the media. They can't afford the apparatus of press agentry, they are not a part of media beat structure, and they do not have offices, phones, and easy contact with the media. But they are, I believe, also seen as inherently trivial and hence not typically worthy of coverage anyway.

When, for example, a high public official or corporate executive speaks, it tends to be news. When a lowly victim complains, it is not news. Because women do not hold dominant positions in society, women lack access to news making and hence the likelihood of becoming newsmakers. Women are not in control of society's institutions. Traditional dependence by the media for spokesmen from the top of such institutions means that the sexism which blocks women's mobility in other realms accumulates to block women from even knowing that they exist as a public phenomenon.

I carried out a small exercise in content analysis to check my impressions against what had been happening lately in the news pages. I pored over dozens of dailies looking for stories in which women were present—either as movers and shakers, critics, respondents, or in any other dignified role. The pickings were slim.

Let me provide some illustrations that are not extreme cases but rather typical. A recent Friday edition of the *St. Louis Post-Dispatch* carried, on its first three newspages, a total of fourteen stories. Twelve had to do with actions taken by named males (for example, a Supreme Court justice's opinion, a Bar Assocation official's actions helping indigent clients, and physicians' threats regarding malpractice insurance). Only two stories were *not* about named males—stories recording the collapse of South Vietnam and descriptions of the battle victories of the Vietcong.

The *San Francisco Chronicle* of March 21, 1975 looked much the same: of fourteen news stories, eight were exclusively about the activities of named males (as Senator Mansfield, David Sarnoff, and General Bradley). Four stories were neuter (for example, regarding Vietcong and Vietnamese refugees), and one story involved both sexes: Jack Scott's commentaries on Patty Hearst. The *Chronicle* did run one story on a woman: her body, unclad, was found lifeless in a Bay Area suburban field.

Of all papers I examined, the most attention to women on the newspages came from the *Oakland Tribune*. Of the fourteen news stories published that day, three were about women. I want to describe them in some detail because I feel they have something in common with the "bra-burning" kind of coverage provided the women's liberation movement.

Story number one (appearing front-page) was headlined, "Gypsy Ruled Guilty in $89,500 Bilking." This young woman was involved in a scheme that used "trickery" in order to get other women to write her large checks. Among her reported tricks was the "muttering of incantations" over such items as a tomato, an egg, and a banana.

The second women's news story in the *Tribune* was a prominent above-the-masthead item that involved a Vietnamese woman's "want-ad wedding proposition." She had taken out an ad promising to marry anyone who would get her out of her war-torn country. The interviewer was concentrating on the angle of a woman who would marry anyone, even if she didn't like him, rather than from the angle of a trapped human being in terror, or of a woman who has the serious problem of only being able to survive (like so many other women) through the beneficence of a man.

The final *Tribune* story was very different from the other two. It covered the protests of an environmental activist who was a woman. The coverage was substantive, and she was treated with dignity (no description of her physical shape, for example). But clearly the most common type of story is not represented by this conservationist item. The biggest single woman newsmaker I ran across, in all the papers I looked through, was Jacqueline Kennedy Onassis, who was more or less accused through the angle of the coverage of having responded improperly to her husband's death. By innuendo, the coverage suggested that she married the old man for the money, danced on his grave, and robbed his daughter of part of her inheritance.

What do I make of this general pattern in which women appear as soap-opera figures, fantasy-role players, and not as people who do things in the world—even those things that are virtually reserved for them in their traditional wife-mother roles? Seldom do women appear at all in the newspages. There is no affirmative action in the content of the news print media. When women do appear, it is from a man's perspective of what is interesting: woman as sex objects, as quasi-promiscuous; women who undress, who are out for a man only for his money; or women who use their exotic wiles (gypsies) to steal from other women (impressionable, incompetent, overly trusting, superstition-ridden). Sex stereotypes are reified in the news but it is worthwhile to understand how and why. All of these stories are about events that may have happened, but they are *news* primarily from a man's perspective. It is locker-room talk. The incidents which, when reported from the proper angle, can serve to perpetuate sex stereotypes tend to be inherently interesting because they serve the news needs of those who own, control, and write the newspapers. That such stereotyping should persist even in the face of recent gains by women is not curious; it is constituted through the work of men in the news business and parallels and is built upon the general news work of men living their daily routines, whether in or out of the news business. Seeing the world in this way, in a sexist way, helps a guy get through the day and that is a project in which we all need all the help we can get.

Chapter 11

*GAYE TUCHMAN**

The Newspaper as A Social Movement's Resource

Proponents of a variety of social reforms and social interests have argued that news coverage can aid their cause: It can disseminate knowledge of their ideas to potential supporters and recruits. Ultimately, these proponents and such academicians as Molotch and Lester (1974) have claimed that the ability to define events as news is the expression of raw political power. The ability to define news, the publicists and politicians have cried, must be wrested from the hands of the powerful or the rich or the Democrats or the Republicans or the liberals or the capitalists in order to ensure that a new message can crash past existing gatekeepers identified as serving the powerful, the rich, the liberals, or whomever.

Much effort has been expended to implement the theory stated above. Vice-President Spiro Agnew and other members of the late Nixon administration declared a field day for attacking the media. The C.I.A. expended vast sums to use the Chilean news media to overthrow Allende's socialist government (Landis, 1975). Franz Fanon (1963) reminds us that capture of radio and television stations is a high priority in wars of liberation. Indeed, Hans Magnus Enzenberger (1974), the German poet and political theoretician, announces that illegal political action demands both maximum security and maximum publicity. Yet, it may be possible to gain publicity for some social movements, particularly reformist movements, by treating the news organization as a resource to be exploited, rather than as an obstacle to be attacked.

This article considers the women's page of metropolitan newspapers as a resource for the women's movement. It argues that the disinclination of male editors to treat events of the women's movement as general news opened the way for some women editors to include movement news in their preserve. But the women's pages have not been a constant resource since the resurgence of the women's movement in the mid-1960s. Rather, because newspapers interact with their environment, they are themselves affected by the very changes in the social world that they claim to record. Some women's pages have been a resource for the women's movement at some moments, but not at others.

Several examples involving coverage of women and items of interest to women may help to clarify the nature of this interaction. Each example depends upon the idea that news is a social construction: No event can be news unless members of a news organization identify it as separate from the "glut of occurrences" in the everyday world, gather information about it, process that information (transforming the event into a story) and disseminate the story. Donna Allen reports that during the heyday of the suffragettes the *New York Times* routinely covered the annual conventions of the League of Women Voters on its general pages.* Then, although the annual conventions with their keynote speeches continued to be held, the coverage ended; the news media had rung the death knell of the feminists. That declaration of death helped to advance the early movement's demise.

* Personal communication, 1975.

Similarly, the *Times*—like radio with its bond drives and the movies with their patriotic hoopla—sought to support American interests in World War II. Not only did stories on the women's pages announce the military's need for nurses, but more significantly, the daily *Times* introduced recipes as an aid to the homemaker. The recipes were intended to teach her to cope with shortages and rationing by providing imaginative ways of producing tasty dishes with available ingredients. Rather than merely reporting about society, the *Times* as social institution sought to tell members of society how to behave under wartime conditions.[1]

A third example of the interaction between medium and environment is contemporary. Influenced by the women's movement that their own employers hesitated to cover, women at such places as the *Ladies' Home Journal, Newsweek, Time-Life,* and the *New York Times,* to name but a few, organized women's caucuses to obtain their own rights as workers. They also insisted that the women's movement be treated as news. By their actions, these women reporters also created news. For example, a demonstration by a caucus at the *Ladies' Home Journal* gave a reporter at the *New York Times* an event involving women's issues for which she could demand coverage.[2] The political importance of these reported actions was considered so great that they became the subject of sociological (Freeman, 1975) and historical (Hole and Levine, 1971) reports on the women's liberation movement. That is, the news reports came to be treated as an example of the impact of the women's movement upon institutions, even while feminists (Ruckleshaus, 1975; Pogrebin, 1975) continued to deplore news coverage of women's issues.

In their attitudes (Enzenberger, 1974), in their social organization (Tuchman, 1974), and in their identifications of events as news (Molotch and Lester, 1974), the news media are part and parcel of the society they serve. Although they claim to be merely a mirror to the world, that "mirror" might be better described as part of a reciprocal relationship between the news media and their environment.[3] The news media are both "a cause" and an "effect."

NEWSPAPERS AS A MOVEMENT RESOURCE

Like all other goods in the society, access to the news media and the ability to use the media as a resource are stratified. The news media are more accessible to some social movements, interest groups, and political actors than to others. Those holding recognized reins of legitimated or institutionalized power clearly have more access to the media than those who do not. Lower-class groups are particularly cut off from the media as a resource unless they recruit middle-class supporters who have routine media contacts (Jenkins, 1975), attack those who attract media coverage,[4] or recruit reporters to join their cause as "advocate journalists." After studying the access of four community groups to Boston's three daily newspapers, Goldenberg put it this way. "The reporter is the key media person for resource-poor groups, the major filter in the access process. However, the reporter is also an organization person who works for a newspaper with goals, structure, standard procedures and policies that somewhat limit and shape the discretion that individual reporters have in news-gathering and reporting" (1975, p. 145).

From its "official" inception with the birth of the National Organization for Women in 1966, the women's movement has not been a resource-poor group. Its original members, drawn to a 1965 Washington meeting to pressure government to improve women's lot, were professional and largely upper middle class. Early press releases were cranked out on congressional mimeograph machines by well-paid executives whose contacts extended to borrowing these facilities. The press releases were designed by the top women in public relations in New York, especially recruited by Betty Friedan to convert the news media into a movement resource. On the advice of these advisers, the press conference announcing the formation of N.O.W. was held in the living room of Friedan's home, and Friedan posed on an antique chair. The novelty of the setting, it had been supposed, would attract all the New York based media. Friedan herself had been a reporter, had fairly extensive media contacts in part developed during a promotional tour for *The Feminine Mystique* (1963), and was hired to write a monthly column in a woman's magazine. When she wanted a public forum, she learned to call press conferences about the "controversial" topics of her monthly column. Friedan, in turn, was backed up by groups of talented free-lance writers who hawked articles on the ideas of the nascent movement to the New York based magazines. Like any professional community, the world of New York free lancers and staff writers is essentially a small one. It extends from the magazines, with their continual search for new topical materials that "everyone is talking about," to the world of daily news. Those worlds overlap, for some daily reporters also write magazine pieces. Feminism was one topic circulated and assessed by this group.

Instead of suffering from a dearth of contacts, the women's movement was beset by an excess of mirth: male editors joked and simply refused to take seriously "women's lib," to use the slighting nickname conferred by the media. As Morris (1973, p. 527) points out, news treatments characterized by ridicule and ostracism indicates public definition of the women's movement as peculiar. The *New York Times*'s coverage of the 1965 White House Conference on Equal Opportunity provides one well-known example of ridicule. Hole and Levine (1971) report that at the conference "one person wondered if the law required Playboy Clubs to hire male bunnies. Almost immediately [a section of Title VII providing for valid exceptions from the law] became known as the 'bunny law.' A *New York*

Times front page story on the Conference was headlined: 'For Instance, Can She Pitch for the Mets?'; the bunny problem was referred to throughout" (p. 34). Editors at the *New York Post* had proposed the headline "It's Ladies Day on Fifth" to characterize the mammoth march of August 26, 1970, although they were discouraged by the newsroom's feminists (Interview with *Post* reporter, July 1975).

Sometimes, the "jokes" were invented by women reporters to satisfy the attitudes they attributed to their editors. Lindsay Van Gelder of the *New York Post* regrets her coverage of the 1968 Atlantic City demonstrations about the Miss America pageant. Although she was "really turned on" by the WITCH (Women's International Terrorist Conspiracy from Hell) group and "could identify with" the demonstration, she says

> it didn't occur to me at the time that I should insist upon its being taken seriously. [Other demonstrators] were burning draft cards at the time and I featured overmuch the burning of bras, girdles, and curlers. I tried to be light and witty so it [the story] would get in [the paper]. I was afraid that if I reported it straight, it wouldn't get in at all (Interview, July, 1975).

GETTING IN THE PAPER: BEING NOTICED

To become news, an event must be noticed. This means more than that an event or issue must come within a reporter's or a news organization's purview. Being "merely" physically and temporarily part of a reporter's "here and now" (to use Schutz's [1966] term) is not sufficient. Rather, an issue or event must be sociologically or psychologically pertinent to a reporter's grasp of the world, including his or her purposes and practical activities (see Molotch, Chapter 10). Public definition of the women's movement as peculiar tended to limit coverage of the movement, since male editors shared that view (Morris, 1975) and tended to reinforce it by their patterns of selective blindness toward women. Bernard (1973) points out that power, politics, and stratification are male concerns; traditionally they are also first-page concerns. That is, the professional ideology to which "newsmen" subscribe identifies male concerns as *the* important news stories and accordingly relegates topics traditionally characterized as "feminine" to a peripheral status as news.

Dorothy Smith has argued that today's dominant ideologies are male. As she puts it: "The control by men of the ideological forms which regulate social relations . . . is structured socially by an authority they hold as individuals by virtue of their membership in a class . . . as men, they appear as representatives of the power and authority of the institutionalized structures which govern the society" (1975, p. 362; see also Daniels, 1975; Smith, 1973). Smith's notion may be extended to the professional ideologies that govern the behavior of reporters. They also operate to maintain male authority by insisting upon the rectitude of male concerns.

One way in which this happens is that professional ideologies identify *events,* not *issues,* as the stuff and substance of hard news. Hard news is itself the stuff and substance of daily news coverage (as discussed by Tuchman, 1973b; see also M. Fishman, 1977). Deemed factual, hard-news stories about events take precedence over other stories, both in their evaluation as potentially newsworthy items and in their internal processing through a news organization. Particularly during the period when the so-called radical wing of the movement emphasized consciousness raising (described by Carden, 1973; Freeman, 1975), much of the movement's political emphasis was upon thinking about issues, women's place in the world, and "changing people's heads." To say the least, this is not an observable political event as are such traditional events as canvassing, caucusing, campaigning, and voting. Because it was not observable, it was relatively easy to dismiss as "not newsworthy." As one New York reporter who covered the movement in the late 1960s put it, "I think that news is what's in people's heads. But that's not the traditional view." A reporter for another New York paper was more explicit: "There were a lot of interesting things going on, but I couldn't nail things down. There was formless kind of talk." She continued, "I could see things changing, but it was hard to put my finger on it and say to the metropolitan desk, 'This is what's happening.' And to be covered by the metropolitan desk, a story has to be of general interest to everyone" (interview, August, 1975).

To be more explicit, consciousness raising does not provide observable events that may be held to symbolize the progress, purposes, or problems of organized institutions. It does not provide, for instance, speeches that may be predistributed, quoted, and, analyzed for new (but not radically new)[5] statements about the condition of the world. Inasmuch as consciousness-raising groups are militantly egalitarian in efforts to eradicate traditional "male" leadership roles, including the role of public spokesman, any *one* consciousness-raising group cannot provide the name of one woman who can *always* speak for the group about women's issues. More importantly, *nobody* could speak for *all* consciousness-raising groups. If a reporter wanted to know what members of such groups thought and of whom they were representative, there was no one person who had been elected to speak for the group or whom they recognized as their legitimate spokesperson.

Consciousness raising and its "issues" could not be covered by professional formulas. Yet, the professional ideology of newswork insists that social transformation must be located and brought to the attention of the news consumer. To mediate between and to satisfy these seemingly conflicting expectations, newspersons turned to established ritualistic practices (Tuchman, 1972; Halloran *et al.,* 1970). Some of these tended to elicit critical assessments of feminism. Newspersons would interview a "first" (for example, the first woman to head a coed university, the first woman to head a multinational corporation, the first woman to be a professional jockey, and so on) and ask her opinions about issues raised by the women's movement. Particularly in the early days of the movement, politicians and "firsts" lent, at the most, moderate approval of some of the aims of the women's movement. As research on women who have achieved greatly in the professions has demonstrated (Hochschild, 1974) they tend to view themselves as exceptional women who have succeeded because of their abilities, and they tend to have little sympathy with the plight of those whom they feel to be less talented.

Another ritualistic practice encouraged reformist statements by media-nominated leaders. This practice is termed writing a "reaction story." When editors judge an event to be more newsworthy than usual, particularly if it might reasonably be expected to bear ramifications for future events, they seek to learn the "reactions" of public figures. Gathered in a "reaction story," these opinions may introduce issue-like elements to the story about the event,[6] particularly if the reporters question people who are known to disagree with one another. A leader of the women's movement could be asked to give a "feminist" reaction, when the opinions of political and civic leaders are being sought. Writing about the views of a leader obviously undermines the radicals' attempt to remain leaderless.

Moreover, to ask a leader her view, the reporters had to locate someone who would at least admit to being a leader. (That role was eschewed by some radicals.) Frequently, those who were noticeable to newspersons had satisfied the notions of accomplishment designed by men for male spokespersons. To use the traditional sociological distinction between "to do" and "to be," such women as Betty Friedan, Kate Millett, and Germaine Greer had accomplished their own achieved status rather than "merely" being wives and mothers, and so newspersons could notice them as individuals. Each of these three women had written books. Millett's had served as her doctoral dissertation at a major American university; Greer taught at a well-known British university; Friedan had founded N.O.W. The nature of each woman's accomplishment would encourage her to accept the publicity garnered by a media-nominated leader: Publicity sells books, as well as ideas.[7]

That the media's nomination of spokespersons favors reform rather than radical ideas is also indicated by the fate of two women whom the media had once exploited. Millett (1974) abandoned her role after finding that the constant publicity not only estranged her from radical friends but also interfered with her ability to maintain her radical life-style. In the mid-1960s Betty Friedan might have thrust forward the then well-dressed and lady-like Ti-Grace Atkinson to speak to the press at demonstrations. But by the mid-1970s, Friedan and Atkinson had quarreled about N.O.W.'s stance toward lesbianism, and Atkinson had participated in founding the Radical Feminists and declared herself a lesbian. Ti-Grace Atkinson was abandoned by the media. The news media could not condone such announcements in a "legitimate" or "representative" spokesperson.

Professional ideologies also contribute to a male vision of the women's movement by inadvertently disparaging events disruptive of social order. The practical task of locating a spokesperson again dominates. As Goldenberg (1975) points out, repeated access to the news media requires ongoing contacts between a reporter and a news source. Those who plan disruptive events do not have these contacts, because they are frequently suspicious of the media or may have other reasons, such as possible arrest,[8] for *not* cultivating them. In such cases, to learn about the event, reporters turn to their routine sources of information:

those who because of their institutionalized status are in a central position[9] to know what's going on. Such routine sources are, of course, the people in power who are being attacked and are more than willing to disparage their attackers. Standard reportorial practice favors those with institutional power.

Finally, inasmuch as reportorial ideology searches for sources of power and other male concerns, it may transform the revolutionary potential of such groups as the Women's Political Caucus into a reformist thrust. To cover a caucus is to cover an event. Since a caucus is explicitly concerned with the distribution of political power or with other legitimated institutions, reporters can rely on known ways of covering conventions.[10] As one informant put it, "Take the women's political caucus; they [the men][11] are used to covering things like that. They can do it from the old formulas, but talk about women in front instead of men." A powerful[12] and very professional reporter who has covered such conventions gave an idea of those formulas in her critique of coverage by a Texas newspaper: "My favorite horrifying example of coverage of the caucus is from 1974 in Houston [a national convention]. Three thousand women were there for three days. Sissy Farenthold, a hometown girl, was elected head of the whole shebang. Everyone was there—black, white, Friedan, Chisholm" (Interview, August, 1975). But, rather than covering "the hometown girl," the celebrities in town, the racial angle, the internal scuffle for power and for unity, "Their only story on page one was a two-column box about a workshop on sexual privacy—a codeword for lesbianism."[13] To this reporter, at least, nonprofessional coverage (the kind produced by what she terms "rotten rags") ignores issues by sensationalizing; professional coverage focuses upon leaders, their interactions, and concrete group actions. Again the emphasis is upon events, not issues.

Of course, a professional ideology can sometimes be used to serve a social movement. For instance, women reporters, whom their male colleagues recognize as people who subscribe to professional ideologies, may make *issues* in the movement *noticeable as stories*. Grace Lichtenstein, head of the *New York Times* Rocky Mountain bureau and first female head of a national *Times* bureau, gave an example of one such story: "Several months ago, I initiated a story carried on page one about changes in the rape laws across the country as it looked in every state. I used Colorado, where it was being discussed in the legislature, as a peg and it got a lot of space. There have been times when I found editors unaware of things happening, like the rape laws. Only women think in terms of rape laws; the men [who are editors] know about capital punishment" (Interview, August, 1975).

Lichtenstein credits Eileen Shanahan, the *Times*'s Washington-based economics reporter, with instituting coverage of the fight for the Equal Rights Amendment, N.O.W. conventions, and W.P.C. meetings. Shanahan herself explains: "In 1971, the first time E.R.A. was in the House, I became aware of it, and I became aware that no one else was interested in covering it and they thought it peculiar that I was interested. If you volunteer for work, you're allowed to do it. I created a national women's rights beat here" (Interview, August, 1975). Of course, Shanahan is a very well-established reporter. Proud of the professionalism of her paper, she can also state, "I have never, well very rarely, done a piece that didn't run pretty much as I wrote it and the length I wrote it. [The national editor] is happy to have me telling him, 'This is good, we have to cover this.' My ability to define stories is because of professionalism." Ironically, feminist reporters who can get stories noticed because of professionalism ask hostile questions of feminists at news conferences. Judy Klemesrud, also a well-known *Times* reporter, explains, "The hardest part of the job [of covering feminists] is not sounding like one of them. I have to be objective, a gadfly"[14] (Interview, July, 1975).

GETTING IN THE PAPER: MAKING THE DEADLINE

Even when recognized professionals such as Shanahan or Lichtenstein can make women's issues noticeable as stories, problems occur in using the newspaper as a movement resource. One problem is the difficulty of converting an issue or even a sequence of issues and stories into a beat, a routine round of institutions and persons to be contacted at scheduled intervals for knowledge of events (M. Fishman, 1977). Shanahan, in part, can run her self-created women's beat while continuing to cover economic news, because the Washington groups are heavily institutionalized. Like other lobbying operations, E.R.A. and N.W.P.C. (National Women's Political Caucus) each has an office; they are open at specified hours; they are administered, so to speak. When Nancy Hicks, the *Times* Washington-based education reporter took over covering the equal rights provisions of Title 9 of the Civil Rights Act from Shanahan, she had both the time available, some sources who would be routinely familiar with the bill, and a knowledge that political activities and lobbying activities in Washington fall into temporal patterns that can be made convenient for newswork.

However, particularly in the early days of feminism's reemergence and to a large extent today, the scheduling of the activities of feminist groups is in conflict with, even directly opposed to, the schedules that govern newspapers. In one interview after another, New York-based feminist reporters insisted, to quote one, "I find a lot of feminists are ignorant of the realities of working in a newsroom" (Interview, August, 1975). In part, they mean that beat reporters for morning papers tend to report for work in the late morning and leave in the early evening. To make the early edition, their copy must be filed by the early evening. Deadlines for the mammoth Sunday papers are even earlier, at some papers occurring in mid-Saturday afternoon. However, many members of the women's movement have jobs outside the home, just as these feminist reporters do. In consequence the movement tends to schedule meetings for the evening, after work and when baby-sitters are available. Conferences, including for instance, the convening meeting of the New York City's chapter of the Women's Political Caucus, are held on weekends. Like other working people, most reporters, including beat reporters, are off on weekends. Those who go to cover women's weekend activities must have their stories filed by mid-Saturday afternoon. The activities themselves may have barely started by that time. A general assignment reporter assigned by the *New York Times* "to keep an eye on" the women's movement (as opposed to having it as a beat), insists, "My main problem was Sunday, weekends and night meetings, conferences and things like that" (Interview, August, 1975).

To be sure, newsrooms are geared to handle late-breaking news. In other studies I have noted that as much news as possible is processed well ahead of time to provide for "emergencies," and that staffing patterns anticipate the transformation of other institution's crises into newsroom routines (Tuchman, 1973b). Special provisions are made for perenially late standard items, such as theater reviews. For example, a hard-news story judged of only marginal news value may be run in the first edition to occupy the space saved for a review. Provisions, including an elaborate system of stringers, are also made for the sports department as a department, since scores are not final until the late evening and key games are played on weekends. But to make those expensive provisions, a publisher and his or her editors must be convinced that the expected coverage is vital to the newspaper as a consumer product. Reviews of cultural events and coverage of late-breaking sports are held to be of clear economic value to the news as product. Not so news of the late-breaking events of the women's movement.

There is, however, one place in a newspaper that seems at least topically related to news of the women's movement and can be geared to handle those stories. That is the women's page, in particular the women's page of such quality metropolitan dailies as the *New York Times* and the *Los Angeles Times*. In each of these cases, a diligent editor with an adequate budget runs an alert staff that produces its own copy; it does not draw from syndicated items and wire services.[15] Although no longer called the women's page and labeled "life-style" or "food, family, furnishing, fashion," these pages are a clear outgrowth of the traditional women's page that Van Gelder (1974) still finds typical of American newspapers.[16] They may be seen as a resource for the women's movement.

GETTING IN THE PAPER: THE NEW YORK TIMES

Drawing on interviews with female editors and reporters for the *New York Times,* the rest of this article will consider the *Times*'s "family/style" section (its women's page) as such a resource. The data also include discussions with New York feminists about the *Times*'s coverage. The *Times* was selected because it is a nationally prominent newspaper whose women's page was said to have introduced a new type of journalism in the 1960s.

One of its women's page reporters characterizes that section as "the most feminist-oriented cross-country," although she notes that they "go through periods when the [page] editors say 'We've had too many women's lib stories lately' " (Interview, August, 1975). Credited by her staff with believing that the section is not to be written by feminists for feminists, Joan Whitman, the section's editor, insists it should carry "news about women, not news for women." That necessarily includes some news about the women's movement, in particular some news about "the changes in women's lives and the effects of the women's movement." Whitman says that her section covers the movement "by my choice." When she replaced Charlotte Curtis who had been promoted to editor of the Op-Ed page, she asked neither the managing editor (her boss) nor her colleague, the metropolitan editor, if she could assume responsibility for the coverage. Rather, "I just started to do it," in part because the women's page could provide better coverage than the general pages. The *Times*'s women's page is a movement resource because its editor chooses to let it be one. An experienced professional, she may be likened to the professionally respected women reporters who introduce movement news into the general news columns. As long as her page meets professionally respected criteria, such as having an interesting layout, it is hers to run.

Whitman, members of her staff, and members of the metropolitan staff are all quick to cite four characteristics that make the women's page an ideal spot for news of the women's movement. The most important of these is that the columns don't cover much "breaking news." Although an occasional story, perhaps ten or twelve a year (to use Whitman's figure), may be so topical or so tied in with that day's world events that it starts on page one and jumps to "family style," most news on that page is "soft." By "soft" is meant that knowledge of the event was not gleaned by a routine (perhaps daily) interaction with a recognized news generating institution and the knowledge is not viewed as being dated by the passage of one or more days. In short, one can ignore late-night and Saturday afternoon deadlines and hold a story over for another day's paper, if desired.

In practice, of course, classifying any one event as hard news or soft news may be difficult. Let me offer three examples involving the *Times*'s women's page. In 1965, it ran a brief story in which Betty Friedan announced the formation of N.O.W. Placed between a recipe for turkey stuffing and an article announcing that Pierre Henri was returning to Saks Fifth Avenue, the article clearly indicated that Friedan had been interviewed at least several days before. The founding of N.O.W. was treated as soft news.

A women's page reporter was assigned to cover a press conference held by Julie Nixon Eisenhower when she was to serve as Barbara Walters' television replacement for a week. After Eisenhower made comments about her father, the story was reassessed. Hard news now, it started on page one.

A third ambiguous example involves the *Times*'s coverage of International Women's Year. Some stories about it were written by the U.N. correspondent (who reports to the foreign editor) and were carried on the general pages. Some were written by Judy Klemesrud, one of the two women's page writers who keep an eye on the movement, and were carried on the women's page. Coverage of the Mexico City conference was provided by Klemesrud and carried by both general and women's pages.

One is tempted to say that if "facts" are emphasized, the story is "hard news" and if the "facts" are transformed into issues ("what's in people's heads"), the story is soft news. But it appears more accurate to conclude that by agreement the women's pages do not handle stories of daily topicality. But once an item becomes part of their preserve, for any reason, it may be reconstituted as "soft news." The pages' editor may exercise her autonomy to treat it as hard news; or she may offer the story to another editor to be treated as hard news. Each day Whitman attends the department editors' conference with the managing editor. At that meeting, the department editors assess their available material and may offer stories for page one.[17]

Second, because most of the page's items are held to be feature stories, news of the women's movement takes on added news value. Reporters and editors think of events-as-news (events transformed into stories) as competitive items. Not only do reporters compete to be assigned to good stories and editors compete to get their own reporters' stories in the paper, but also the events themselves are said to vie for attention. On her page, Whitman noted, stories about the women's movement don't have to "compete with Watergate." To be sure, Whitman has taken as an example of contrast a story that newspersons would identify as one of the most important of the decade. But others echo her assessment. Klemesrud says, "If the feminist stories didn't run on our page, they wouldn't run anywhere." Van Gelder of the *New York Post* says, "Whitman ran a story on that woman minister in France; if she didn't run it, it wouldn't have run at all" (Interview, July, 1975). Lichtenstein suggests, "Half of where a story goes has to do with the kind of news day it is. If it's slow, the story [one of her feminist stories] may be on page one." But "if it's heavy [that is, if the story must compete with many others], it goes inside and may be offered to the women's page" (Interview, August, 1975).[18]

Defined as important on the "soft news" women's page, a story may take on two more valued characteristics, informants note. It can be longer than it would be if run on the general pages and it can receive a better display, including pictures. National bureau reporters, Washington reporters, and metropolitan reporters are all oriented toward page one. Indeed, a Washington reporter may become more oriented toward page one of the *Washington Post* than to the women's page of the *Times*. Yet, a national reporter volunteered, the women's page "is the most revolutionary page in the paper. I never mind a story of mine appearing there [instead of on page one]. You get good play, sensitive editing, and it will be well read" (Interview, August, 1975). One women's page reporter points out, "There are space limitations for other [pages]" (Interview, August, 1975). The coverage of International Women's Year offers a good example. The U.N. correspondent filed a story about a U.N. conference. It was terse, ran on an inside page, and was primarily a "shopping list of speakers." Klemesrud filed a story on that same topic for the women's page. It occupied several columns, discussed the content of speeches, and analyzed the political interaction among conference planners, American feminists, and Third World women.

In this context, Whitman's assessment of her page's role becomes theoretically pertinent. She says, (August, 1975) "I always get flack from women in the movement" who think stories about their activities should be run on the general news pages. "I just think they're wrong. It's better to have lots of space and good display [pictures] than to be in a four-paragraph story and," to repeat an example, "compete with Watergate" for editorial and reader attention. Indeed, Whitman's assessment raises two issues. The first is: What are the comparative merits of publishing a story on one page instead of another? (This topic is discussed by Epstein in Chapter 12.) The second is more complex: How does the eventual site of publication constitute an event as a topic? In the next section, I will tackle the second issue.

CONSTITUTING THE MOVEMENT AS A TOPIC

Like other institutions that process knowledge, such as universities and publishing houses, a newspaper is a bureaucracy. A major metropolitan daily, like the *Times,* not only has such gross divisions as "advertising" and "editorial," but in addition its large divisions are subdivided into areas of discrete responsibility, each with its own department head (or editor) and, most important, its own budget. Department heads may jockey among themselves for power within the bureaucracy, as documented by Talese's (1966) account of the *Times.* And this jockeying may include sexual politics. Talese reports (p. 111) that an assistant managing editor mocked the "wasted" columns of the women's page to criticize a more highly placed editor's notion of importance.[19] One informant advised me that Charlotte Curtis was one of two powerful women who refused to join the *Times*'s women's caucus when it started, adding that at that period Curtis's promotion from editor of the women's page to editor of the Op-Ed page was being considered.

Department heads include such personnel as the foreign editor, the national editor, the metropolitan (New York) editor, the financial page editor, the sports page editor, the women's page editor, and the culture editor. Each editor is in charge of either a geographical or a topical preserve. For instance, the national editor is in charge of a string of national bureaus (excluding the Washington, D.C. bureau, which is a separate preserve). The foreign editor oversees bureaus scattered outside the United States as well as the United Nations in New York. The metropolitan editor is responsible for New York City and its environs, except for the United Nations. Thus, if the secretary of the treasury gave a news conference at his Washington office and then flew to New York to confer at the United Nations, technically (geographically), he would be moving from the responsibility of the national desk to that of the foreign desk. At no time would he be the responsibility of the metropolitan desk. Of course, if the secretary were scheduled to confer with New York City officials or if he commented upon New York City's financial condition, lines of authority and responsibility would be murky.[20] And the metropolitan desk would be in charge anywhere in Manhattan but the U.N. Lines of authority are also murky if, for instance, the music critic wants to survey the state of European opera houses. All trips outside the United States are charged to the budget of the foreign desk; the music critic reports to the culture editor.

The divisions used at the *Times* (and most papers) build in the possibility of murkiness and conflict, since one group of editors (the higher-status group) has geography-specific responsibilities with a topical overlay and the other lower-status group appears to have topical responsibilities regardless of geography.

In practice, the activities of the "topic" group may need the approval of the "geography" group. In the seeking and giving of approvals, and in the interactions between and among the editors, the character of news is made.

Daily, the "geography-based" and the "topic-based" editors meet as a group with the *Times*'s managing editor to review the day's stories and tentatively decide what will be slotted for page one. For instance, at one meeting Whitman "offered" a story on black-market adoptions. At another, she suggested that a piece on the impact of the recession on the divorce rate be carried on Monday. Whitman estimates her offers are accepted ten or twelve times a year.[21] Much of the product of such meetings is as much a result of practical reasoning and internal practical politics as it is an indicator of the state of the world. Sigal (1973, p. 30) provides a demonstration. He devised a crude but serviceable measure[22] to determine whether the local, national, and foreign desks of the *New York Times* and the *Washington Post* evenly divided their newspaper's first page over the course of a year. Despite that crudeness, Sigal's findings are more than suggestive. In 1970, the three desks equally divided page one of the *Post* 12.9 percent of the time and of the *Times,* 16.4 percent. For the *Post* 83.1 percent and for the *Times* 94.5 percent of the first pages were within three stories of a perfect tripartite division.

These data indicate how much news is an artifact of daily bureaucratic negotiation; for, to say the least, it is difficult to believe that each day, approximately one-third of the "important" events in the world occur outside the United States, one third occur at the location of national and internal news bureaus, and one third occur either in the metropolitan New York or metropolitan Washington area. Whitman notes that her "page" has more stories starting on page one than in previous years—at least in part because of social changes that involve women but are pertinent to all. But, in part, it is due to changes at the *Times:* "There's greater interest in some things; [the other editors] are realizing the importance" of topics covered by the staff of the women's page. After all, the media and the society affect one another.

Discussions between and among the editors may also determine the disposition of any story. On occasion, though very rarely, the national editor may offer the women's page editor a story "he thinks will be good" for that section of the paper. The previously mentioned article (written by a national reporter) on the impact of the recession upon the divorce rate is one example. The coverage of the Mexico City conference of International Women's Year is another. In the first example, offering a story to the women's page "buys" more space elsewhere in the paper.[23] (That is, it leaves more room for stories in the general page.) But, in editorial conferences, Whitman will argue that stories about women and the changing family belong on her page. She says, "I fight for these stories. I request of whatever [province it may fall into], this is coming up and I would like to cover it for my page." Whitman requested that one of her reporters, Klemesrud, be assigned to International Women's Year after Klemesrud had herself asked Whitman for the assignment.

The International Women's Year Conference is particularly interesting because its Mexican location makes clear the extent to which editorial discussions determine the disposition of a story. Technically, all stories in Mexico are in the province of the foreign editor. Travel arrangements for a reporter assigned to a story outside the United States are charged to his budget. And a United Nations correspondent (a member of his staff) had filed some stories on International Women's Year. Klemesrud had filed more stories and longer ones on events and issues relating to International Women's Year. An award-winning journalist who also writes for magazines on a free-lance basis, Klemesrud could claim expertise on women's issues and some familiarity with the diplomatic issues that might be expected to crop up and had surfaced at previous I.W.Y. meetings. Faced with Whitman's recommendations, the managing editor and foreign editor agreed that Klemesrud should cover the Mexico City event. But, it was specified that: (1) it was to be "the foreign editor's story; he would get all running news stories about the Conference and Tribune [a special meeting for feminist nondelegates held simultaneously with the Conference]"; and (2) "we [the women's page] would rake-off stories that were not hard news, like stories about delegates" (Whitman interview, August, 1975). Some of Klemesrud's running news stories started on page one and were fairly lengthy. All of her women's page stories received a good display.

The principle of territoriality and budgetary priority continued to be invoked to explain the *Times*'s coverage after the Mexico City conference had ended. Jill Ruckleshaus, head of the American delegation, and other American delegates called a news conference to protest the stories carried by the American media. They noted that the stories had emphasized the disorganization of this woman's conference without adding that all international conferences are disorganized. Thus, the delegates claimed, the stories blamed the women for the disorganization. Klemesrud, who felt their critique to be justified, covered the press conference (a hard-news story) for the *Times.* Her story was on the women's page; hard news connected with the conference had ceased to be the foreign editor's preserve when Klemesrud returned to her desk at the "family style" department. And, as hard news carried on the women's page, this story received a fair amount of space.

In essence, the practical reasoning associated with bureaucratic bargaining and bureaucratic budgets helps to constitute a topic. For, just as any event in the world may or may not be constituted as a story, depending upon whether it is noticed and deemed newsworthy, so too the practical reasoning associated with bureaucracies may determine: (a) which aspects of a phenomenon are noticed and deemed newsworthy; and (b) how those aspects will be treated, both (c) in their written style and

(d) in their display, including the length and use of eye-catching pictures.[24] These attributes may be considered the essence of a topic. Indeed, one might even say that an event serves as the occasion of a topic. One informant claimed that editors will do a story on the women's movement, if "they think a story on that topic is due and an event comes along."

By identifying a hard news "general" story on International Women's Year with a story on the women's page, one may miss the fact that each story concerns a different topic: The event may occasion different accounts (Altheide, 1974; Lester, 1975), different plots (Darnton, 1975; Hughes, 1940), and different treatments.[25] That different topics should result is particularly probable, since reporters tend, over time, to adopt the outlook of the news sources with whom they are associated: They ask the questions appropriate to their sources' world. Inasmuch as questions contain their own answers, for they guide where one may look for an answer and so what one may find, these questions may be said to reconstitute not only a topic, but a world.

CONCLUSIONS

The answer to the practical question, "Can newspapers be used as a resource for social movements?" is necessarily complex. To answer it, I have tried to isolate several factors that influenced use of the news media by the women's movement. I have argued that although the sexual ideology (chauvinism) of male editors militated against such use, women newspersons were able to lessen the opposition to the women's movement by acting as journalist-advocates. Such advocacy was particularly effective if accompanied by male recognition of the advocate as a more than competent professional whose judgment was to be respected. Since professional ideologies are themselves frequently conservative and are both extensions and expressions of male authority, one finds that women who have most identified with those ideologies are those who are most likely to be successful in internally combatting them. The men most accept the women who have met their standards.

Additionally, at the *New York Times,* reporters and editors were able to develop a definition of "women's movement news" as desirable news by invoking professional distinctions. Among these is a distinction between hard news and soft news. Treating news about the women's movement as concerned with social issues and changes in women's lives enabled women's page staffers to define stories as soft news. So defined, they could ignore the deadlines and problematic scheduling of events that had beset general metropolitan reporters who tried to keep an eye on the movement. Ultimately, such redefinition and the practical reasoning associated with bureaucracies constitute the women's movement as the topic of news stories. And, in the hands of sympathetic reporters, they enable the *Times*'s women's page to serve, upon occasion, as a resource for disseminating knowledge of the women's movement.

To some extent, the circumstances I have described are idiosyncratic. Not only may some of their elements be peculiar to the *New York Times,* but also some elements are characteristic of the women's movement itself. (1) One is not surprised to learn that *Times* reporters started a women's caucus and acted as movement advocates. Other social movements may not have had as many potential members employed in news rooms. There are more women journalists than there are black journalists or native American journalists or journalists who identify themselves with the no-growth ecology movement. (2) The caucus may have been an artifact of the times. According to Goldenberg (1975), young proponents of advocacy journalism are rarer now than in the late 1960s. Advocate journalists are increasingly mistrusted, even on liberal metropolitan dailies such as the *Boston Globe.* So, it might be more difficult to found an effective caucus today. (3) The movement also had a traditionally autonomous department (the women's page) as a resource, and this department was particularly well respected and in a position to protect its autonomy and improve its power. Other social movements have not had this kind of resource at their disposal. For instance, the pages in southern newspapers that specialized in "black news" in the 1950s and early 1960s could not be used as a movement resource.

Of course, a social movement might not want to convert an existing institution into a movement resource. Some informants noted that using the women's page as a resource may be detrimental to the women's movement. General reporters, as well as New York City feminists cited by Whitman and some of her staff, objected that women were being shunted into a ghetto or reservation;[26] all aspects of women's life should not be segregated as the responsibility of one department or one general or beat reporter. Rather, they insisted, stories about women should be integrated into all aspects of the world of news just as women should be integrated into all aspects of the world. Such integration, however, cuts off the power and autonomy of those women who run the "women's news reservation," the women's page.

Favorable publicity, such as that provided by the *Times*'s women's page, may have been irrelevant to the growth of the women's movement, particularly in its consciousness-raising phase. Carden (1973) reports that even bad publicity, such as ridiculing movement members who were attacked on television talk shows, brought telephone calls and inquiries about membership in N.O.W. Morris (1974) makes a similar suggestion when she notes that the number of women's groups in Los Angeles snowballed during a period of press ridicule and ostracism. Perhaps, she supposes, one should look elsewhere than the news for a public definition of a social movement or assume the existence of more types of social movements than those provided by the sociological theory with which she worked.

As Ellul (1964) points out, there may be more effective ways of spreading information and combatting and implanting ideologies than the use of the mass media. He discusses "horizontal propaganda," a technique associated with the Chinese. It is the organization of small groups to discuss problems and practices with ideological implications. American T-groups and encounter groups may be viewed as engaging in "horizontal propaganda," spreading our particular blend of individuality and conformity to a competitive ideal. Consciousness-raising groups are another medium of "horizontal propaganda," challenging male hegemony and offering emotional support for those who seek to continue the challenge. During the early period of the rebirth of the women's movement, news that the challenge existed could be carried from friend to friend and consciousness-raising groups may have been a more valuable ideological medium than the press.

In all probability, that is no longer the case. The era of consciousness-raising is waning. So questions raised in the 1960s continue to be important: Should the movement be covered on the women's page? How can one assess that page as a sexual ghetto? Does it decrease the likelihood of women's news appearing elsewhere? Equally important is a strategic issue: Can one convert the pages described by Van Gelder (1974)? Can they be transformed into resources for the women's movement, if that movement should find them a desirable ally? Part and parcel of the society they claim to serve, cause and effect of social change, accounts on the women's page present women to themselves.

NOTES

* I am grateful for the cooperation of my informants, New York reporters, editors, and feminists, some of whom remain unnamed. Most were interviewed in August, 1975.

[1] The social meaning of these recipes was transformed from aid

during wartime rationing to part of the "feminine mystique" (see Friedan, 1963).

[2] Viewing themselves as important institutions, the media frequently deem themselves newsworthy. For example, the *New York Times* carries a disproportionately large number of newspersons' obituaries. Such magazines as *Time* and *Newsweek* have separate sections on the press, television, and movies. Banks and the steel industry are grouped under "Finance."

[3] That reciprocal intertwining may be viewed as indexical (Garfinkel, 1967). That is, the news both reports and creates social realities.

[4] In this case, their enemies may be said to determine their tactics.

[5] Turner and Killian (1957) suggest, as Morris (1974) reminds us, that revolutionary ideas may be ignored as a means of social control. This goes beyond the mechanism of social control described by Lazarsfeld and Merton (1948). At least one editor interviewed in an earlier study (Tuchman, 1969), forbade his reporters to publicize radical ideas that appear rational, lest they draw "converts."

[6] Cater (1959) gives an example of a reporter who created an issue by searching for a senator willing to criticize a bill most senators had been thought to favor.

[7] I do not mean to imply that greed motivated these women. Millett (1975) writes of being overwhelmed by media attention. Friedan (conversations with author, Spring 1975) sought publicity for N.O.W.; her finances were and are intertwined with her political position, for it brings paid speaking engagements and media appearances.

[8] Thorne (1970) reports that members of social movements suspect that persons identifying themselves as reporters may instead be government agents. Reporters interviewed for a previous study (Tuchman, 1969) identified some "reporters" seen at news conferences as "ringers": They were held to work for the F.B.I. or other investigative agencies.

[9] M. Fishman (1977) reminds us that reporting as an activity is organized around locations in which information is centralized. Bernstein and Woodward's (1974) investigation of the Watergate affair may be viewed as a progressive search for centralized data. This also characterizes activities of the Senate Watergate Committee as their witnesses progressed from secretary to cabinet member to presidential assistant.

[10] For a discussion of coverage of conventions, see Altheide, 1974; see also Becker, 1974 for a more general view.

[11] Traditionally, men have covered politics. Women who were political reporters have been few and far between.

[12] Several colleagues identified her as "powerful," meaning she could choose her own stories. An editor did not tell her what to do.

[13] At least one feminist reporter sought to protect the movement from charges of lesbianism. She said with pride, "We did not capitalize

on differences within the movement. The lesbian thing, it could have torn the movement apart. We haven't turned it into something divisive." This reporter used professional ideology to justify her action. Professional ideology identifies news as information of general interest. She was proud to have protected the movement from male editors by ignoring schisms, since "internal divisions within the movement are not of general interest" (Interview, August 1975). Whether such an assessment is correct is irrelevant to this discussion.

[14] For a discussion of objectivity as professional ideology, see Tuchman, 1972, 1973a.

[15] Each of these papers runs its own wire service and includes stories from its women's pages in its distribution.

[16] She suggests that a Martian reading a traditional page "would conclude that every female earthling spent at least several days every month getting married" (p. 113).

[17] To the best of my knowledge, such meetings are unstudied.

[18] She continues, "Perhaps it's unconscious discrimination."

[19] "[Editorial critics] say that the women's page gets too much space, and they particularly oppose the publication of lengthy stories by the women's-page editor . . . [who describes] the activities of wealthy wastrels from Palm Beach to New York at a time when most of America is moving toward the goal of a more egalitarian society. Clifton Daniels likes to read [her work]." Talese adds that the women's page mocks the "society people" whom it covers.

[20] A similar issue arose at the *Washington Post* as it became clear that the Watergate office building promised to raise a political scandal. The national editor sought to have a member of his staff replace metropolitan reporters Bernstein and Woodward (1974). They kept the story when it was argued they had developed sources vital for uncovering more information (Bernstein and Woodward, 1974).

[21] A woman's page reporter estimated three or four such stories at the *Times* each month. Whitman gave a lower estimate.

[22] Sigal (1973) counted the number of stories on page one and divided by three to learn how many stories each desk might be expected to have if they evenly shared the page. He then observed how many stories each desk had and added the differences between observation and expectation. Unfortunately, Sigal does not report the *number* of stories on the typical first page, so one doesn't know how to assess a balance variation associated with a specific number.

[23] It is in the interests of the metropolitan, national, and international editors to have their stories jump to the women's page. Such "jumps" leave free columns in the general pages they share for more of their own news. The women's page has its own "space budget." However, appearance on the women's page may be viewed as decreasing the article's importance and the writer's glory. Klemesrud acknowledged

this past meaning of appearing there when she suggested reporters who "mind" when their work is on that page "don't like women."

[24] Who chooses the pictures to be used on a page is an indicator of power. The women's page editor selects her own. Other departments have picture editors.

[25] Several examples involving ex-President Nixon are pertinent. In each, a reporter unaccustomed to covering the president noted items designed to be ignored. Noticing them changes the topic of each story.

Wise (1973) reports that Latham of the *Times*'s metropolitan staff was sent to cover Thanksgiving dinner at the White House, an event in which Nixon was scheduled to host wounded veterans of the Indochina War. Since Latham had never covered the president, he did not have a White House identification card and was kept for twenty minutes at the building's gate. "As a result, Latham missed the opening glimpse of dinner afforded other reporters and cameramen; by the time he got through the gate, they were back in the White House press room watching football on TV." They were bored by this routine event; Latham was excited. So, he requested the list of men who had sat at the president's table, phoned them about the dinner-time conversation, and learned that the president had discussed an American raid on a military base near Son Tay. The existence of that raid had previously been denied by the State Department.

Berstein and Woodward (1974), the metropolitan reporters assigned to Watergate, attended a Nixon news conference well after their disclosures had crumbled some of Nixon's powers and thus enabled them to request assignment to his news conference in the place of the regular reporter. Toward the end of the story they wrote, they noted that Nixon's hands shook throughout the news conference. Beat reporters assigned to the White House routine omitted this observation. In both cases, Wise & Woodward-Bernstein the *Post*'s editors rescued Nixon.

[26] Gerbner (this volume, Chapter 1) points out that television ghettoizes minorities including women.

Chapter 12

CYNTHIA FUCHS EPSTEIN

The Women's Movement and the Women's Pages

SEPARATE, UNEQUAL, AND UNSPECTACULAR

Four years ago, I was invited to compile a book of articles on women and their changing roles, as part of a series published by Quadrangle Press, presently owned by the *New York Times.* The articles were to be drawn from some previously published in the *Times,* particularly its Sunday magazine section. A content analysis of twenty years of the *Times* indicated there were too few articles for a book: From 1940 to 1960, only a few articles discussed women's position in the world. Those few did not consider minority women, older women, working women, or any other subcategory now considered important. Even during World War II, when one would have expected stories about the hundreds of Rosie the Riveters in the factories and women in the armed services, only two or three articles appeared in the *Times* magazine. A few articles on the WACS and WAVES reported the dispute between those maintaining that women who entered the service were immoral or would become corrupted, and those defending their virtue. A medium designed to deal with serious news, the *New York Times* excluded coverage of women, treating them as if they didn't exist.

Since the 1960s, there has been some change in the kind of attention that newspapers give to women. A local wit recently observed that perceived change in public attitudes had permitted *Times* editors to comment on women and menstruating on the women's page and men masturbating on the Op-Ed (or opinion) page. But this insider noted that there was considerable blue pencilling of any attempt to interchange the two topics, or to place them anywhere else in the newspaper. This brief essay is addressed to the ghettoization on the women's page of stories categorized as women's news and to the social consequences of the positioning of news about women's changing status in newspapers.

Every newspaper editor and writer knows that where a story is placed means the difference between public notice and oblivion. Categorizing by section (i.e., sports, general news, women's news) makes a large difference in how messages are heard and experienced. Placing news about women on the women's page even reinforces the still-current view that the material is only appropriate for women and that it is less serious and important than news highlighted as general news. Even if men read the women's page (and what men wish to be seen by work or traveling companions peering down on that section?) they may well decide the material to be outside their acknowledged sphere of competence. They are therefore not accountable for knowing the information available from reading those pages. And they are not provoked to discuss those stories. For women, the positioning of news about women only reinforces other messages they receive from society: that if a woman demonstrates competence in some important sphere, it is an idiosyncratic event, not worthy of general notice and not to be judged by a universal standard—that is, a male standard.

Additionally, there is a problem of "mix" on the women's page. Modern treatment lumps together news on women astronauts, the Equal Rights Amendment, recipes for lobster newburg, and the length of skirts. I suggest that the mix of news about women and the women's movement with food, fashion, and furniture news violates the very notion of news. By "news" I mean information about important events in the world—the definition used by newsworkers and news organizations. Putting movement news on the women's page with items about food and fashion diffuses its impact. Further, it violates the very canons of journalism that newsworkers use to justify their professional decisions.

Both Molotch and Tuchman point out in this volume that newspaper presentations are not, and can never be, synonymous with everyday reality. At best, newspaper reports are abstractions from the daily reality of events and institutions. They tell of some events, but other events are deemed not worth reporting. Such a process of inclusion and exclusion occurs in all aspects of life. As Molotch says, the process occurs even in terms of the *kinds* of things that people consider worth talking about to each other. Every system—the sciences, gossip networks, newspapers—have formal and informal rules about what information should be included or excluded. According to the general canons of journalism, news of the women's movement—"hot news"—should be included in general news.

Once the women's movement started, its issues and networks should have been high-priority news, yet decision makers in the news world of newspapers and television attempted to undercut the meaning of movement events by the use of derision and humor (Morris, 1974). The events reported in greatest detail invariably were trivial and idiosyncratic. Notions that objectivity means equal presentation (Tuchman, 1972) were invoked to give equal time and space to the tiny number of women's groups who were dissenters to the movement (for example, the Pussycat League) and who maintained that women ought to stay in the home. Leaders of the feminist movement were portrayed as curiosities. Some were characterized as strident, masculine, aggressive types through news editing and picture selection (on women and news pictures, see S. Miller, 1975). Betty Friedan and Bella Abzug were presented as prototypes of that strident image. Furthermore, the message of the media undercut the messages of movement women; it made their ideas appear absurd and characterized the movement leaders in such a way that women in their audiences were not likely to identify with them. The message was trivialized and made banal. Mundane issues, such as whether equality meant that men ought still to doff their hats or hold doors open for ladies, were often posed as central to whether one ought or ought not to be allied with the women's movement. Steinem got as much attention for her hair style and miniskirts as for her message.

The *New York Times*'s policy of reporting news about the women's movement on the women's page contributed to that trivialization. A particularly apt example involves their women's page coverage of a 1970 fund-raising event in support of a mass march of women. Charlotte Curtis, a society reporter since promoted to editor of the women's pages and then editor of the *Times*'s Op-Ed page, was assigned to cover the fund raiser. Famed for cynical stories about society parties, she applied her sardonic eye to a feminist party being held at the home of a prominent art collector. The resulting article made humor its theme. Curtis reported that while Betty Friedan spoke about the need to support the women's movement, a sleeve slipped off one shoulder and that Friedan appeared to have had too much to drink. Curtis mockingly reported Jill Johnston's act of bravado as she took off her shirt to take a dunk in the swimming pool of the opulent home. Although this was a funny story, it missed the point of the fund raiser. The fund raiser was news of a sort: It was termed feature news appropriate for the women's pages. The August 1970 march marking the anniversary of women's suffrage itself did not get even as much space on the general pages as did the Columbus Day or St. Patrick's Day parades. The symbolic action of the women's movement had been defined by the newspaper as women's news only.

The practices that typed news as women's news are curious.

Newspapers like to be first in coverage. They also like to get *all* the news. But newspapers did *not* apply these values in reporting when the women's movement began to gain impetus. Their failure to do so emphasizes how closely the news media maintain a collective view with other sources of information in our society. Media representatives can only "see" news stories developing in already well-defined frameworks. By viewing the women's movement as women's business only, newspapers take the moral position that men don't need to know about this phenomenon.

Judgment about what men need to know was more accurate in the *Wall Street Journal,* which led in good reporting of women's movement activities. It did better reporting of litigation and legal issues affecting women's rights and the accumulating landmark decisions in the courts about sex-discrimination legislation and the machinery for its implementation. Still, reporting was poor on events that could be construed as news items. For instance, the important cases of stewardesses who fought, with movement support, to retain their jobs after marriage and the cases of working-class women with children fighting to keep their jobs (such as *Phillips* vs. *Martin Marietta*) got poor coverage. The significance—for the economy as well as the society—of the fight to end sex discrimination in employment was not yet grasped. Only when the E.E.O.C. suit against A.T.&T. was won in 1973 did women's news become corporate and business news. Enormous fines or settlements are big business; they justify the move from the women's page to general news and business pages. Perhaps it is not surprising then that throughout that time span of coverage, the *Wall Street Journal,* concerned about the consequences of the women's movement for business, often did more accurate reporting of women's activities than did the *New York Times* and the news magazines.

One last social meaning attaches to the pattern of reporting that I have described. It acts on the assumption that men do not have emotional needs or interest in events having to do with human concerns. This view assumes that men's concerns have been met once their occupations and political and sports activities have been given attention. It suggests, among other things, that men don't have families or love affairs with their attendant problems. Ghettoizing discussions of such matters on women's pages reinforces outmoded views that men should not be concerned with families and their own and others' emotional needs.

In the last analysis, the encouragement of sex divisions in newspapers also indirectly colors the reality of news coverage. After all, when South Vietnam fell, millions of women's lives were affected even though most reporters were unobservant of them. Starvation in Biafra and throughout central Africa also affected women. Not documenting the consequences of these events for women creates a message for all women and for all men as well. It says that women don't count for much in social and national life. It suggests that, like the sediment in wine, they sink to the bottom in a brew that doesn't mix. Such a view, though, ignores the fact that the sediment is vital in imparting to wine its characteristic zest, sophistication and taste.

4

Television's Effect on Children and Youth

INTRODUCTION

Relatively little is known about the effects of the mass media's sex-role stereotypes upon attitudes and behavior. The sparse information available focuses upon television's influence on children. This section includes two empirical studies of the effects of television upon children's sex-role stereotypes. Each emerges from a different research tradition. The work reported by Joyce Sprafkin and Robert Liebert in Chapter 13 is based on work done in the experimenters' laboratory. In Chapter 14, Larry Gross and Suzanne Jeffries-Fox offer a theoretical discussion and preliminary results of a longitudinal survey.

Although complimentary findings in laboratory and survey data may be seen as validating one another, that is *not* the case with these two research reports. First, each essay discusses a different problem. Second, each deals with a different age group. Thus, each chapter should be read as an example of the kinds of research undertaken to learn about the impact of television upon sex-role stereotypes.

Sprafkin and Liebert (Chapter 13) want to know whether boys and girls pay more attention to members of their own gender when they watch television. They are interested in this question, because television programmers claim that both boys and girls respond to male-oriented children's shows, but boys don't like female-oriented programs. Television programmers use this justification to schedule more male-oriented than female-oriented children's shows.

Sprafkin and Liebert also want to discover how closely children pay attention to boys and girls engaged in sex-typed or neuter activities and whether the children identify with the television characters. Here, Sprafkin and Liebert's interest is more theoretical. Attention and identification are two components of the modeling process through which gender identity is formed.

To study these issues, Sprafkin and Liebert invited girls and boys to watch television in a laboratory designed to look homelike. The room contained toys for children to use if they wished to watch the programs televised from time to time. And the children were shown carefully selected programs known to be popular with their age group. Each program featured a family including boys and girls, and the young viewers were given the opportunity to select one of two episodes from the same series. The different episodes revolved around either a boy or a girl; the television characters were involved in behaviors appropriate to a boy (in the case of male actors), or a girl (female characters), or activities that were neuter. Sprafkin and Liebert monitored the behavior of the young viewers and videotaped their behaviors for further analysis. Then they interviewed the youngsters. Their findings directly and forcefully contradict the programming rationale of the television industry; Sprafkin and Liebert find that members of each sex prefer to watch characters of their own gender. Chiefly, their data suggest that children model their sex-role behaviors after stereotyped television portrayals.

Gross and Jeffries-Fox invoke a different theoretical rationale in their preliminary report (Chapter 14). Rather than testing a theoretical model of how children learn from television, they assume that children do in fact learn from it. They raise the theoretical issues: Does television compliment or contradict other lessons from the child's social world, or does it exert an independent influence? Empirically, the child's social world is captured by such variables as grades in school, parents' education, parents' participation in the labor force and their social class, and the child's intelligence as measured by IQ. Lessons learned from television may be many and varied, from antisocial and prosocial behavior to specific skills. In Chapter 14, the "lessons" relate to educational desires, educational aspirations, and the adoption of sexist attitudes. In essence, Gross and Jeffries-Fox want to know, does heavy television viewing raise or lower children's educational desires and aspirations? Or, are those desires and aspirations embedded in other aspects of their social world? Does television generate sexist attitudes? Or does it compliment or contradict aspects of children's social world? These questions cannot be answered yet because the longitudinal data are still being gathered.

The answers given here are preliminary and incomplete. Gross and Jeffries-Fox present data only about the association between television viewing and specific lessons. They ask how much of those associations are explained by other background variables. They do not claim that television is the cause of lowered educational aspirations in children who are heavy viewers. Nor do they claim that television causes sexist attitudes. Additionally, the associations reported are relatively weak, compared with those generally viewed as theoretically interesting by social scientists. But the statistical significance of their data indicates that the variations are not the result of happenstance. Rather, they say: (1) the more television children watch, the lower their educational desires and expectations, although some of this variation is accounted for by IQ and indicators of social class; and (2) television is associated with sexist attitudes in boys more than in girls. Most of the variation in boys is explained by intelligence, but girls' intelligence appears virtually irrelevant to the association of television viewing and sexist attitudes.

Later phases of Gross and Jeffries-Fox's research may say why these patterns exist. For now, their work enables us to make the tentative statement that television viewing and sexist attitudes may, on occasion, go hand in hand.

Chapter 13

JOYCE N. SPRAFKIN and ROBERT M. LIEBERT

Sex-Typing and Children's Television Preferences

Throughout the entire life span, an individual's gender is one of the most important determinants of interpersonal behavior and attitudes. As early as school age, children recognize the concepts "male" and "female," and express socially prescribed preferences for behaviors and activities considered "gender-appropriate" (Kohlberg, 1966). It is widely accepted that these sex-typed attitudes and behaviors are gradually acquired during early and middle childhood. Accordingly, the process by which this learning takes place has been addressed by a number of developmental theorists. A cognitive interpretation (Kohlberg, 1966) assumes that children develop the realization that their gender is unchangeable, and then in order to maintain a sense of self-worth they positively evaluate attributes of their own sex and model their own behaviors and values after same-sex models. A social-learning view (Grusec and Brinker, 1972; Mischel, 1970) asserts that children are reinforced for imitating same-sex models, and, therefore, they attend more closely to and learn more from same-sex models. Consistent with both views is the idea that children will emulate same-sex models because rewards are maximized, whether they be self-worth or social or tangible benefits.

Sex-role socialization has many sources, the most important of which are parents, teachers, siblings, and peers. In addition to these primary sources, the contemporary child has available a multitude of compelling models via the entertainment media, particularly television. Television is clearly the most pervasive communication medium in the United States today. Regardless of economic status, virtually every American home has at least one television set, and children watch on the average between two and three hours each day (Lyle and Hoffman, 1972). This amounts to considerable exposure; in fact, by the time the average child is fifteen years of age, he or she will have spent more time watching television than in school (Liebert, Neale, and Davidson, 1973).

Given the pervasiveness of television, parents and special-interest groups have reasonably asked: What are the sex-role behaviors and attitudes that children can learn from television? Researchers have explored this issue by examining the nature of televised sex-role portrayals and their influence.

A framework for understanding the influence process has been suggested by Clark (1972), who states that the way the television viewer develops attitudes toward social groups involves a two-step process. First, the group has to gain *recognition* through sheer representation on television. If a viewer sees a particular social group very frequently on television, he or she presumes they are at least a relevant segment of society, while a group never (or hardly ever) presented communicates that the group must be insignificant. If a group is represented, the viewer's impression is further influenced by the degree of *respect* the group is given. Respect for a group comes from both the formal social class or occupational roles it is assigned as well as the personalities its members project. A group seen frequently on television can still be relegated to an inferior status if its members occupy a low socioeconomic class or display undesirable characteristics. In short, recognition addresses *how often* a group is represented, and respect, *how* it is portrayed.

The accumulated evidence from a number of content analyses strongly suggests that in terms of both recognition and respect, portrayals of females on television are extremely biased. First, females are grossly underrepresented on television. Unlike their forty-nine percent proportion in the population, males repeatedly have been found to occupy between sixty-six percent and seventy-five percent of all television roles in studies spanning two decades (Gerbner, 1972a; Head, 1954; Tedesco, 1974). Aside from conveying the message that females are less significant than males, this underrepresentation results in female viewers having available a disproportionately small number of sex-appropriate models relative to male viewers.

In terms of the formal social roles, television males are generally employed and enjoy highly prestigious occupational roles (for example, as physicians, lawyers, and law-enforcement officials). In contrast, most television women are assigned marital, romantic, and family roles; only one-third of television roles having a definite occupational activity are held by women and those jobs are rarely prestigious ones (DeFleur, 1964; Gerbner, 1972a; Tedesco, 1974).

Aside from their formal occupational or social status, television males and females project very different personal attributes. For one thing, the nature of the roles given to females and males are quite different—females are more often cast in light or comic roles and males in serious roles. Almost seventy-five percent of female television characters are found in comedies or similar shows, whereas more than fifty percent of the male characters are in crime, western, and action-adventure shows (Tedesco, 1974). Within these roles, females are portrayed as more attractive, fair, sociable, warm, happy, peaceful, and youthful than males, and males are portrayed as more powerful, stable, rational, and smarter than females (Tedesco, 1974). Studies that quantified specific social behaviors also reveal very different portrayals for males and females. Donagher, Poulos, Liebert, and Davidson. (1976) found that on bi-racial prime-time programming, females are more likely than males to help, share, and cooperate with others, to sympathize and explain their feelings to others, to repair damage caused to others, and to resist the temptation to break societal rules. In contrast, males were found to be more aggressive, but also better able to delay gratification and to persist at tasks. On children's programs, females are generally passive, deferent, and very likely punished for emitting high levels of activity, while males make plans, are constructive, and generally are rewarded for their efforts (Sternglanz and Serbin, 1974). Overall, parallel with the societal stereotypes, television portrays females as kind and altruistic and males as aggressive and successful.

Two recent studies suggest that children's sex-role attitudes are influenced by televised sex-role portrayals. Frueh and McGhee (1975) found that children (kindergarten through sixth graders) who were heavy television watchers (twenty-five hours or more per week) maintained more stereotypic sex-role values than a comparable group of light television watchers (ten hours or less per week), a finding which very likely suggests a causal influence. In a series of experimental studies, Atkin (1975) varied the apparent occupational role of the spokeswoman giving a testimonial in a commercial for eyeglasses that influenced viewers' perceptions of the appropriateness of that occupation for women. For example, children who saw the spokeswoman dressed as a court judge subsequently perceived this occupation as more appropriate for women than did children who saw her presented as a television technician and vice versa. Atkin also found that the sex of the children who appeared in a commercial for toy racing cars influenced young viewers' attitudes regarding the sex appropriateness of playing with this toy; viewers of the commercial in which girls were seen playing with the cars were subsequently more likely to perceive this activity as appropriate for girls than were children who saw the same commercial, but with boy characters. Thus it would seem clear that children's sex-role attitudes may be influenced by programs and commercials.

The notion that television affects children's sex-role attitudes is further strengthened by the impressive evidence of television's influence on other areas of functioning. The effect of violent programming on children's subsequent behavior has been extensively researched and soundly supported (Ellis and Sekyra, 1972; Leifer and Roberts, 1972; Liebert and Baron, 1972; Stein and Friedrich, 1972; Steuer, Applefield, and Smith, 1971). On the positive side, it has been found that exposure to socially desirable content can increase child viewers' prosocial interpersonal behaviors (Stein and Friedrich, 1972), their willingness to help (Sprafkin, Liebert, and Poulos, 1975), and to cooperate (Liebert, Sprafkin, and Poulos, 1975; Poulos, Liebert, and Schwartzberg, 1975). Furthermore, television has been shown to influence more subtle areas such as racial attitudes (Graves, 1975) and cultural views (Gerbner and Gross, 1974a). These findings make it quite compelling to believe that the stereotyped sex-role portrayals on television affect child viewers.

Special-interest groups have been quite vocal in their demands for an increase in the representation of and an improvement in the portrayal of females on television (for example, Women on Words and Images, 1975). However, these requests for change have not been well received by the television industry, in part because of conservatism and inertia, but chiefly because of an apparent belief that viewership or capturing an audience will be maximized with a predominance of males and a stereotyping of sex roles.

The standard methods of determining program appeal have been the survey method in which individuals are asked to name their favorite programs and the Nielsen ratings, in which the number of television sets within a representative sample tuned to various programs is indicated. Conclusions about the appeal of various sex-role portrayals based on either of these procedures are questionable due to a number of methodological limitations. First, the survey method relies totally on self-reports, and the validity of such data can be reasonably questioned. Second, the Nielsen ratings merely provide a gross figure of the number of tuned-in television sets, not who is watching television and how consistently the program is attended to. Third, both methods are intended to detect viewership differences between series, but they provide little information about the program attributes contributing to a series' appeal. For example, the relative success of a male character-featured program over a female character-featured program proves little when there is a lack of comparability on plot and program tone.

Designed to avoid the limitations of these methods, we developed an experimental procedure for determining the influence of specific program attributes on children's television program selections and attention. Briefly, the technique involved directly monitoring the child's viewing behavior from behind a well concealed one-way screen, while he or she watched television in a den-like setting in which wall hangings and toys served as natural distractors. The influence of specific program attributes on program selections and attention was assessed by providing the child with a channel changer (which operates essentially like a regular dial changer) and giving her or him the opportunity to choose between previously broadcast, unedited programs selected by the experimenters so as to vary on a particular attribute but to be as similar as possible on all other relevant dimensions. To ensure that the data reflected viewing behavior rather than "tuning in" behavior, a videotape record of the child's attentional pattern to selected programs was made and later analyzed for duration of attention (defined as eyes oriented toward the screen) to the programs and scenes within the programs. Program preferences, selections, and attention were thus measured directly in a more or less natural viewing situation, while experimental control of the programs available permitted us to determine the specific attributes influencing these viewing behaviors. Finally, because children have been found to learn most from characters with whom they identify (Maccoby and Wilson, 1957), at the end of the viewing period, we interviewed the children about the characters with whom they identified; this had been operationalized by Maccoby and Wilson (1957) as the character the child likes, feels he or she is similar to, and wants to be like.

In a recent study (Sprafkin and Liebert, 1976) we used this general method to determine the influence of sex and sex-role portrayals on children's selections of and attention to television programs. From our videotape library of recorded programs, we selected nonviolent programs that featured a child character; programs that featured a girl character were called female character-focused, and those that featured a boy character were called male character-focused. Thirty-two first- and second-grade children, sixteen males and sixteen females, were invited individually to watch television alone in our den setting. All children chose between a male character-focused and a female character-focused program from the same series; half the children saw a pair of programs from the "Brady Bunch" series and half saw programs from the "Nanny and the Professor" series. Inviting children to choose between programs from the *same* series minimized the chances that program differences other than the sex of the featured character could account for the observed program preferences. The sex-stereotyping dimension was included by having half the children watching each series see programs in which the featured character was engaged in a sex-typed activity (a behavior usually performed by members of one sex) and the other half see programs in which the featured character engaged in a nonsex-typed activity (behaviors generally performed by members of both sexes).

The presence of a pattern of sex-typed behaviors permitted us to classify entire episodes as sex stereotyped; for example, a story that revolved around a female character's affection for her doll was a female sex-typed program, and one that focused on a boy character's problems with being a hall monitor at school was a male sex-typed program. Nonsex-typed programs presented less rigid sex-role portrayals; for example, one program was about a child who lost her balloon and another was about a girl entering her father in a "Father of the Year" contest.

It will be recalled that the broadcasters apparently assume that male characters capture a wider general audience than do female characters. However, we found that while the boys selected and attended to the male-focused programs more than to the female-focused programs and attended specifically to male character-dominated scenes more than to female character-dominated scenes, exactly the opposite was true of girls. In all, the girls selected and attended to the female-focused programs and to female character-dominated scenes for approximately two-thirds of the potential viewing time. Girls were *no more likely* to attend to male-focused programs or scenes than were boys to attend to female-focused programs and scenes. Girls attended to 29.4 percent of the male-focused programs and boys attended to 35.8 percent of the female-focused programs. These percentages are not significantly different. Further, girls attended to 38.4 percent of the male character-dominated scenes and boys attended to 38.8 percent of the female character-dominated scenes. These percentages are almost identical. Figures 13.1 and 13.2 graphically show boys' and girls' attention to male- and female-focused programs and scenes. Parallel with these selection and attention findings, boys and girls to the same degree identified with same-sex characters; same-sex characters were named as the favorite for 83.9 percent of the children, as the one most similar to the child by 90.6 percent of the children, and as the one most desired to be like by 96.7 percent of the children. Overall, the data strongly suggest that the broadcasters' economic justification for the underrepresentation of female characters is unwarranted.

In addition to gender, the sex-role behavior of the main child character was found to influence the children's viewing behav-

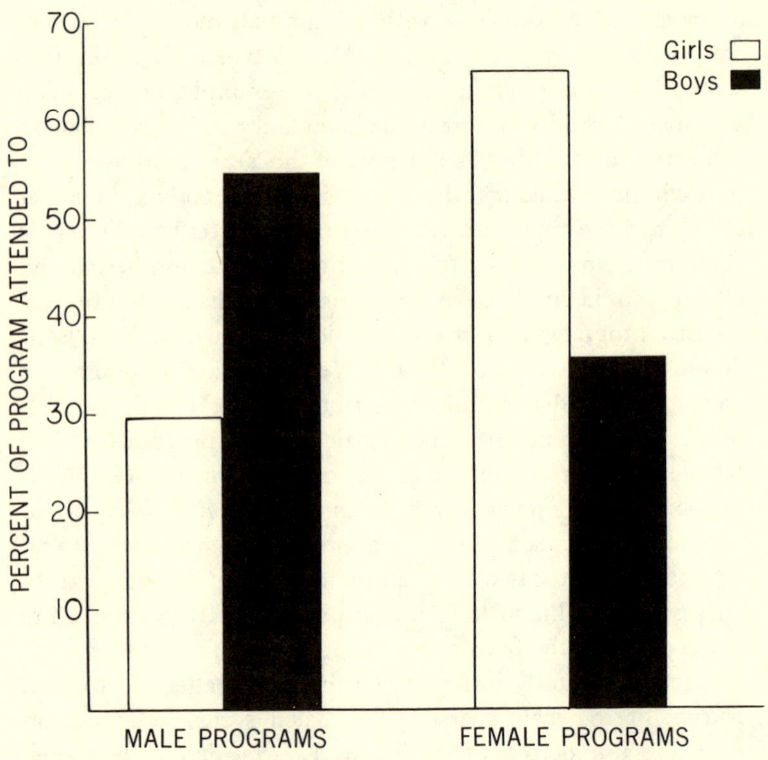

Figure 13.1. Percent Attention to Male and to Female Programs.

ior. First, the sex-typed program pairs were attended to significantly more closely than the nonsex-typed pairs. Further, children's selection of and attention to characters of their own sex, a generally robust phenomenon, tended to be even more strongly evidenced when the characters' actions were sex-typed than when they were not. For example, girls shown the sex-typed programs on the average attended to 77.70 percent of the female-oriented program and to 16.95 percent of the male-oriented program; in contrast, girls shown the nonsex-typed programs attended al-

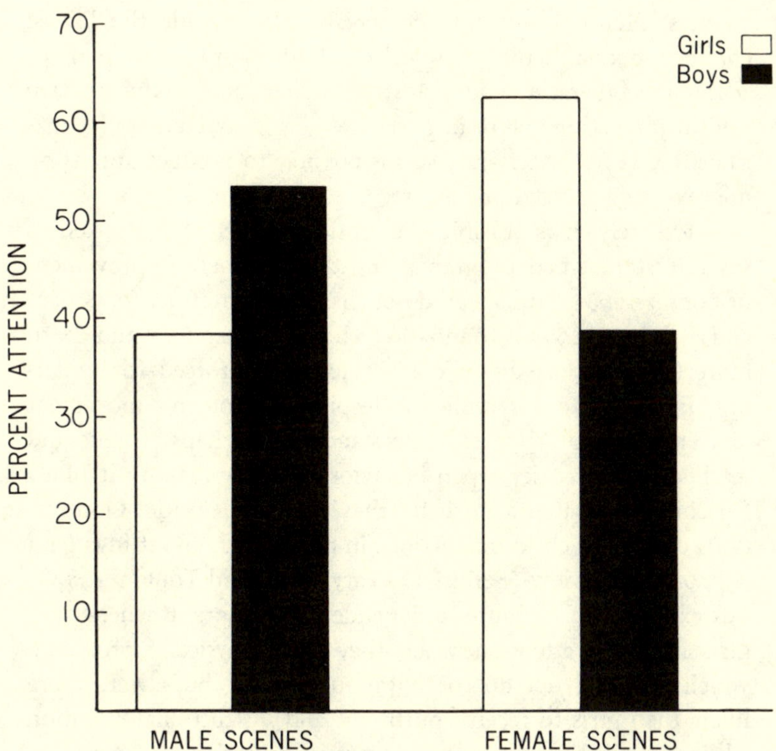

Figure 13.2. Percent Attention to Male and to Female Scenes.

most equally to the male- and female-focused programs (51.74 percent paid attention to the female-oriented program and 41.89 percent paid attention to the male-oriented program).

There are at least two plausible explanations for the greater appeal of sex-typed programs. First, the finding may be a reflection of program writers' and producers' creative skills. In trying to reach the largest possible audience, the most obvious formula is to rely on stories and characters that are simplified and exaggerated so as to be instantly recognizable to a wide range of viewers. Hence stereotypic portrayals may provide the lowest common denominator on which to build story lines; perhaps without exaggerating and distorting, writers and producers have difficulty creating interesting yet credible characters and situations. However, it certainly seems possible to produce appealing nonsex-typed entertainment fare.

Alternately, it is feasible that children might be attracted to sex-role stereotyped programs, and that the mere improvement of nonsex-typed scripts would not change this preference. Grusec and Brinker (1972) found that children attend to and learn more from models they were previously reinforced for imitating. In regard to our findings, despite the women's movement and an easing of rigid sex-role standards, perhaps parents and teachers reinforce sex-typed behaviors, thereby making it likely for children to attend to such behaviors on television. Observations of teacher-child interactions in nursery school settings lend support to this view (Serbin, O'Leary, Kent, and Tonick, 1973). For example, in response to dependent behaviors, teachers gave girls increased attention when they were physically proximal, which they did not do for boys; in contrast, boys were more likely than girls to receive nurturant and instructional attention while participating appropriately in class activities.

While sex-role viewing preferences may reflect sex-role socialization practices, it is likely that they in turn influence the development of children's sex-role attitudes. The findings of our naturalistic experiment suggest that when children are left to choose their own programs (which is the case for the overwhelming majority of children), they tend to select programs that feature characters of their own sex behaving in stereotypic ways. They attend closely to those same-sex characters and identify with them; and both attention (Yussen, 1974) and identification (Maccoby and Wilson, 1957) are known to enhance the amount learned from a model. Beyond that, the potential of the child viewer to acquire and incorporate the sex-typed behavior is great in the light of television's demonstrated power to influence children's behaviors and attitudes. Our society is gradually moving in the direction of liberating both males and females from following rigid standards of sex-role behavior, and the confining and outmoded sex roles viewed on television may undermine, or at the least retard, that progress.

Chapter 14

LARRY GROSS and SUZANNE JEFFRIES-FOX

"What Do You Want To Be When You Grow Up, Little Girl?"

APPROACHES TO THE STUDY OF MEDIA EFFECTS

The aims and limitations of this report require some prefatory clarification. Our intention is twofold: (1) to consider how the effects of television on viewers might be identified and measured; and (2) to present a progress report on the initial stages of a project attempting to formulate and investigate that question. The theory we are detailing and the progress we are reporting are part of a larger enterprise, the Cultural Indicators project at the Annenberg School of the University of Pennsylvania where George Gerbner and the senior author are co-investigators. The concepts and concerns embodied in this report would not have come into being were it not for Gerbner's initial inspiration and continued collaboration.

We must also note that we are reporting here on only a small part of the aims and accomplishments of the Cultural Indicators project, specifically the early phases of that part of the project that is particularly relevant to the problem of assessing the role of television drama in the cultivation of sex-role related beliefs, values, and aspirations among children.

CAN WE MEASURE THE EFFECTS OF TELEVISION?

"ROUND UP THE USUAL SUSPECTS"

The accumulated wisdom of social-science research offers a clear and respectable method for the identification and measurement of the effects of exposure to messages, namely to assess the differences between the state of the receivers before and after exposure and to compare these differences with those obtained from a control group who have not received the message. One may then venture to draw conclusions about the consequences of exposure to that message, at least for certain kinds of receivers.

When the message whose effects we wish to identify and measure is television drama, however, this traditional approach may be inappropriate. Indeed, for reasons outlined below, we believe that any attempt to conceptualize, isolate, and assess the consequences of exposure to television drama must begin by categorically abandoning approaches based on either comparison of pre- versus post-exposure groups or experimental versus control-group viewers.

A fond hope of researchers in this area has been to locate an island of unexposed (or, as it usually happens, about-to-be-exposed) potential viewers in order to achieve scientifically valid measures of the effects of exposure to television. The researchers might attempt to gather data on the pre-exposure state of nature for comparison with the later, post-exposure beliefs and behavior of these new viewers; or, if possible, even attempt to maintain (or locate) a group who remain unexposed long enough to serve as a control comparison for the newly exposed. The problem, however, is how such fortuitous natural experiments can tell us anything about the effects of exposure to television in a society where television has been ubiquitous for the entire lifetime of half of the population. The results of this type of research may answer a host of theoretical and practical questions about the introduction of television to the few remaining unexposed corners of the earth; they have nothing useful to say, however, about the effects of television on the beliefs and behavior of adults or children in our society.

Another popular research route we believe inappropriate is the experimental or quasi-experimental test of the consequences of exposure to a particular sample of television programming. Much of the research on the effects of television media violence has focused on the observation and measurement of viewers' behavior after exposure to a particular television program. All such studies, however, no matter how clean the design and clear the results, are of limited value because they ignore the fundamental feature of television drama, namely that it consists of a vast, complex, and integrated system of characters, events, and relationships and that its effects cannot be measured by any single program (or set of programs) seen in isolation.

THE SYSTEM IS THE MESSAGE

How, then, can the effects of television be conceptualized and studied? We believe that one must begin with a fuller understanding of the total phenomenon of television. We begin with two fundamental and related assumptions. The first is that television is a cultural arm of the established industrial order and as such serves primarily to maintain, stabilize, and reinforce rather than to alter, threaten, or weaken conventional conceptions, beliefs, and behaviors. Because media messages are commodities manufactured for sale, their perspective reflects institutional organization and control. The goal of greatest audience appeal at least cost demands that these messages follow conventional social morality. The second assumption is that in most relevant respects television drama is not essentially different from other forms of mainstream cultural entertainment.

These assumptions require us to question many of the common arguments and concerns raised in discussions of television's effects. An important example is the concern over the consequences of violence on television. In contrast to the worries that are most often expressed, we do not believe that the primary result of television violence is the stimulation of violence or aggression on the part of viewers. As Gerbner and Gross have stated: "Fear may be a more critical concomitant of a show of violence than aggression. Assumptions about life and conceptions of social reality may be more telling indicators of what violent representations cultivate than any individual behavior. Acceptance of violence and passivity in the face of injustice may be consequences of great social concern" (1974, p. 4).

The invention and development of systems that produce and disseminate mass-mediated fictional images have historically raised a specter of subversion, corruption, and unrest being encouraged among the various lower orders—poor people, ethnic and racial minorities, children, and women. Whether the suspect and controversial media are newspapers, novels, and theater, as in the nineteenth century, or movies, radio, comic books, and television in the twentieth, concern tends to focus on the possibilities of disruptions that threaten the established norms of belief, behavior, and morality. Therefore, in our view the primary function of these symbolic images is the demonstration of power and authority—often through the dramatic use of violence. Moreover, the lessons are generally effective; the social order is only rarely and peripherally threatened. The system is the message, and, as our politicians like to say, the system works.

PRIMUS INTER PARES

The reality of television drama does not differ in its basic assumptions from the reality of our public (and often false) consciousness; indeed, given television's corporate and institutional sources and economic imperatives, how could it? Public protest and scientific research may bring about adjustments in the cruder, more controversial, or repellant aspects of television's fictional fare; they are unlikely to challenge its central principles and lineaments.

At this point, however, we may appear to have eliminated any possibility of success in our task, that is, the identification and assessment of the effects of television drama. If it is the case that television functions to prevent or minimize changes in beliefs and behavior, and if it is the case that television drama performs this function in concert with all other major cultural institutions, how can (and why should) one hope to isolate its effects, let alone presume to measure them? Clearly, this is a dilemma for policymakers as well as for researchers, a favorite rejoinder on the part of the television industry being, "Why pick on us?"

THE MEDIUM OF THE MASSES

First, television may be credited with an unprecedented ubiquity that makes it potentially much more effective than the other branches of mass culture. It reaches ninety-six percent of U.S. households, is available literally round-the-clock for most of the population, and is watched over five hours per day in the average household. Gerbner and Gross say of television's pervasiveness:

> [We] cannot emphasize too strongly the historically novel role of television in standardizing and sharing with all as the common norm what had before been more parochial, local, and selective cultural patterns. We assume, therefore, that TV's standardizing and legitimizing influence comes largely from its ability to streamline, amplify, ritualize, and spread (to previously unreached groups) the conventional capsules of mass-

produced information and entertainment (Gerbner and Gross, 1974, p. 6).

Second, the nature of the medium itself contributes to the degree and the depth of television's cultural penetration. Unlike the print media, television does not require literacy from its audience. Unlike the movies, television is free (at least one doesn't pay by the show—we all pay over the counter, whether or not we watch television). Unlike radio, television can show as well as tell. Each of these characteristics is significant in itself, and the combined force of all three is overwhelming. This constellation of medium-specific characteristics endows television with a dangerously seductive credibility. It seems to us indisputable that television's predominance can be attributed to its transparent intelligibility as well as to its omnipresence. In fact, it is probable that the former has helped make the latter possible.

THE MESSAGE IS THE SYSTEM

We are arguing that the appropriate stimulus or treatment is not any specific program or type of program, nor any particular hero, or villain, or action. The important stimulus is the entire world of television drama. We are concerned with the *system* of messages to which total communities are exposed and which provide bases for interaction and common assumptions and definitions (though not necessarily agreement) among large and heterogeneous publics. Gerbner states: "The dominant agencies of communication produce the messages that cultivate the dominant image patterns. They structure the public agenda of existence, priorities, values and relations" (1972b, p. 159).

By contrast, public concern about the content and effects of other symbolic message systems is generally directed towards specific and limited aspects of content, particularly if such content could instill in audiences ambitions and notions inappropriate to their stations in life. In the terms of our analysis such concerns are missing the point. The ground, as well as the figure, is crucially important.

FICTIONAL FIGURES ON "REAL" GROUNDS

As Gross has written elsewhere:

> The dominant stylistic convention of Western narrative art—novels, plays, films, TV dramas—is that of representational realism. However stereotyped television plots are, viewers assume that they take place against a backdrop of the real world. Characters must behave as normal people would in most situations. When the impossible does occur, it will often be treated as if it, too, were part of a natural order in which nuns can fly and horses speak (1974, p. 86).

Nothing impeaches the basic "reality" of the world of television drama. Television offers the viewer an apparently rich array of windows through which he or she can glimpse apparently diverse images and actions, but the diversity is only in the shape of the window and the angle of the glimpse—the basic topography of the fictional world is the same. Television is also highly informative, offering a continuous stream of "facts" and impressions about the way of the world, the constancies and vagaries of human nature, and the consequences of actions it seems to offer realism. "The premise of realism is a Trojan horse which carries within it a highly selective and purposeful image of the facts of life" (Gross, 1974, p. 86).

Can we assume, however, that viewers absorb these facts of life from the world of media fiction? More important, can we determine whether and to what degree they assimilate these "facts" into their images and beliefs about the real world?

A normal adult viewer is not likely to be unaware of the fictiveness of television drama. No one calls the police or an ambulance when a character in a television program is shot. Still, one may wonder how often and to what extent viewers suspend their disbelief in the reality of the symbolic world. Surely viewers know that Robert Young is not a doctor and that Marcus Welby is an M.D. only by poetic license. Yet in the first five years of the program, Mr. Young (or should we say Dr. Welby?) received over a quarter of a million letters from viewers, most containing requests for medical advice.[1]

The naiveté that leads viewers to ask Dr. Welby for medical advice, however, is a misleading minor example of the phenomenon we are interested in. After all, many of these viewers may simply have assumed that Robert Young had picked up a lot of medical knowledge or that he has a staff of medical experts working on the show. Underlying either of these explanations, however, is the real crux of the issue—the apparently convincing naturalism of the Dr. Welby program that could give a viewer grounds for making either of those exculpatory assumptions. In the newspaper story cited above, the Pennsylvania Insurance Commissioner was reported to have blamed Dr. Welby for causing the public to expect much more of doctors and to have claimed the series might be one reason for the increase in malpractice suits!

Doctor shows are not the only targets of such accusations. A former New York City police official has complained that jury members have formed images and expectations of trial procedures and outcomes from television that often prejudice the police in actual trials.

Isolated anecdotes and examples should not, however, confuse or trivialize the real point—that even the most sophisticated among us can find many large and important components of our knowledge of the real world which, upon reflection, are found to derive in whole or part from fictitious symbolic representations. How often, in fact, *do* we un-suspend our disbelief as we attend to the action figure (which we know is not real) and at the same time assimilate the setting and premises (which are, after all, "realistic")?

Most viewers have never been in an operating room, a criminal courtroom, a police station or a jail, a corporate boardroom, or a movie studio. Much of what they "know" about these diverse spheres of activity, about how these various kinds of people live and what they do—much of their "real" world—has been learned from fictional worlds. To the extent that viewers see television drama (the foreground of plot or the background of the television world) as naturalistic, they may derive a wealth of incidental knowledge. This incidental learning may be effected by bald "facts" and by the subtle interplay of occurrence, co-occurrence, and nonoccurrence of actors and actions.

The premise of realism is a major promoter of such tacit learning because it predisposes us to assess falsely the status of the images we observe. To recognize an event as symbolic is to see it as intentionally articulated in accordance with known conventions of communicative behavior (Worth and Gross, 1974, p. 27). However, if we assess that event as natural we make a very different assumption—natural events are governed by the facts of life, not by the conventions of art. The naturalistic conventions of television realism, while far from natural in any sense of objective truth, are perilously susceptible to such assessment errors. We may therefore have grounds for apprehension that all of us are fooled some of the time and some of us may be fooled all of the time.

In addition to the subtle patterns against whose influence we may all be somewhat defenseless, television provides another seductively persuasive sort of imagery. In real life much is hidden from our eyes, motives are often obscure, outcomes ambiguous, personalities complex, people unpredictable. The world of television, in contrast, offers us clarity and resolution. Problems are never left hanging, rewards and punishments are present and accounted for; the rules of the game are known and rarely change. Not only does television "show" us the normally hidden workings of many important and fascinating institutions—medicine, law enforcement, and justice, big business, and the glamorous world of entertainment—but we "see" the people who fill important and exciting roles. We see who they are in crude terms of sex, age, race, and class and we also see them as personalities—dedicated and selfless, ruthless and ambitious, good-hearted but ineffectual, lazy and shiftless, corrupt and corrupting.

From the myriad of images, events, and patterns a world emerges that is often intermingled with our "real" world. In an interview with a middle-aged Philadelphia man, one of our researchers was told that the police he saw on television were "more real" than those in real life, because in real life one occasionally found a bad apple who wasn't, therefore, a "real" policeman. While that opinion seems relatively rare, this viewer was joined by many others in justifying his belief in the realism of television police shows by saying, "Well, if it wasn't real they wouldn't be allowed to show it, would they?"

THE SEDUCTION OF THE INNOCENT

Finally, however generous we may be in granting adults a degree of sophisticated immunity to many of the subtle lessons of television's hidden curriculum, it is not possible to be as sanguine about the ability of children to distinguish the accurately realistic from the improbable and the downright misleading "facts of life" they see on television, since those "facts" are presented realistically.

There are several reasons for thinking that children may be particularly susceptible to those aspects of television drama that cultivate systems of belief and "knowledge" that may be assimilated into their basic world view. In the first place, they simply have less opportunity to contrast the world of television with the real world. Much of what they see on television is no more directly familiar to them than are the depictions of cowboys and Indians in the Old West (from which most of us have also learned many false "facts"). Moreover, much of what they watch, Saturday morning cartoons in particular, presents the lessons of television in starkly blatant form.

Children also have a particularly strong belief in the inherent reality and truth of photographic and filmic images. Worth and Gross (1974) have proposed a theoretical model of the ways in which we learn to assess and interpret natural and symbolic events. Studies conducted by them and their students have shown that children will respond to a story shown them in the form of photographic slides by stating that it was real—that it really happened. The reasons the children give for these judgments are based precisely on the assumption of realism: They know the story is real because, after all, photographs show reality and don't lie.

Our concern over the likelihood that children are the most vulnerable consumers of television's messages is heightened by the research of Melvin and Lois DeFleur. The DeFleurs set out to assess the relative influence of television on children's occupational knowledge (1967). Utilizing an analysis of the portrayal of occupational roles on television (DeFleur, 1964), they selected groups of occupations in three categories—those the ordinary child finds in direct contact, those rarely seen directly but frequently portrayed on television, and those neither encountered directly nor seen on television. When they asked children of various ages to identify, describe, and assess the relative prestige of these occupations, the influence of television was obvious and powerful: "[It] seems safe to conclude that, within the limits of the present sample of children and occupations, television is a more potent source of occupational status knowledge than either personal contact or the general community culture" (DeFleur and DeFleur, 1967, p. 787).

Moreover, the DeFleurs reported an effect that is even more supportive of our approach. Television was indeed a "potent source of 'incidental' learning for children concerning adult occupational roles," but what were they learning? The DeFleurs noted that the television portrayals were, in fact, stereotyped and that their data showed a homogenization effect—both among and between the children, their parents, and experts—in "ranking the occupations for which TV was the major learning source." They concluded with an expression of concern about television's influence:

> Given the limited amount of objective research data on incidental learning which has been assembled at present, we can do little more than note that television appears to be an important agency of socialization for children concerning the adult world. However, there is ample reason to suspect that the information it presents is often distorted in a variety of ways.
>
> [It] can be suggested that TV provides children with much superficial and misleading information about the labor force of their society. From this they acquire stereotyped beliefs about the world of work (p. 789).

"WHAT'S A RESEARCHER TO DO?"

Television drama functions primarily, we have argued, to stabilize and reinforce rather than challenge or alter established norms, conventions, and behavior. For this reason, one might think that the question of effects would be better addressed by focusing on those not exposed to television rather than on those who are. But then, it will be objected, surely such people must differ from the general population on many grounds and dimensions at least as important in determining their beliefs and behavior as not watching television.

In fact, the causal question is fundamentally insoluble. The arguments that lead us to reject the orthodox effects-research approach do not at the same time suggest any easy alternative solutions. If television is all of a piece, and if that piece is itself interwoven into a wider net of social institutions and values, how can we possibly hope to isolate, let alone measure, its effects? The very title of our project—Cultural Indicators—embodies the belief that television drama can be taken, and studied, as a reflection and manifestation of a culture that it may also help shape and maintain.

Our views of the nature of the medium and of the content and function of its messages lead us to begin the study of television's effects with the delineation of the central and critical facts of life in the world of television. Once we describe and enumerate many of the elements, relationships, and emphases of this system we should be able to tackle the problems of assessing their contributions to the beliefs, behavior, and values of viewers.

It has been noted that if everything people knew was learned from television drama their perceived world would differ sharply from the so-called "real" world. Beliefs about population parameters, the chances of people like themselves for success and happiness, their chances of meeting with violence—all are portrayed differently by television than by statistics. Which version of the world is the real one for most people?

One of our strategies is to pick out of our analysis and description of the content of television drama instances that exemplify its distortions and question viewers about their beliefs and perceptions on such issues. While no member of society can remain unaffected by an influence so pervasive as television, those who spend more of their time in the world of television facts may be more likely to perceive the world in terms of its lessons. Responses to our questions allow us to assess how often the more-frequent television viewers may be more likely than less-frequent viewers to give answers reflecting television's image of the world. These patterns can then be examined in light of various controls—age, sex, education, occupation, and so forth—in order to determine the extent to which it is possible to view television's influence as independent, complementary, or contrary to these other major social variables.

This strategy is least appropriate when we study the role of television in shaping or cultivating images and beliefs in areas where viewers have considerable first-hand knowledge and where television presumably presents an oversimplified but not exactly distorted view of reality. This is certainly the case in the area of sex-role portrayals and patterns.

As a purveyor of sex-role images television drama can be indicted on at least three distinct grounds. There are ways television presents a false image that can be attributed to the indirect consequences of its dramatic conventions and plot stereotypes. These conventions limit and restrict the roles and characters portrayed by women for reasons that have little or nothing to do with the true state of the world. We are all in some sense the stars of our own life stories but very few kinds of stories are ever presented in fiction and most of them feature male heroes. The fact that most television programs have male heroes derives entirely from the conventions of fiction.

In addition to distortions attributable to story-telling conventions presumably reflecting the basic values of the culture, there is a second form of bias that is characteristic of mass-media portrayals. When women are shown in the fictional world (and they comprise only about twenty-five percent of the characters in prime-time television drama) they are usually depicted in a fashion that mirrors stereotypes. This type of distortion is functionally separate from the first kind we mentioned in that even when a program has a female hero she is generally presented as a "typical" female.

To cite one example, Mary Tyler Moore is the lead character in a very popular show, yet the way she is shown manages subtly to undermine her status as the star character. Although officially the fictional Mary works as an associate producer of a television news program, the viewer who knew only what he or she actually saw on the screen would be likely to think Mary is a secretary, an impression that is reinforced by the fact that her boss calls her "Mary" and she calls him "Mr. Grant" while all the males on the staff call him "Lou."

The third sort of bias is in some moral sense more ambiguous than the others. Many of the more stereotyped features of the portrayal of women on television are also accurate reflections of the sexist reality of our society. This should not be taken in any sense as a justification for the existence or the continuation of such patterns; it does, however, complicate the process of identifying and studying the consequences of such stereotypes for viewers' conceptions of the world.

At this point it must be clear that we do not have any simple or satisfactory answer to the question of how to proceed. Our rejection of many orthodox attempts to formulate and investigate the question of television's effects does not reflect the smugness of those who possess the final solution to the problem. We feel strongly, though, that any hope of achieving even a partial solution must rest upon the kinds of considerations we have detailed. In the remaining sections of this chapter we shall describe and briefly illustrate an ambitious, but still embryonic, effort to pursue, illuminate, and possibly confirm the DeFleurs' conclusion that "television appears to be an important agency of socialization for children concerning the adult world."

PLUS ÇA CHANGE . . . ?

In the spring of 1955, the Kefauver Committee, investigating juvenile delinquency, held hearings on the effects of television. One of the prominent witnesses was Paul Lazarsfeld and his testimony was later published under the title, "Why is so little known about the effects of television on children and what can be done?" (1955). These questions are still asked and still lack definitive answers. Part of Lazarsfeld's testimony is especially relevant to our enterprise:

> We in the universities, with our limited funds, can do only short-term studies. We put kids into laboratories, have them listen to programs and then find out what they think or feel a few minutes later. But the real problem is the cumulative effect of television, what it does to children six years, not six minutes, later. . . .
>
> . . . What I am trying to argue is that we probably have to follow up all sorts of children for a period of 4 to 8 years to get a real picture of what role television plays in the development of personality. . . . I submit that only such long-term studies would give us a realistic picture of the role of television in a child's personality development (p. 246).

One of the larger ambitions of the Cultural Indicators project is to investigate longer-range effects of television.

We have noted that there are many things most of us have learned exclusively or primarily via the mass media. In contrast to these arguably media-derived images, however, there are many more things we know and believe in whole or large part as a result of our personal experiences and observations of the real world around us. Some of the most fascinating and critical questions facing us in our attempt to identify and assess the effects of television drama lie primarily in this second area. Questions of what children (or adults) think and believe about the nature of men and women—their differences and similarities, their potentials and proper roles in society—cannot be answered without attending to a complex of familial, social, mass-mediated, and other influences.

The attractions of longitudinal research, therefore, go far beyond our distrust of and disinterest in the demonstration of effects that are observed six minutes after a child is shown a particular television program. By gathering information on a variety of dimensions and variables and tracing patterns and relationships over time, we may be able to achieve insight into the intricacies of association, correlation, and perhaps even causes and effects.

SETTING THE STAGE

Our faith in the theoretical importance and potential empirical riches of a longitudinal study of television's effects on children has yet to be subjected to the inevitable trials and disappointments that lie ahead. Our willingness even to contemplate such an undertaking has derived in large part from the raising of our collective consciousness by Professor Frank Furstenberg of the Sociology Department of the University of Pennsylvania. Having helped us to realize the critical necessity of asking the right questions, he has contributed generously to our attempts to achieve some answers.

We have also enjoyed the unstinting cooperation of the public-school officials through whom we were able to initiate a three-year panel study involving approximately 250 children now in the eight, ninth, and tenth grades of a school serving both suburban and rural communities. At present we have concluded administering five of the six questionnaires (begun in December, 1974) and are now engaged in the complexities of coding, classifying, compiling, and cautiously contemplating the responses. Consequently, the most we can offer in this report are a few of the simpler, preliminary results. Our discussion will also reflect the primary goal of this initial analysis—the delineation of patterns and relationships that can serve as the baseline levels for our projected longitudinal comparisons and interpretations.[2]

TOO MUCH, TOO EARLY?

One of the first things we wanted to examine was the amount and the pattern of television viewing in our sample. Those readers who have not been exposed to previous research in this area are likely to be somewhat surprised by the sheer amount of television children report watching. The distribution of reported television viewing by sex and grade is given in Table 14.1. Only ten percent of the children reported spending less than two hours a day watching television, while forty percent of the children reported watching television for five hours or more a day.

While the amount of viewing seems obviously important it may be that most adults will not fully comprehend some of the implications of this phenomenon. Let us suggest, therefore, to those readers who were born before 1950 or thereabouts, that they consider the following. Imagine the response of your parents had you, at the age of twelve, developed the habit of coming home from school every day, grabbing a quick bite, and going off to spend about three hours at the movies then returning home for supper and going back for another three hours at the movies (not to mention spending even more time at the movies on the weekends). Not only would most parents not have permitted such behavior, but most children would not have contemplated the possibility. Yet, in our sample twenty-five percent of the children reported watching six or more hours of television daily.

Even without considering other important data and control comparisons or analyses, these data seem to have important im-

TABLE 14.1 Mean Reported Hours of Daily Television Viewing by Grade and Sex

GRADE	BOYS	(N)***	GIRLS	(N)	T	TOTAL	(N)
Sixth	4.6	(27)	5.2	(39)	−1.55	5.0	(66)
Seventh	4.2	(121)	4.7	(136)	−2.54**	4.5	(257)
Eighth	4.0	(102)	4.4	(123)	−1.89*	4.2	(225)
Ninth	3.1	(29)	3.3	(25)	−0.54	3.2	(54)
TOTAL	4.2	(279)	4.5	(323)	−3.12**	4.3	(602)

* Significant at .05 level or better.
** Significant at .01 level or better.
*** Number of respondents.

plications. One of these is the strong possibility that besides whatever effects the *content* of television may be accused of, a critical consequence of viewing may be the diversion of time that would otherwise be spent in other pursuits. Sections of our still-unanalysed data include many questions about time budgeting and how much our respondents engage in a variety of activities (including those that may accompany the watching of television). Our suspicion that television does drive out other activities is strengthened by the findings of a study (described by Wright, 1975). This work escapes the range of our somewhat shotgun condemnation of most research in this area by combining independent before-and-after surveys with a panel design in investigating the impact of the introduction of television on adolescents in Sydney, Australia (Campbell, 1962). Finding that television viewing reduced the amount of time spent on other leisure activities, "They observe that the most striking change occurred in a sharp reduction in social interaction" (Wright, 1975, p. 206).

ANTECEDENTS AND ASSOCIATIONS

A primary issue in the investigation of television as a factor in the development and shaping of sex-role images and beliefs is whether one can determine the extent to which it essentially supports and reinforces the life-style patterns, values, and expectations that the child's family and social environment embody, manifest, and transmit. Alternatively, can television be shown to exert an independent and potentially divergent influence that may complicate, confuse, or even alter the expectations and aspirations of some of its viewers? Although this is precisely the sort of question we feel must be held in abeyance pending longitudinal evidence, some of the groundwork must be initiated at this stage.

Literally as well as analytically, light, medium, and heavy

viewers are different prior to becoming television viewers. If we want to ask about the possible consequence of television viewing for their beliefs and behavior we must begin by attending to some basic antecedent characteristics of our respondents. Many of these are neither subtle nor unexpected. As Table 14.2 shows, IQ is strongly correlated with the children's television viewing. In fact, multiple-regression analyses have shown that IQ is a better predictor of television viewing behavior than grade, sex, father's occupation, or father's education. (Analyses not presented here divided the children into three groups of equal size on the basis of their IQ scores. The children in the highest IQ group were found to watch an average of 3.4 hours of television daily, while those in the lowest IQ group watched television an average of 5 hours a day.)

Table 14.2 shows that both the occupation and educational attainments of the father are strongly correlated with children's television viewing behavior.[3] Although this finding is not surprising, it does alert us to certain possible questions. We are assuming that the probable influence of television is the strengthening and reinforcement of conventional values and beliefs. To

TABLE 14.2 Correlations of Television Viewing[1] with Demographic Variables by Sex

	BOYS (N = 204)	GIRLS (N = 227)	TOTAL (N = 431)
	r	*r*	*r*
Grade	–.15*	–.10	–.13**
IQ	–.31**	–.20**	–.26**
Father's occupation[2]	–.31**	–.09	–.20**
Father's education[3]	–.15*	–.12*	–.14**

[1] Reported hours of television viewing per day.
[2] Measured by Duncan scale of occupational prestige.
[3] College/no college dichotomy.
* Significant at .05 level or better.
** Significant at .01 level or better.

the extent that the more educated parents can be assumed (and it is a tentative assumption) to be somewhat less likely to manifest and transmit conventional values in the realm of sex-role related matters, we should be particularly interested in the correlates of television viewing among their children. The low viewers in this group might comprise the segment of our sample most insulated from the complex of those conventionalizing influences that might result in more traditional sex-role conceptions and lower aspirations among the girls.

Another variable, which is arguably a correlate (or even consequence) as well as an antecedent of television viewing is the child's level of educational aspiration and expectation. Table 14.3 shows the correlations between viewing behavior and the level of schooling the children said they hope to achieve and the level they expect to achieve. Again, unsurprisingly, these are inversely related to the amount of television they report viewing. (Clearly, educational desires and expectations are highly correlated; they are also correlated with parental education.) These relationships hold for both boys and girls, and are not strongly affected by the introduction of controls for grade, IQ, father's occupation, and father's education.

Having granted the obvious fact that our heavy, medium, and light viewers were different (within as well as between groups) conceptually as well as chronologically prior to being exposed to television, we also may ask whether they are different in any interesting ways after (conceptually if not, in this case, chronologically) such exposure. Specifically, in the areas on which we are reporting, can we find consistent and interpretable differences between sex-role related beliefs and aspirations of our heavier and lighter viewers of television, holding our antecedent control variables constant?

The question is deceptively simple and possibly misleading. While we have argued that television's influence should reinforce and support (and, in some possible instances, introduce) conventional beliefs and traditional aspirations, we must recog-

TABLE 14.3 Partial Correlations of Television Viewing[1] with Educational Desires and Expectations by Sex

	EDUCATIONAL DESIRES			EDUCATIONAL EXPECTATIONS		
	BOYS (N = 204)	GIRLS (N = 227)	TOTAL (N = 431)	BOYS (N = 204)	GIRLS (N = 227)	TOTAL (N = 431)
	r	*r*	*r*	*r*	*r*	*r*
TOTAL	—.22**	—.20**	—.21**	—.16*	—.17**	—.17**
Controlling for:						
Grade	—.23**	—.20**	—.21**	—.16*	—.17**	—.17**
IQ	—.15*	—.15*	—.14*	—.10	—.12*	—.11*
Father's occupation[2]	—.15*	—.19**	—.17**	—.11	—.16*	—.12**
Father's education[3]	—.19**	—.18**	—.18**	—.12*	—.15*	—.13**

[1] Reported hours of television viewing per day.

[2] Measured by Duncan scale of occupational prestige.

[3] College/no college dichotomy.

* Significant at .05 level or better.

** Significant at .01 level or better.

nize that in the realm of sex-role images television is but one among many powerful symbolic and social forces. Many of these, as other research has demonstrated, share the same distorted sexist biases we have ascribed to television; but at the same time all—television included—are beginning to show at least tokens of change to a more egalitarian and even-handed portrayal of the sexes. Our content analysis of television drama has so far not shown signs of change that can be considered more than token, but that may not be true in the future (although we have found the more subtly insidious stereotypes quite resilient—see also Gerbner *et al.*, 1977); and it is difficult to estimate the short- or long-term impact of even a few highly visible token improvements.

Further, although our conceptual model requires us to predict that high levels of exposure to television should be correlated with more traditional aspirations among the girls in our sample, even the most powerful controls will not allow us to infer from our data causal directions from such relationships. In part these may eventually emerge from our longitudinal analyses, but regardless of the outcome of such assessments we do not believe that the question is meaningfully posed in that way. Certainly, we might discover that our dependent variables of attitudes and behavior are overwhelmingly attributable to the complex of life-style dimensions that we have termed the antecedents of television viewing. This could lead us to question the influence of television in cultivating the conceptions and values of the parents which, in turn, are embodied and transmitted via the life-style and environment in which they raise their children. When the burden of the message system is the maintenance and stabilization of conventional patterns, however, it may be both wrong-headed and fruitless to define or search for change (within or across generations) as the way of demonstrating effects. Accepting these limitations, let us look at some patterns which suggest that we may be able to make some headway.

SEXIST VIEWS

In order to assess the relationship of television viewing to the expression of sexist views we constructed an index of five questions that ask about the nature of men and women, how they are treated by society, and why it is that women have fewer top jobs than men. The five questions are given below, and the sexist answer is underlined:

1. True or false—Women have less chance than men to get the education for top jobs.
2. True or false—Men are born with more drive to be ambitious and successful than women.
3. True or false—By nature, women are happiest when they are making a home and caring for children.
4. True or false—Our society discriminates against women.
5. True or false—Women have just as much chance to get big important jobs, but they just aren't interested.

We expected that television viewing would be associated with a tendency to give sexist responses to these questions and, as Table 14.4 shows, this is the case, particularly for the boys. This relationship is not strongly affected by the introduction of controls for father's occupation and education. The correlation is significant for boys, but the table shows that this is mainly attributable to IQ. For the girls the correlation of sexist responses with television is much weaker, but IQ is a less important factor than for boys.

TO BE CONTINUED . . .

It would be neither necessary nor appropriate to end this report with a concluding discussion or summary—unnecessary be-

TABLE 14.4 Partial Correlations of Television Viewing with Scores on an Index Based on Sexist Answers to Questions about Women's Nature and Role in Society by Sex

	BOYS (N = 204) *r*	GIRLS (N = 227) *r*	TOTAL (N = 431) *r*
TOTAL	.19**	.10	.14**
Controlling for:			
Grade	.17**	.08	.12**
IQ	.07	.08	.08*
Father's occupation[1]	.12*	.09	.11*
Father's education[2]	.16**	.08	.12**

[1] Measured by Duncan scale of occupational prestige.
[2] College/no college dichotomy.
* Significant at .05 level or better.
** Significant at .01 level or better.

cause the theoretical and methodological analysis has been stated at great length; inappropriate because the data presented are from what is very much work still in progress. In place of a summary or conclusion, then, we offer a parable.

Suppose that your doorbell rang and you opened the door to find a very pleasant, well-dressed, and respectable-looking man standing there. You smile inquiringly at the man (he doesn't look like a salesman or an F.B.I. agent) and ask what you can do for him. He replies that, on the contrary, he wants to do something for you. He still doesn't look like a salesman, so you wait, still smiling, to hear what he has to say. He has a very simple proposal. He wants to come and visit your house every day for a few hours (particularly in the daytime while you are working and on weekend mornings when you want to sleep late) and tell stories to your children. He has no ulterior motive, he just likes to tell stories to children (maybe, just occasionally, he will tell them about some toy they might like to have or some new cereal they would like to eat), and he would love to baby-sit for your children and keep them happily entertained while you are busy or when you want to get away from the kids.

It is really a very simple, tempting offer. What would you do?

NOTES

[1] *Philadelphia Bulletin,* July 10, 1974.

[2] Although the makeup of our sample will permit cross-sectional as well as longitudinal comparisons, we have, for a variety of practical and theoretical reasons, concentrated in this paper on identifying baseline variables and patterns. Data presented were collected in the second year of the study (1975–76).

[3] Two caveats: At this stage in our data gathering and analysis we have only indirect, incomplete, and not necessarily valid data on parental education (derived from the children's reports) and we have also left out of some initial comparisons those cases in which only the father (nineteen percent) or the mother (eight percent) was reported to have gone to college. A possible artifact we cannot rule out at this moment is that the children of college-educated parents may be more likely to underreport the amount of television they watch.

Conclusion

JAMES BENÉT

Will Media Treatment of Women Improve?

Media professionals would probably agree that there has been change for the better over the past decade, but they would differ widely on whether the change has been significantly large and whether it is a promise of more change to come. Nor do students outside the media agree about the future. In Chapter 1 of this volume, George Gerbner takes a pessimistic view, expecting the media to dig in for a last-ditch stand. But Alan Pifer, the president of the Carnegie Corporation, in a recent report contends that "new societal values . . . will not come painlessly, but they must come. . . . The broadcast media, especially television, could be particularly helpful in publicizing the entry of men and women into fields conventionally associated with the opposite sex" (1977, p. 14).

Of course, much will depend on continuing efforts. Laws against discrimination and requiring affirmative action must be enforced and improved. Women's organizations need to become even stronger and more skillful. Individual women will have to continue their determined efforts to get the jobs, the recognition, and the power that will make them fully equal.

There is still far to go, as the research collected here convincingly demonstrates. Its insights are still confirmed daily by events; only a few days before this was written, the public broadcasting station where I work was celebrating network acceptance of its program called "Womantime," exactly confirming Cantor's contention (Chapter 4) that in public as in commercial television, women "are seen as members of a special category, not as one-half of the population."

As members of this special category, they are relegated to secondary as well as special statuses within the society. And so, it seems worthwhile to attract attention to one as yet unmentioned aspect of the issue: the scarcity of women who exercise ownership powers over newspapers, magazines, or broadcasting stations.

This is not, of course, peculiar to the media, but a general characteristic of American economic life. There are a few industries where active women owners are not unusual, but they are generally industries producing goods almost exclusively for women—fashions, cosmetics, and perfumes—and where, therefore, women may be thought specially qualified in judgment simply because of their sex. One segment of the media, the specialized feminist press, may be regarded as a mini-industry of this kind. Outside these areas it is rare to find active women owners.

And yet there are, of course, many very wealthy women who could, if they chose, acquire media properties or simply exert the power over present holdings that they now delegate to male managers. Mills (1956, p. 109) estimated that in 1950, seventy percent of America's very rich rentiers were women. But, as he remarks, "The history of the very rich is, in the main, a patriarchal history; men have always held from eighty to ninety percent of great American fortunes" (p. 110). The implication of these figures is that wealthy men tend in the main to pursue active careers, but wealthy women avoid business though many patronize the arts, are busy philanthropists, or find other useful outlets for their energies.

The principal reasons for women's reluctance to take over the direction of businesses of all kinds are undoubtedly cultural, very old, and very deep-rooted. Both men and women of the ruling class perceive business as "a man's world," and arrange women's upbringing for other roles, so that it doesn't even prepare them for business as well as middle-class women may be prepared. As Domhoff notes in Chapter 9, while the ruling-class men attend business meetings, the women organize social and entertainment life. They may aid their husband's career if they "play the committee game, work hard at charity things and make a good impression." While middle-class girls nowadays mostly attend the same elementary and high schools and the same colleges that their brothers attend, in many upper-class families it is still customary for girls to attend girls' schools and women's colleges. Mills's description of the upper-class girl's education remains true for many. It concludes: "She will marry soon after finishing school or college, and presumably begin to guide her own children through the same sequence" (1956, p. 63). Among many—perhaps most—upper-class families that is still regarded as a woman's normal career.

Hence it is not surprising that lists of the most powerful individuals in national life simply assume that such individuals are male, and don't bother to explain the absence of women's names (Domhoff, 1975, p. 112ff.). In the highest echelons of power they do not appear. Weber (1920; rpt. 1956, p. 258) remarked with a glancing reference to Nietzsche, that "economic supermen who have stood 'beyond good and evil' have always existed." Even so careful a scholar didn't think that superman might be a woman (though a case might be made for Catherine the Great and Elizabeth the First).

In the world of the mass media there are a few exceptions to the general absence of top-level women. Arthur Hays Sulzberger, the late publisher of the *New York Times,* exemplified the usual rule; he was accustomed to explain that he became the publisher by "marrying the boss's daughter," Iphigene Ochs.

But Katharine Graham runs her *Washington Post,* Oveta Culp Hobby heads the *Houston Post,* and until very recently Dorothy Schiff of New York was the third publisher of a big newspaper. Currently, the third-generation of the *Oakland Tribune* are divided into two antagonistic groups; the woman president of the family holding company heads the majority and a male cousin, the minority.

Even in this exceptional group, however, the general tendency to defer to the male is strong, as may be seen in the career of Katharine Graham. When she inherited the *Washington Post* from her father, Eugene Meyer, even though she was trained and experienced in newspaper work—she had served an apprenticeship on the *San Francisco News* and the *Post* itself, very much in the customary style for a male heir—she left the formal leadership of the paper to her husband, Philip L. Graham, until his death in 1963. It was only then that she assumed the presidency of the company.

Similarly Dorothy Schiff, also a wealthy heiress, assumed the presidency of the *New York Post* in 1942 after her divorce from her second husband, George Backer, who had previously run the paper. From then on, for more than thirty years, she was the publisher of a major New York newspaper.

Here the similarity of the two women's careers ends. Dorothy Schiff was a member of none of the organizations of the nation's powerful, listing only the American Society of Newspaper Editors and, for clubs, the Washington Press Club. It is instructive to compare the position of her brother, John M. Schiff of the Kuhn, Loeb banking firm. A director of numerous large corporations, including Kennicott Copper, Atlantic & Pacific Tea Co., Westinghouse, and Uniroyal, his clubs include the Metropolitan in Washington and the Piping Rock in New York.

Unlike Dorothy Schiff, Katharine Graham has achieved a remarkable degree of acceptance in high business circles. She is a director of the Associated Press and the American Newspaper Publishers Association, and a trustee of the Committee for Economic Development, a leading policy-forming organization of the business and political world. Yet she, too, of course, is excluded from the upper-class men's clubs, which play an important part in communication among the nation's top leadership (Domhoff, 1975, pp. 86–91), and so she cannot play her part as a leader as fully as a man might do.

One can only speculate whether the impact of the present movement for women's rights will produce more women chiefs in the mass media and other business sectors. One must assume that currents of thought will have their effect on upper-class individuals. But it may be that the ruling class will be the last bastion of the traditional view of the woman's role. So far there seems to be no evidence of a change, though we have little information on the inner thoughts of people in the highest circles of power.

There can be no remedy through law. To require that women should somehow become owners of half—or more—of business and industry can't be reconciled with private-property rights. And if women who acquire ownership choose to delegate their power to men, that is their right as owners.

Yet without far wider control by women who hold the ultimate power of decision, the mass media will continue to have its policies decided on the whole by men—with all the possibility of misunderstanding or deliberate distortion that that implies. As Molotch remarks in Chapter 10, much of what passes for news today is "locker-room talk," catering to men's interest only.

Nor will this be prevented by any number of women in high staff positions. For, as nobody with experience in the mass media can doubt, active owners do make their views felt throughout their staffs. A single owner may with that single vote decide an issue against a large majority of his or her staff.

The problem is important not only for the media but for the society in general. A leading contemporary student of American ruling groups, E. Digby Baltzell, has written that "the American upper class, whose white Anglo-Saxon-Protestant members may still be deferred to and envied because of their privileged status, is no longer honored in the land. For its standards of admission have gradually come to demand the dishonorable treatment of far too many distinguished Americans for it to continue, as a class, to fill its traditional function of moral leadership" (1966, p. 381).

Baltzell's reference was to the exclusion of Jews from upper-class society. "Dishonorable treatment" may seem too strong a term to apply to the treatment by the ruling class of its own women, especially since the women themselves appear in the main to accept their prescribed role. Yet as egalitarian ideas become stronger and more secure among both women and men generally, the paradox will surely become apparent that the most "privileged" women are among the least equally treated.

If they should then begin to exercise their powers as owners, the effect on the media's image of women could be profound.

*The Image of Women in Television: An Annotated Bibliography**

INTRODUCTION

Image has a bad name. To many, it is reality's cunning antagonist, something the public-relations expert creates for products or politicians who cannot bear the glare of candor. An image is therefore created to portray as glamorous that which, in reality, is plain, or dull, or even sordid. It is unfortunate that the notion of falsity has become so strongly attached to the word "image," but it is understandable, for many images are false in that they severely depart from reality.

Televised images of women in large measure are false, portraying them less as they really are, more as some might want them to be. The articles annotated here—reporting portrayals of women in adult entertainment programming, in news and public affairs, in commercials and, in children's programs—document that portrayal and suggest that it has changed very little in the last twenty years. Some highlights: The ratio of female characters to male characters in television drama is approximately 30 : 70 although women constitute over fifty percent of

* This bibliography was compiled in 1975.
It is still the most up-to-date annotated review available.—Eds.

the population. Television women are predominantly in their twenties although American women are found in all age groups and there are increasing numbers of them who are in their sixties, seventies, and eighties. Television women are portrayed primarily as housewives although close to forty percent of the women in this country are in the labor force. The occupations in which television women are portrayed are restricted primarily to stereotyped positions such as nurses and secretaries. Women are portrayed as weak, vulnerable, dependent, submissive and, frequently, as sex objects.

Television is a dominant force in American society and has great potentiality for impact on those of us who watch it a great deal. This impact is particularly likely for those of us who have a tendency to believe that television is a realistic medium, a tendency that is found in children and in heavy viewers of television.

There has been almost no research on the role that television plays in the development of sex-role attitudes or on behavior. The few studies annotated here that have tentatively explored this issue, however, suggest that the portrayal of women on television has an impact on the development of career goals in girls and on beliefs about a woman's vulnerability to violence. The need for a thoroughgoing research effort in this area is indeed great, and we have hardly begun to do it. Women's groups—listed at the end of this bibliography—and academic women and men interested in the portrayal of women on television have a challenge: Acknowledge that we now know just about all we need to know about the portrayal of women on television. Let us redirect research and action efforts to the impact of television's image on women and men, girls and boys.

I. PORTRAYAL

A. ADULT ENTERTAINMENT PROGRAMMING

1. RESEARCH STUDIES

Downing, Mildred. "Heroine of the Daytime Serial." *Journal of Communication,* 24 (1974), 130–37.

Method: Content analysis of 300 episodes of 15 daytime serials broadcast in the summer of 1973. *Results:* Of the 256 characters, 129 were women; 127 were men. Less than 3% were not white. Most characters were young and good looking (women were younger than men). 58% of all male characters were "professionals"; in contrast only 19.4% of the females were professionals; 29.5% were full-time housewives. Women have more visibility in soap operas than in other television genres.

DeFleur, Melvin. "Occupational Roles as Portrayed on Television." *Public Opinion Quarterly,* 28 (Spring, 1964), 57–74.

Method: Content analysis of occupational portrayals in 250 half-hour time periods broadcast between 3:30 and 11 p.m. weekdays and 10 a.m. to 11 p.m. on weekends. *Results:* 83.9% of the televised workers were male; 16.1% were female. Males were portrayed in higher status jobs than they actually hold; blue-collar workers being almost totally absent. Children's incidental learning about occupations from television author believes is sufficient to elicit concern.

Gerbner, George and Larry Gross. "Progress Report on Cultural Indicators Research Project." Annenberg School of Communications, University of Pennsylvania, Philadelphia, January 1974.

Method: 656 television plays, 1,907 leading characters and 3,505 episodes coded from one week of television for a six-year period make up the units for analysis. *Results:* Males outnumber females four to one; children's cartoons portray even fewer women. More females than males are young, but women age earlier and faster than men. The televised world victimizes females and nonwhites, even among cartoon animal characters.

Head, Sydney W. "Content Analysis of Television Drama Programs." *Quarterly of Film, Radio and Television,* 9 (1954), 175–94.

Method: Content analysis of 209 regularly scheduled network drama programs randomly selected over a thirteen-week period from March to May of 1952. *Results:* Of 1,023 major characters, 68% were male. 75% of the characters had identifiable occupations; of those, 17% were in police or protective work, 17% were criminals, 11% were housewives, and 10% were in the professions. Occupations were not reported by sex. Crucial life events—birth, health failure, and natural death—were almost completely avoided. Rape was never portrayed.

Katzman, N. "Television Soap Operas: What's Been Going on Anyway?" *Public Opinion Quarterly,* 35 (1972), 200–12.

Method: Various measures of soap opera's popularity—viewers per hour per day, average audience per minute, number of minutes broadcast daily by year, audience demographics—and content analysis of fourteen serials broadcast during the week of April 13, 1970. *Results:* Of 371 characters, 192 were male and 179 were female. Age, marital status, occupations, and conversations of characters reported.

McNeil, Jean C. "Feminism, Femininity, and the Television Series: A Content Analysis." *Journal of Broadcasting,* 19 (1975), 259–69.

Method: Content analysis of forty-three prime-time network programs aired in a one-week period in March–April, 1973; 279 major, sub-major, and supporting roles were coded. *Results:* 69% of *all* characters were male (60% in comedy and 74% in drama). 78% of all *major* characters were male (63% in comedy and 95% in drama). 72% of all males and 44% of all females were employed. Among married characters, 78% of the males and 21% of the females were employed. Only one of thirteen married mothers held a job. Other data on stereotyped occupations, as well as female weakness and passivity are reported.

Miller, M. Mark and Byron Reeves. "Dramatic TV Content and Children's Sex-Role Stereotypes." *Journal of Broadcasting,* 20 (1976), 35–50.

Method: Content analysis of one week of prime time November 1974 television shows. *Results:* Males still predominate in prime-time television: 72.2% of 449 characters in 51 shows were male. Males made up 98% of all criminals, 95% of all self-employed, 92% of all police, 79% of all professionals, 69% of all labor/service occupations, and 60% of all students; women made up 100% of all homemakers, secretaries, and nurses.

Seegar, John F. "Imagery of Women in Television Drama: 1974." *Journal of Broadcasting,* 19 (1975), 273–81.

Method: Content analysis of 50% of all television dramas broadcast between 3:30 and 11 p.m., Monday through Saturday for five weeks in February and March of 1974. Data collected for all female characters (946) and male *major* characters (142). *Results:* 87 (9%) of the female characters were regarded as major; 11% had supporting roles, 15% minor roles, and 65% were in bit parts. Of the major roles held by women only 7% featured minority women. Women were portrayed in stereotyped occupations, were portrayed as less competent than males, were more likely to be dominated by males in interaction, were more likely to be shown as married and as fashionably dressed, and were portrayed as better-off financially than were their male counterparts.

Seegar, John F. and Penny Wheeler. "World of Work on TV: Ethnic and Sex Representation in TV Drama." *Journal of Broadcasting,* 17 (1973), 201–14.

Method: Two hundred fifty half-hours of programming between the hours of 3:30 and 11 p.m. daily and 10 a.m. to 11 p.m. on weekends during five weeks in February and March 1971. 1,830 characters portrayed in occupations were coded. *Results:* 81.7% characters were male; 18.3% females. 14% of all characters were white females; 1% were black females. Minority women were portrayed in higher prestige occupations than white females. Occupational categories for women were primarily service and entertainment oriented: nurse, secretary, maid, actor/dancer were most frequent.

Tedesco, Nancy. "Patterns in Prime Time." *Journal of Communication,* 24 (1974), 119–24.

Method: Major characters from four-year, 1969–1972, sample of prime-time dramatic programming coded from videotape by two-person teams. *Results:* 28% of all leading roles were played by women. More than half the females were married compared with less than one-third of the males; one-third of the females were employed; 63% of males were. Females were killed three times as often as they killed; males killed twice as often as they were killed. Male characters are more powerful, smart, rational, tall, and stable, while females are more attractive, sociable, warm, happy, peaceful, and youthful.

Turow, Joseph. "Advising and Ordering: Daytime, Prime Time." *Journal of Communication,* 24 (1974), 138–41.

Method: Twelve hours daytime, twelve hours prime time were analyzed. Sex of adviser/orderer and advisee/orderee were coded. *Results:* In prime time, 70% of characters were male; 70% of the directives were made by males; only 22% of the interactions initiated by women were related to a professional, action-oriented milieu; even women whose occupations related to business gave directives on typically "feminine" topics. In daytime, 54% of all characters were male. Women gave 44% of the orders.

U.S. Commission on Civil Rights. *Window Dressing on the Set: Women and Minorities in Television.* Washington, D.C.: U.S. Government Printing Office, 1977.

Method: Content analysis of one week of prime-time television drama from 1969 to 1974, emphasizing the portrayal of women and men of five racial and ethnic groups. *Results:* White males predominated, constituting 65.3% of all characters; white females, 23.8%; nonwhite males, 8.6%; and nonwhite females, 2.3%. Proportionately, nonwhite females were least often seen. Measures of age, marital status, occupational role, victimization, and seriousness of role resulted primarily in sex differences. Secondary race differences occurred so that nonwhite females were least well portrayed.

Women on Words and Images. *Channeling Children: Sex Stereotyping on Prime Time TV.* Princeton, N.J. Women on Words and Images, 1975, $2.50.

Method: The sixteen most popular programs broadcast between 7:30 and 9:30 p.m. in November of 1973; three episodes per program were coded by two-person teams off the air plus audio tape. *Results:* 61% of all major characters were male; in adventure shows, 85%

were male. Males were portrayed in twice as many occupations as females. Independent financial status is left to single women. Males and females relatively equal in display of competent behaviors; females displayed twice as much incompetent behavior as males. Detailed discussion of stereotypes in each program.

2. PUBLIC-INTEREST REPORTS

"Analysis of Male and Female Participation on WRC 'Quiz Show' Programming." *Women in the Wasteland Fight Back: A Report on the Image of Women Portrayed in TV Programming.* Washington, D.C.: National Organization for Women, National Capitol Area Chapter, 1972, pp. 139–46.

Method: Content analysis of sixteen hours of quiz shows broadcast between late May and mid-June, 1972. *Results:* None of the seven programs was hosted by a woman. Seventy-six of the eighty-four male contestants were identified by occupation. Female contestants were younger. Females were treated condescendingly by hosts; examples given.

"Comparison of Treatment of Females and Males in Dramatic Programming and Variety Shows Aired by WRC-TV." *Women in the Wasteland Fight Back,* op. cit., pp. 147–89.

Method: Eighteen hours of dramatic programming, two hours variety shows aired in late May and June, 1972. Coded off the air with audio tape. *Results:* 70% of all characters male; 75% of all lead characters male. 40% of all males were over forty, 15% of all females were. 21% of characters with occupational roles traditionally female. Females depicted as dependent, helpess, and emotionally unstable. Detailed tables on occupations for each program; plot summaries.

"Comparison of Treatment of Females and Males in Soap Operas Aired by WRC-TV." *Women in the Wasteland Fight Back,* op. cit., pp. 52–90.

Method: Content analysis of twelve and one-half hours of soap operas aired during a composite week from late May to mid-June of 1972. *Results:* Males were shown in occupational roles in 52.7% of their appearances compared with 17.7% for females; 93% of the male occupations were as doctors, lawyers, or businessmen; over 80%

of the female occupations were as nurses, secretaries, waitresses, or housekeepers. Men were portrayed as authority figures, females as dependent.

Komisar, Lucy. "Turning Off the Tube." *Ms.,* August 1972, pp. 4–8.

Report on N.O.W.'s challenge of WABC-TV's license; hints on how to file a license challenge.

Kopecky, Gina. "You're Under Arrest, Sugar." *New York Village Voice,* December 9, 1974, p. 106.

Report of a recent monitoring project under the auspices of the National Organization for Women in conjunction with plans to challenge the licenses of New York television stations. The writer discusses her monitoring experiences and reactions to a number of programs.

Mills, Kay. "Fighting Sexism on the Airwaves." *Journal of Communication,* 24 (1974), 130–53.

Report of activities, strategies, and results of license challenge brought by National Organization for Women and E.E.O.C. complaints brought by individual women against WRC-TV in Washington, D.C.

"More Women's Thinking about Broadcast Legislation: Who Is To Be Heard?" *Media Report to Women,* September 1, 1974, pp. 6–8.

Testimony from: Patricia Johnson, Director of Communications, Ohio Council of Churches; Mrs. Kazu Obayaski, Asian Americans for Fair Media; Martha Allen, Memphis Women's Media Project; Edna Mosley, Community Relations Coordinator, Colorado Civil Rights Commission; Polly Baca Barragan, Raza Association of Spanish Surnamed Americans; Bishetta Merrit, Concerned Citizens of Columbus, Ohio; Elizabeth S. Cowles, Women for Constitutional Government. Took place before Senate Commerce Committee's Subcommittee on Communications considering a bill to extend the length of broadcast licenses from three to five years.

"NBFO Lists TV Complaints and Protests 'That's My Mama.' " *Media Report to Women,* December 1, 1974, p. 16.

National Black Feminist Organization demands "immediate and ongoing action be taken to improve the quality of television programming, particularly as it reflects the lives of black people." Six specific complaints are listed including: "Few black women in TV programs are cast as professionals, paraprofessionals, or even working people." "That's My Mama" is described as beyond redemption in its perpetuation of racist and sexist stereotypes.

"Screen Actors Guild Documents Use of Women and Minorities in Prime-Time TV Shows." Press Release, October 31, 1974. Contact Paul Sargent, SAG, 7750 Sunset Blvd., Hollywood, Calif.

Method: Content analysis of all prime-time network shows broadcast during the month of February, 1974. *Results:* 71.8% of all roles were played by males. Men outnumber women by three to one on ABC and NBC; two to one on CBS. Minorities played in 12.7% of all roles; blacks, 5.8%; Asian Americans, 1.6%; Native Americans, .29%; Mexican Americans, .83%; others, 4.2%. There is a one-to-one ratio of men to women in age categories under twenty-five; men outnumber women four to one in the over-fifty category.

Stanley, Nancy. "Federal Communications Law and Women's Rights: Women in the Wasteland Fight Back." *Hastings Law Journal,* 23 (1971–72), pp. 15–53.

Application of communications law to the portrayal, programming for, and employment of women in television. The article is based on "the conviction that [television's discrimination against women]—the creation of a highly prejudicial sex stereotype, force-fed to millions of Americans by the mass media—is at least as damaging to women as discrimination in education and employment. For it is the image of what we see of ourselves, day after day, that largely dictates what we are and what we become."

3. POPULAR ARTICLES

Bernstein, Paula. "Women Rap Media's Messages." *New York Daily News,* December 10, 1974.

Report of a conference on women and television sponsored by the Media Women's Association and New York University. Marlene Sanders of ABC-TV stated that images of women in the media "are severely limited by the imaginations of men. Are we only prostitutes and victims, and occasionally, Mary Tyler Moore? We have limitless possibilities, but you'd never know it on TV."

Bordewich, Fergus M. "Why are College Kids in a Lather Over TV Soap Operas?" *New York Times,* October 20, 1974, p. D-31.

Interviews with New York City college students who are avid soap-opera viewers suggest that they like to watch soaps because they are "relevant" and "real"; because they are "unreal"; or in order to concentrate on the problems of others.

Cameron, Sue. "Police Drama: Women are on the Case." *Ms.,* October 1974, pp. 104ff.

Report of new television shows featuring women ("Policewomen," and "Get Christie Love"). Discusses their characters and focus of each show.

Funt, Peter. "Game Shows Now Dominate Daytime TV." *New York Times,* July 7, 1974, pp. D-1ff.

Discussion of new trend in game shows. Economy is presented as major reason they are dominant. Soap operas are reported to have run their course, according to one network VP.

Gardner, Paul. "Hollywood Is Crossing the Last Racial Barrier." *New York Times,* October 6, 1974, p. D-13.

Discussion of black actors, primarily males, who are now being allowed to appear sexy on the screen. Concern is expressed about crossing the line into portrayal as superstud.

Gross, Larry. "The 'Real' World of Television." *Today's Education,* January–February 1974, pp. 86ff.

Popular report of Annenberg "Cultural Indicators" study. Summarizes the findings: Power and success are the province of the white, male, middle and upper class. Such power is held by whites against non-whites and by males against females.

Gross, Leonard. "Why Can't a Woman Be More Like a Man?" *TV Guide,* August 11, 1973, pp. 6ff.

Prime-time women continue to be portrayed as they always have been—in subordinate roles. There are no dramatic heroines because the men who manage television say they are only reflecting the times. Author suggests that there is a network bias against women. Other arguments are considered: women like to watch men; audiences wouldn't find it realistic or comforting to see a strong woman. Gross believes change will come in time.

Gutcheon, Beth R. "Look for Cop-Outs on Prime Time, Not on 'Soaps.' " *New York Times,* December 16, 1973, p. D-21.

Soap operas are the only programs that do not patronize women; issues are dealt with more realistically. Contempt for soap operas "has obscured the fact that the soaps are the only place on television where you may see adult topics—rape, alcoholism, frigidity, the plight of the professional woman who doesn't want children, racism, sexism, even incest."

Gutcheon, Beth R. "There Isn't Anything Wishy-Washy About Soaps." *Ms.,* August 1974, p. 42.

Analysis of soap opera's attempts at relevance and realism; the influence of ratings on content; their impact on their audiences.

Harrington, Stephanie. "Women Get the Short End of the Shtick." *New York Times,* November 18, 1973, p. D-21.

Describes television comedy programs in which women are made the laughing stock. Notes that migrant workers and Indians are not made the butt of jokes. Argues that women are the only group about which it is safe to make jokes.

Kinzer, Nora Scott. "Soapy Sin in the Afternoon." *Psychology Today,* August 1973, pp. 46–48.

Soap operas are about white, middle-class professionals who are highly involved in pre- and extra-marital relationships that almost always result in pregnancy.

Klemesrud, Judy. "TV's Women are Dingbats." *New York Times,* May 27, 1973, p. D-15.

Discusses leading women of the 1973 and the then upcoming 1974 season. Describes some pilots that didn't get purchased that portrayed women in strong, intelligent roles. Expresses concern about the negative aspects in the Edith Bunker and Mary Richards roles, among others.

MacKenzie, Bob. "When the Soap Bubble Burst . . ." *TV Guide,* February 9, 1974, pp. 26–28.

Massive viewer protest reported after "Secret Storm" was taken off the air. Brief analysis of the show's popularity; report of viewer efforts to get it back on the air.

"The New Giant-Size Soaps." *Newsweek,* February 18, 1974, p. 86.

Report of one soap opera's expansion to ninety minutes. Discussion of unreal neighborhood which was almost exclusively WASP. Sex invariably leads to pregnancy; marijuana smoking leads to permanent derangement.

O'Connor, John J. "Some Liberation Music, Please." *New York Times,* April 28, 1974, p. D-15.

"Aspects of the 'new consciousness' are gradually seeping through to general TV content." Favorable critique on new hour-long magazine program CBS aired monthly during daytime hours. (The program, produced and written by women, was taken off the air.—Eds.)

Rock, Gail. "Same Time, Same Station, Same Sexism." *Ms.,* December, 1973, pp. 24–28.

Discusses each of the major television shows that features a woman and discusses the sexism or lack of it in each show. Reports how few women producers (one), script consultants (one), and writers (three) there are for the sixy-two shows of the season, only six of which have female protagonists.

Roiphe, Anne. "The Waltons." *New York Times Magazine,* November 18, 1973, pp. 40f.

Critique of the unreality of "The Waltons." Lengthy discussion of Olivia Walton as the perfect wife and mother who gave up her dreams of becoming an opera star to bear and care for a large family.

Rosen, Diane. "TV and Single Girl." *TV Guide,* November 6, 1971, pp. 13–16.

Discusses Mary Tyler Moore and Rhoda as single women.

Von Hoffman, Nicholas. "Cher: Laughing All the Way in a Step Beyond Chauvinism." *Washington Post,* February 28, 1975, pp. B1–2.

There are more women in the production unit on Cher's show than is usual. According to producer George Schlatter, "Until Cher, women have been the joke, not done the joke. Cher will be the first female star to carry a show in the same way that many men have."

B. PUBLIC AFFAIRS

1. RESEARCH STUDIES

Corporation for Public Broadcasting. *Report of the Task Force on Women in Public Broadcasting,* 1975.

Method: Content analysis on one week of general adult (public affairs) programming distributed through the Public Broadcasting System (PBS) in January 1975. *Results:* Female participants totaled 15% of twenty-eight programs, eleven had no female participants.

U.S. Commission on Civil Rights. *Window Dressing on the Set: Women and Minorities in Television.* Washington, D.C.: U.S. Government Printing Office, 1977.

Method: Content analysis of one week of network news sampled during 1974 and 1975 emphasizing the portrayal of women and men of five racial and ethnic groups as news reporters and newsmakers as well as news about them. *Results:* Most of the news was about white males and they constituted almost all newsmakers and reporters. With one exception, women's issues provided the only context for stories featuring women in an authoritative context. Typically, white women appeared as the wives of government officials, public figures, or private individuals. Minority women appeared primarily as recipients of government assistance.

2. PUBLIC-INTEREST REPORTS

American Association of University Women. "The Image of Women in Television." Sacramento, Calif., 1974. Carolyn Flatt, 27 Greenway Circle, Sacramento, Calif. 95831, $1.50.

Method: Content analysis of news stories on all three channels in Sacramento in April 1974. *Results:* 5,353 straight news stories; 523 were about women; 253 were reported by women; and 222 had an element of sexism. 1,668 feature stories examined; 273 were about women; 208 were reported by women; and 155 had an element of sexism. Discussion of findings for each station.

"Survey of WRC-TV Public Affairs and News Programming Since February, 1972." *Women in the Wasteland Fight Back,* op. cit., pp. 4–18.

Method: Content analysis of news programs broadcast during Spring 1972 on WRC-TV. Comparison of news coverage of events of importance to women in local newspapers with coverage on WRC. *Results:* 190 half-hour news programs were monitored. Only half the local programming consisted of local news. Events of importance to women were almost never covered. Of 4,179 minutes, only 12.5 minutes (.3%) pertained to women's rights, women's changing role, or events important to women as a group. When these events were reported, they were trivialized.

"Survey of WRC-TV Public Affairs and News Programming Since February, 1972," *Women in the Wasteland Fight Back,* op. cit., pp. 1–4.

Method: Content analysis of ninety-hours of public-affairs programming broadcast Spring 1972 on WRC-TV. *Results:* 71% of all hosts were male; 79% of the interviewers were male; 77% of the guests were male. 81% of the males but only 26% of the females were identified by occupation.

B. POPULAR ARTICLES

"Barbara Walters—Star of the Morning." *Newsweek,* May 6, 1974, pp. 55–61.

Appreciative report on Barbara Walters and the reasons for her success. Some discussion of the barriers she has faced because of sexism.

Hennessee, Judith. "Some News is Good News." *Ms.*, July, 1974, pp. 25–29.

Report on the relative sparsity of network newswomen compared with number of newsmen—roughly 10%—and the difficulties they face getting on the air with their stories. Subsequent letters from several newswomen in the December 1974 issue criticized the article claiming that it was outdated and unfair to them. (Interestingly, the updated statistics still translate, as of 1976, into 10% of all network newspeople are women.)

C. COMMERCIALS

1. RESEARCH STUDIES

Akamatsu, Muriel. *Liberating the Media: Advertising.* Freedom of Information Center Report No. 290. School of Journalism, University of Missouri, September, 1972.

Report of stereotyped portrayal of women in a wide variety of advertising, including television. Based on other published reports.

Courtney, Alice E. and Thomas W. Whipple. "Women in TV Commercials." *Journal of Communication,* 24 (1974), 110–18.

Comparison of four studies (Dominick and Rauch, N.O.W.–N.Y., N.O.W.–Washington, D.C., and Toronto Women's Media Committee) demonstrates that despite differing samples over a two-year period using differing methodologies with differing levels of expertise, the results are substantially similar, suggesting that the image of women in television commercials changed little over the two-year period.

Dominick, Joseph R. and Gail E. Rauch. "The Image of Women in Network TV Commercials." *Journal of Broadcasting,* 16 (1972), 259–65.

Method: Nine hundred and eighty-six commercials broadcast during April 14–20, 1971, from 7:30 to 11 p.m., coded directly from the air. Inter-rater reliability of two independent coders ranged between .85 to .92. *Results:* Data on occupational portrayal, settings, and sex-object portrayal indicate that women are most frequently portrayed as "sex object/decoration"; second, as "wife/mother"; voice-overs are predominantly male. Occupational portrayals are primarily in service roles.

Silverstein, Arthur Jay and Rebecca Silverstein. "The Portrayal of Women in Television Advertising." *Federal Communications Bar Journal,* 27 (1974), pp. 71–98.

Method: Commercials shown on three major networks, from 8 to 11 p.m. on week nights in October and November 1973, allowing a successive four-day period to each network. *Results:* Data on giving and needing advice, and help and directives by sex; for example, 100% of the explicit directives given to one sex or the other to use or buy a product were directed toward women. Data on occupational portrayals, physical, and psychological appearance. Authors infer a relationship between the nature of the product and portrayal of women.

Verna, Mary Ellen. "The Female Image in Children's TV Commercials." *Journal of Broadcasting,* 19 (1975), 301–9.

Method: Commercials broadcast from 9 a.m. to 12 noon on three consecutive Saturdays in October (one for each network). One hundred seventy-three commercials were coded. Ads were coded for orientation toward males, females, or neutral orientation. *Results:* One hundred one ads directed toward males, twenty-four directed toward females, forty-eight were neutral. Activity levels, independence, cooperativeness, aggressiveness, and loudness of sound tract were significantly higher in ads directed toward males than in ads directed toward females. All ads directed toward males had a male voice-over or male actor; twelve of the twenty-two ads directed toward females had a male voice-over or male actor. Passivity and quietness characterized ads directed toward females.

2. PUBLIC-INTEREST REPORTS

American Association of University Women. "The Image of Women in Television," op. cit.

Method: Content analysis of commercials on news programs on three channels broadcast in April 1974. *Results:* Of 4,501 commercials,

751 had women announcers; 1,312 were products for women; and 591 had an element of sexism. Criteria for sexism in appendix.

Cantor, Muriel. "Comparison of Tasks and Roles of Males and Females in Commercials Aired by WRC-TV during Composite Week." *Women in the Wasteland Fight Back,* op. cit, pp. 12–51.

Method: 2,755 commercials aired between 7 a.m. and 1 a.m. (excluding Sundays from 7 to 9 a.m.) for three weeks in May and June 1972 monitored off the air (audio-taped) by two coders. *Results:* Women were portrayed primarily as housewives, mothers, and daughters. Occupational portrayals limited primarily to service-oriented jobs such as waitresses, secretaries, and nurses. Thirty-three nonwhite male and twelve nonwhite female product representatives in entire sample.

Faust, Jean. *Women's Roles in Contemporary Society,* Testimony before the New York City Commission on Human Rights. New York: Avon Books, 1972, pp. 689–90.

Part of a statement on the image of women in the media. Females learn from commercials "that a women is a wife, mother, laundress, scrubwoman, cook, but, above all, consumer." Stereotypes are discussed with examples.

Hennessee, Judith Adler and Joan Nicholson. "N.O.W. Says: TV Commercials Insult Women." *New York Times Magazine,* May 28, 1972, pp. 12–13.

Report of the monitoring study associated with the N.O.W.—New York challenge of WABC-TV's license. Sample included 1,241 commercials monitored off the air in the spring of 1972. Women were portrayed primarily as sex objects or as housewife-mothers. Thematic portrayals: women as domestic adjuncts, demeaned housekeepers, dependents, and as unintelligent and submissive creatures. Voice-overs are predominantly male.

National Advertising Review Board. "Advertising and Women." 850 3rd Ave., New York, N.Y. 10022, March, 1975.

Summary of published research findings regarding the image of women in television commercials and a checklist of do's and don'ts directed toward advertisers who wish to eliminate sexism from their ads.

A Redstocking Sister. "Consumerism and Women." In Gornick and Moran, op. cit., pp. 658–64.

"The chief function of media stereotypes of women is not to sell goods but to reinforce the ideology and therefore the reality of male supremacy."

Screen Actors Guild–New York Branch Women's Conference Committee. "The Relative Roles of Men and Women in Television Commercials." Screen Actors' Guild, 551 Fifth Avenue, New York, N.Y. 10017. November 13, 1974.

Method: Content analysis of 656 commercials randomly selected from Clio Award entries for 1973. *Results:* Females make up 32% of all people in the commercials; 37% of on-camera speaking principals; 40% of on-camera nonspeaking principals; 7% of off-camera speaking principals; 29% of off-camera singing principals; and 33% of extras. Data related to product category and a number of other variables.

Wormley, Wallace. "Images of Women in Media Advertising." *Cablelines,* November 11, 1974, pp. 4–5.

The image of adult women may be changing, but the image of the little girl remains the same: passive, feminine, and subordinate. The portrayal of little girls should not be overlooked.

3. POPULAR ARTICLES

Embree, Alice. "Media Images I." In Robin Morgan (ed.), *Sisterhood is Powerful.* New York: Vintage Books, 1970. pp. 175–91.

Women are exploited by commercials in two ways: urged to play consumer role and to play the sex object while selling the product. "The mass-media created woman . . . must view herself not as the controller of the technology surrounding her, but as the one controlled. She must be the object, not the subject, of her world."

Florika. "Media Images 2: Body Odor and Social Order." In Morgan, ibid., pp. 191–97.

The aerosol spray can is a major symbol of popular culture. Its message: "An impinging and elusive environment (enemy)" must be exterminated. In the case of deodorants the enemy is oneself.

Komisar, Lucy. "The Image of Women in Advertising." In Vivian Gornick and Barbara K. Moran (eds.), *Women in Sexist Society.* New York: Basic Books, 1971, pp. 304–17.

A wide variety of stereotypes are presented using examples from commercials and other forms of advertisement. It is suggested that the stereotypes are so insulting that they may form the basis of consciousness raising for many women.

Martin, Judith. "Washing the Sexism Right Out of Those Ads?" *Washington Post,* March 28, 1975, p. B1.

Report of a National Advertising Review Board study of "Advertising and Women, a Report on Advertising Portraying or Directed to Women." The report finds that working women are underrepresented and that housewives are portrayed as stupid, inadequate, guilty, mean, catty, envious, and boastful. Advertisers asked to comment did not take *Washington Post* reporter or NARB report seriously.

D. CHILDREN'S PROGRAMS

1. RESEARCH REPORTS

Busby, Linda. "Defining the Sex-Role Standard in Commercial Network Television Programs Directed toward Children." *Journalism Quarterly,* 51 (1974), 690–96.

Method: Content analysis of twenty network cartoon programs videotaped in 1972 and 1973. *Results:* Fourteen major female characters and thirty-four major male characters; seventeen minor female characters, sixty-six minor male characters. Data on occupations, activities, appearance, roles, and personality characteristics by sex.

Corporation for Public Broadcasting. *Report of the Task Force on Women in Public Broadcasting,* October, 1975.

Method: Content analysis of six series of children's programs aired during the 1974–75 season. *Results:* The number of male characters exceeded the number of female characters by two to one. Females were less likely than males to be portrayed in occupational roles; the roles in which they were portrayed were stereotyped. Males talked more, were more active, and initiated more action. "Sesame Street" had the fewest number of female characters and portrayed them the most traditionally.

Long, Michele and Rita J. Simon. "The Roles and Statuses of Women on Children and Family TV Programs." *Journalism Quarterly,* 51 (1974) 107–10.

Method: Content analysis of twenty-two programs shown on Saturday mornings and late afternoon and early evenings that featured an adult female character. *Results:* Fourteen of the twenty-four women are married and eleven are mothers. Of the ten unmarried, six hold jobs. Twelve of the married women are portrayed as deferring to husbands. Almost all are young and exceptionally physically attractive. Overall image: dependent, concerned with bodies and home, stereotyped occupations.

2. PUBLIC-INTEREST REPORTS

Hoffman, Heidi. "Monitoring of Children's Television Programming Aired by WRC-TV: A Comparison of Male and Female Roles." *Women in the Wasteland Fight Back,* op. cit. pp. 91–104.

Method: Monitoring of ten and one-half hours of programming designed for children, primarily on weekends. *Results:* Twenty-one male and eight female characters in live action shows. The only female lead was a witch; other women shown performing domestic tasks. Males in a wide variety of occupations. In cartoons, thirty-five characters were male, eight were female. Twenty males initiated action. One female did. Overall, 70.6% of characters were male; 29.4% were female.

3. POPULAR ARTICLES

Cathey-Calvert, Carolyn. "Sexism on Sesame Street," KNOW, P.O. Box 86031, Pittsburgh, Penna. 15221, $.60.

"Sesame Street" stereotypes females as passive, quiet, domestic, beautiful, and ladylike. Detailed examples from program segments.

II. IMPACT OF PORTRAYAL ON ATTITUDES AND BEHAVIOR

A. RESEARCH REPORTS

Gerbner, George and Larry Gross. "Violence Profile No. 6. Trends in Network Television Drama and Viewer Conceptions of Social Reality, 1967–1973." Annenberg School of Communications, December 1974.

Method: Telephone survey using a purposive quota sample of 607 households in Philadelphia, Chicago, Los Angeles, and Dallas and interview survey of a national probability survey of 2,052 men and women. Respondents were subdivided by sex and heavy versus light viewing. Error-choice questions focused on perceived violence in society. Respondents could give a "TV answer," which greatly exaggerated the degree of violence in society or an answer that was closer to reality. *Results:* Heavy viewers, particularly heavy female viewers gave TV answers. Light female viewers gave TV answers, more than did light male viewers. As women are more likely than men to be portrayed as victims than as perpetrators of violence on television, these results suggest that the TV answers are indicative of its impact.

Greenberg, Bradley S. and Charles Atkin. "Parental Mediation of Children's Social Learning from Television." (A proposal funded by Office of Child Development.) Department of Communication, Michigan State University, 1975.

Research project designed to assess the relative impact of televised social roles; field surveys, field experiments, laboratory experiments, and demonstrations are contemplated. Project is expected to last three years.

Miller, M. Mark and Byron Reeves. "Dramatic TV Content and Children's Stereotypes." *Journal of Broadcasting,* 20 (1976), pp. 35–50.

Method: Survey of 200 third- through sixth-grade Michigan schoolchildren regarding characters on television children would like to emulate and the "OK-ness" of certain nontraditional occupations filled by females in current television programs. Children were also asked to predict how frequently women filled such occupations in real life. The independent variable was the child's awareness of the character and the occupation she filled. *Results:* Boys chose proportionately more males as models to emulate than girls chose females; no boys selected females as models; 27% of the girls selected males as models. Boys tended to choose characters on the basis of their aggressiveness and girls on the basis of the characters' physical attractiveness. Those children exposed to counter-stereotypical occupations held by television women were more likely to believe those occupations were filled by women in real life and that it was all right for them to do so, although most children in the sample were not able to identify these characters or their occupations or both.

Stone, Vernon A. "Attitudes Toward Television Newswomen." *Journal of Broadcasting,* 18 (1973–74), pp. 49–62.

Method: Attitude survey of four audience groups: students and professors from University of Wisconsin; grade-school children from a small town and their parents. Comparison of their attitudes with television news directors' attitudes toward newswomen. *Results:* At least 50% of all audience groups reported that the sex of a newscaster made no difference to them; only 16% of the news directors estimated that it would make no difference to the audience. A female as city hall correspondent was preferred more than a female Viet Nam correspondent. Greater believability of male reporters ascribed to tradition and habit.

Warner, W. Lloyd and William E. Henry. "The Radio Day Time Serial: A Symbolic Analysis." *Genetic Psychology Monographs,* 37 (1948), pp. 3–71.

Method: In-depth study of the audience of soap operas. Sixty-two subjects were regular listeners selected to meet a variety of criteria; five subjects who did not listen to soap operas were selected for contrast. A variety of measures used including Thematic Apperception Test. *Results:* Detailed discussion of subjects' responses to interviews and T.A.T.'s in an effort to discover the function of soap operas in the lives of regular listeners.

Whittaker, Susan and Ron Whittaker. "Relative Effectiveness of Male and Female Newscasters." *Journal of Broadcasting,* 20 (1976), pp. 177–84.

Method: 174 adult men and women from a variety of occupational backgrounds heard two newcasts, one delivered by a male, the other a female.
Results: No significant differences in acceptance, believability, or effectiveness resulted.

B. PUBLIC-INTEREST REPORTS

Screen Actors Guild. "SAG Survey Reveals Public Attitudes, Preferences in TV." Press Release, October 31, 1974.

Method: A nationwide survey of attitudes toward television. Of 14,000 respondents, 83.6% were female. *Results:* 70% of the females and 61.8% of the males said they didn't think the image of women on television is truthful and believable. 67.2% of the females and 62.6% of the males prefer to see women in positions of authority on television. 28.2% of the women and 52.2 % of the men said they like the women they see on television. Numerous other results reported.

United Nations Economic and Social Council, Commission on the Status of Women. "Influence of Mass Communication Media on the Formation of a New Attitude toward the Role of Women in Present-Day Society." January 10, 1974.

Compilation and summary of reports of member nations regarding the role television and other media play in the portrayal of women. Most nations reported that the media lag behind changes in attitude and behavior but that women are making progress despite the media.

C. POPULAR ARTICLES

Bird, Caroline. "What's Television Doing for 50.9% of Americans?" *TV Guide,* February 27, 1971, pp. 5–8.

"Television . . . does not provide human models for a bright thirteen-year-old girl who would like to grow up to be something other than an ecstatic floor waxer." Discusses television's messages. To women and girls it says, You're not really interested in work:

what you really want is a man! Women can't boss men. You are powerful—and smart—only on your own feminine turf.

Freeman, Jessica David. "Heel, Maude!" *Family Circle,* June 1973, pp. 10ff.

Argues that children believe that television families and the sex roles they play are real and that their own families are fantasy.

Peck, Ellen. "Television's Romance with Reproduction." In Ellen Peck and Judith Senderowitz (eds.), *Pronatalism: The Myth of Mom and Apple Pie.* New York: T. Y. Crowell, 1974, pp. 78–97.

Report of themes in prime-time and soap operas programming and commercials that promote parenthood. Objectionable commercials are described and changes are suggested that would make them unobjectionable.

III. ORGANIZATIONS CONCERNED ABOUT THE PORTRAYAL OF WOMEN IN THE MEDIA

Ruth Abram
Linda Small
Women's Action Alliance
370 Lexington Ave.
New York, N.Y. 10017

Donna Allen
Media Report to Women
3306 Ross Place, N.W.
Washington, D.C. 20008

Dr. Gloria Anderson, Chairperson
Task Force on Women
Corporation for Public Broadcasting
1111-16th Street
Washington, D.C. 20036

Pam Curtis
U.S. Commission on the Observance of International Women's Year
Room 1004
Department of State
Washington, D.C. 20520

Betty Fierro
Mexican-American Women's National Association
P.O. Box 656
L'Enfant Plaza
Washington, D.C. 20024

Margaret Gates
Center for Women Policy Studies
803 National Press Building
Washington, D.C. 20004

Mary Hallern
Women in Community Service
1730 Rhode Island Avenue, N.W.
Washington, D.C. 20036

Mim Keller
Media Committee
National Women's Political Caucus
257-7th Avenue
New York, N.Y. 10001

Susan Lowe
Zero Population Growth
1346 Connecticut Avenue, N.W.
Washington, D.C. 20036

Peggy Mellem
General Federation of Women's Clubs
1734 N. Street, N.W.
Washington, D.C. 20036

Mary Lynn Moody
Director of Women's Programs
National Association of Educational Broadcasters
1346 Connecticut Avenue, N.W.
Washington, D.C. 20036

National Council on Negro Women
1346 Connecticut Avenue, N.W.
Washington, D.C. 20036

Marjorie Newman
Women's Equity Action League
805 15th Street, N.W., Suite 822
Washington, D.C. 20005

Ellen Peck
National Organization for Non-parents
2231 Rogene Drive
Baltimore, MD. 21209

Dorothy Eugenia Robinson
National Black Feminist Organization
285 Madison Ave.
New York, N.Y. 10017

Nancy Seifer
Institute on Pluralism and Group Identity
165 East 56th Street
New York, N.Y. 10222

Judy Senderowitz
Population Institute
110 Maryland Avenue, N.E.
Washington, D.C. 20002

Chuck Shepherd
National Citizens Committee for Broadcasting
Room 525
1346 Connecticut Avenue, N.W.
Washington, D.C. 20036

Joyce Snyder
National Organization for Women
55 West 14th Street
New York, N.Y. 10007

Lynne Stitt
American Association of University Women
2401 Virginia Avenue, N.W.
Washington, D.C. 20037

Carmen Votaw
President, National Conference of Puerto Rican Women
c/o Office of the Commonwealth of Puerto Rico
1625 Massachusetts Avenue, N.W.
Washington, D.C. 20036

Women on Words and Images
Box 2163
Princeton, New Jersey 08540

References

Akhminov, Herman
1961 "Obituaries as a key to the Soviet elite." *Bulletin of the Institute for the study of the USSR* 8(7):37–43.

Altheide, David
1974 "The news scene." Ph.D. dissertation. University of California, San Diego.

Argyle, M.
1975 *Bodily Communication.* London: Methuen.

Atkin, C. K.
1975 "The effects of television advertising on children: second year experimental evidence." Report submitted to the Office of Child Development.

Baltzell, E. Digby
1958 *Philadelphia Gentlemen: The Making of a National Upper Class.* New York: Free Press.

———.
1966 *The Protestant Establishment.* New York: Vintage Books.

Bandura, A., D. Ross, and S. Ross
1963 "A comparative test of the status envy, social power and sec-

ondary reinforcement theories of identification learning." *Journal of Abnormal and Social Psychology.* 67(6):527–34.

Bardwick, Judith and Suzanne Schumann
1967 "Portrait of American Men and Women in TV Commercials." *Psychology.* 4(4):18–23.

Barens, F. E.
1971 "Saturday children's television: A report of television programming and advertising on Boston commercial television." Action for Children's Television. Unpublished monograph.

Barret, M.
1973 *A State of Siege.* New York: T. Y. Crowell.

Baumann, Zygmunt
1972 "A note on mass culture: on infrastructure." In Denis McQuail (ed.), *Sociology of Mass Communication.* Baltimore: Penguin Books, pp. 61–74.

Becker, Howard S.
1974 "Art as collective action." *American Sociological Review.* 39:767–76.

Bender, Marilyn
1967 *The Beautiful People.* New York: Coward-McCann.

Benét, James
1972 "The California regents: Window on the ruling class." *Change.* 4:22–27.

Bernard, Jessie
1973 "My four revolutions: an autobiographical history of the ASA." *American Journal of Sociology.* 78:773–91.

Bernstein, Carl and Robert Woodward
1974 *All the President's Men.* New York: Simon & Schuster.

Beuf, Ann
1974 "Doctor, lawyer, household drudge." *Journal of Communication.* 24(2):142–45.

Blumberg, Paul M. and P. W. Paul
1975 "Continuities and discontinuities in upper-class marriages." *Journal of Marriage and the Family.* 37(February):63–77.

Bogart, Leo
1973 "Warning: The surgeon general has determined that TV violence is moderately dangerous to your child's mental health." *Public Opinion Quarterly.* 36(Winter)491–521.

Bowen, William G. and T. Aldrich Finegan
1969 *The Economics of Labor Force Participation.* Princeton: Princeton University Press.

Breed, Warren
1973 "Social control in the newsroom: a functional analysis." In Richard Flacks (ed.), *Conformity, Resistance, and Self-Determination.* Boston: Little, Brown and Co., pp. 153–60.

Broverman, Inge K. *et al.*
1972 "Sex-role stereotypes: a current appraisal." *Journal of Social Issues.* 28(2):60–78.

Busby, Linda J.
1975 "Sex-role research on the mass media." *Journal of Communication.* 25(4):107–31.

Campbell, W. J.
1962 *Television and the Australian Adolescent.* Sydney: Angus and Robertson.

Cantor, Muriel G.
1975 "Children's television: sex-role portrayals and employment discrimination." In *The Federal Role in Funding Children's Television Programming.* Vol. 2. Edited by K. Mielke *et al.* United States Office of Education, USOE OEC-074-8674.

Cantor, Muriel G. *et al.*
1972 "Comparison of the tasks and roles of males and females in commercials aired by WRC-TV." In *Women in the Wasteland Fight Back.* Washington, D.C.: National Organization for Women, pp. 12–50.

Carden, Maren Lockwood
1973 *The New Feminist Movement.* New York: Russel Sage.

Carpenter, Liz
1970 *Ruffles and Flourishes.* Garden City: Doubleday.

Cater, Douglass
1959 *The Fourth Branch of Government.* Boston: Houghton Mifflin.

Clark, C.
1972 "Race, identification, and television violence." In G. A. Comstock, E. A. Rubinstein, and J. P. Murray (eds.), *Further Explorations.* Television and Social Behavior, Vol. 5. Washington, D.C.: U.S. Government Printing Office.

Clarke, P. and V. Esposito
1966 "A study of occupational advice for women in magazines." *Journalism Quarterly.* 43:477–85.

Colle, R. D.
1968 "Negro image in the mass media: A case study in social change." *Journalism Quarterly.* 45:55–60.

Courtney, A. E. and T. W. Whipple
1974 "Women in TV commercials." *Journal of Communication.* 24(2):110–18.

Crouse, Timothy
1973 *The Boys on the Bus.* New York: Random House.

Daniels, Arlene Kaplan
1975 "Feminist perspectives in sociological research." In Marcia Millman and Rosabeth Moss Kanter (eds.), *Another Voice: Feminist Perspectives on Social Life and Social Science.* New York: Doubleday/Anchor, pp. 340–80.

Darnton, Robert
1975 "Writing news and telling stories." *Daedalus.* (Spring): 175–94.

Davis, Margaret
1976 "The *Ladies' Home Journal* and *Esquire:* A comparison." Unpublished manuscript. Stanford University, Dept. of Sociology.

DeFleur, Melvin L.
1964 "Occupational roles as portrayed on television." *Public Opinion Quarterly.* 28(Spring):57–74.

———. and Lois B. DeFleur
1967 "The relative contribution of television as a learning source for children's occupational knowledge." *American Sociological Review.* 32(5):777–89.

Domhoff, G. William
1970 *The Higher Circles.* New York: Random House.

———.

1975 *The Bohemian Grove and Other Retreats.* New York: Harper & Row.

Dominick, Joseph and Gail Rauch

1972 "The image of women in network TV commercials." *Journal of Broadcasting.* 16(3):259–65.

Donagher, R. C., R. W. Poulos, R. M. Liebert, and E. S. Davidson.

1976 "Race, sex and social example: an analysis of character portrayals of inter-racial television entertainment. *Psychological Reports.* 38:3–14.

Downing, Mildred

1974 "Heroine of the daytime serial." *Journal of Communication.* 24(2):130–37.

Ellis, G. T. and F. Sekyra

1972 "The effect of aggressive cartoons on the behavior of first grade children." *Journal of Psychology.* 81:37–43.

Ellul, Jacques

1964 *Propaganda.* New York: Alfred Knopf.

Enzenberger, Hans Magnus

1974 *The Consciousness Industry.* New York: Seabury Press.

Fanon, Franz

1963 *Wretched of the Earth.* New York: Grove Press.

Ferguson, Marjorie

1974 "Women's magazines: the changing mood." *New Society.* 29:475–77.

———.

In progress. "The creation of myth with reference to female roles: The impact of social change on the contents and editorial processes of mass circulation women's magazines, 1949–1974." Ph.D. dissertation. London School of Economics.

Filene, Peter Gabriel

1974 *Him Her Self.* New York: New American Library/Mentor.

Fishman, Mark

1977 "Manufacturing the news: the social organization of media newswork." Ph.D. dissertation. University of California, Santa Barbara.

Fishman, Pam
1975 "Interaction: The work women do." Paper read at the annual meeting of the American Sociological Association, San Francisco, August.

Flora, Cornelia
1971 "The passive female: Her comparative image by class and culture in women's magazine fiction." *Journal of Marriage and the Family.* 33(August):435–44.

Franzwa, Helen
1974a "Working women in fact and fiction." *Journal of Communication.* 24(2):104–9.

———.
1974b "Pronatalism in women's magazine fiction." In Ellen Peale and Judith Senderowitz (eds.), *Pronatalism: The Myth of Motherhood and Apple Pie.* New York: T. Y. Crowell, pp. 68–77.

———.
1975 "Female roles in women's magazine fiction, 1940–1970." In R. K. Unger and F. L. Denmark (eds.), *Woman: Dependent or Independent Variable.* New York: Psychological Dimensions, pp. 42–53.

Freeman, Jo
1975 *The Politics of Women's Liberation.* New York: McKay.

Freud, Sigmund
1959 *Group Psychology and the Analysis of the Ego.* London: The Hogarth Press and the Institute of Psychoanalysis.

Friedan, Betty
1963 *The Feminine Mystique.* New York: Dell.

Frueh, T. and P. E. McGhee
1975 "Traditional sex role development and amount of time spent watching television." *Development psychology.* 11:109.

Gans, Herbert J.
1974 *Popular Culture and High Culture.* New York: Basic Books.

Garfinkel, Harold
1967 *Studies in Ethnomethodology.* Englewood Cliffs, N.J.: Prentice-Hall.

Gerbner, George

1972a "Violence in television drama: Trends and symbolic functions." In G. A. Comstock and E. A. Rubinstein (eds.), *Media Content and Control.* Television and Social Behavior, vol. 1. Washington, D.C.: U.S. Government Printing Office, pp. 28–187.

———.

1972b "Communications and social environment." *Scientific American.* 227(3):153–60.

———, and Larry Gross

1974a "Cultural indicators: The social reality of television drama." Unpublished manuscript. Annenberg School of Communications, University of Pennsylvania.

———, with Michael F. Eleey, Nancy Tedesco, and Suzanne Jeffries-Fox

1974b "Violence profile no. 6: Trends in network television drama and viewer conceptions of social reality, 1967–1973." Unpublished research report. Annenberg School of Communications, University of Pennsylvania.

———.

1976 "The violence profile." *Journal of Communication.* 26 (Spring):17–99.

Gerbner, George, Larry Gross, Michael F. Eleey, Marilyn Jackson-Beeck, Suzanne Jeffries-Fox, and Nancy Signorielli

1977 "TV violence profile no. 8: The highlights." *Journal of Communication.* 27(2):171–80.

Goldenberg, Edie N.

1975 *Making the Papers.* Lexington, Mass.: D. C. Heath.

Graves, S. B.

1975 "How to encourage positive racial attitudes." Paper presented at the biennial meeting of the Society for Research in Child Development. Denver, Colorado, April.

Greenberg, Bradley

1972 "Children's reaction to TV blacks." *Journalism Quarterly.* 49:5–14.

———, Gary Held, Jacob Wakshlag and Byron Reeves

1976 "TV character attributes, identification and children's modeling tendencies." Paper presented at International Communication Association, Portland, Oregon, April.

Gross, Larry
1974 "The real world of television." *Today's Education.* 63 (January–February):86–92.

Grusec, J. E. and D. B. Brinker, Jr.
1972 "Reinforcement for imitation as a social learning determinant with implications for sex-role development." *Journal of Personality and Social Psychology.* 21:149–58.

Guenin, Zena B.
1975 "Women's pages in contemporary newspapers: Missing out on contemporary content." *Journalism Quarterly.* 52(Spring): 66–69, 75.

Halloran, J. D., P. Elliott and G. Murdock
1970 *Demonstrations and Communications: A Case Study.* London: Penguin.

Hatch, David L. and Marya G. Hatch
1947 "Criteria of social status as derived from marriage announcements in the *New York Times." American Sociological Review.* 12:396:403.

Hatch, Marya G. and David L. Hatch
1958 "Problems of married and working women as presented by three popular working women's magazines." *Social Forces.* 37:148–53.

Head, Sydney W.
1954 "Content analysis of television drama programs." *Quarterly of Film, Radio and Television.* 9:175–94.

Hirsch, Paul
1978 "Television as a national medium: Its Cultural and political role in American society." In David Street (ed.), *Handbook of Urban Life.* San Francisco: Jossey-Bass.

Hochschild, Arlie
1974 "Marginality and obstacles to minority consciousness." In Ruth B. Kundsin (ed.), *Women and Success.* New York: Morrow, pp. 194–99.

Hoffman, Abbie
1968 *Revolution for the Hell of It.* New York: Dial Press.

Hole, Judith and Ellen Levine
1971 *Rebirth of Feminism.* New York: Quadrangle.

Hughes, Helen McGill
1940 *News and the Interest Story.* Chicago: University of Chicago Press.

Hume, Brit
1975 "Now it can be told, or can it?" *More.* 5(April):6.

Irving, Washington
1808; rpt. 1962 "Aunt Charity Cockloft," in Henry C. Carlisle, Jr. (ed.). *American Satire in Prose and Verse.* New York: Random House, pp. 4–8.

Isber, Caroline and Muriel Cantor
1975 *Report of the Task Force on Women in Public Broadcasting.* Washington: Corporation for Public Broadcasting.

Jenkins, Craig
1975 "Farm workers and the powers: Insurgency and political conflict (1946–1972)." Ph.D. dissertation. State University of New York, Stony Brook.

Jennings, Ralph and Alan P. Walters
1977 "Television station employment practices: 1976." Mimeo. New York: United Church of Christ.

Johns-Heine, P. and H. Gerth
1949 "Values in mass periodical fiction, 1921–1940." *Public Opinion Quarterly.* 13(Spring):105–13.

Kagan, J.
1958 "The concept of identification." *Psychological Review.* 65(5):296–305.

Katz, Elihu and Paul F. Lazarsfeld
1955 *Personal Influence.* New York: The Free Press.

Katzman, N.
1972 "Television soap operas: What's been going on anyway?" *Public Opinion Quarterly.* 35:200–12.

Kohlberg, L.
1966 "A cognitive-developmental analysis of children's sex-role concepts and attitudes." In E. E. Maccoby (ed.), *The Development of Sex Differences.* Stanford: Stanford University Press, pp. 82–173.

Landis, Fred
1975 "The C.I.A. makes headlines with psychological warfare in Chile." *Liberation.* 19(3):21–32.

Lane, Robert
1959 *Political Life.* Glencoe, Ill.: The Free Press.

Lasswell, Harold
1948 "The structure and function of communication in society." In L. Bryson (ed.), *The Communication of Ideas.* New York: Harper Brothers, pp. 37–51.

Lazarsfeld, Paul F.
1955 "Why is so little known about the effects of television on children and what can be done?" *Public Opinion Quarterly.* (Fall):243–51.

———, and Robert K. Merton
1948 "Mass communication, popular taste and organized social action." In L. Bryson (ed.), *The Communication of Ideas.* New York: Harper Brothers, pp. 95–118.

Lee, S. Y. and Pedone, R. J.
1974 *Status Report on Public Broadcasting, 1973.* Washington, D.C., Corporation for Public Broadcasting.

Leifer, Aimee Dorr
1975. "Socialization processes in the family." Paper presented at Prix Jeunesse Seminar, Munich, Germany, June.

———, and D. Roberts
1972 "Children's responses to television violence." In J. P. Murray, E. A. Rubinstein, and G. A. Comstock (eds.), *Television and Social Learning.* Television and Social Behavior, vol. 2. Washington, D.C.: U.S. Government Printing Office, pp. 43–180.

Leifer, Aimee Dorr, N. J. Gordon, and S. B. Graves
1974 "Children's television: More than mere entertainment." *Harvard Educational Review.* 44:213–45.

Lesser, G. S.
1974 *Children and Television: Lessons from Sesame Street.* New York: Random House.

Lester, Marilyn
1975 "News as a practical accomplishment: A conceptual and empirical analysis of newswork." Unpublished Ph.D. dissertation. University of California, Santa Barbara.

Lichtenstein, Grace
1974 *A Long Way Baby: Behind the Scenes in Women's Tennis.* New York: William Morrow and Co.

Liebert, R. M. and R. A. Baron
1972 "Some immediate effects of televised violence on children's behavior." *Developmental Psychology.* 6(3):469–75.

Liebert, R. M., J. M. Neale, and E. S. Davidson
1973 *The Early Window: Effects of Television on Children and Youth.* New York: Pergamon.

Liebert, R. M., J. N. Sprafkin, and R. W. Poulos
1975 "Television and social behavior: A prototype for experimental programming." Paper presented at the Annual Conference of the American Educational Research Association, Washington, D.C., April.

Lowenthal, Leo (ed.)
1944, rpt. 1961 "The triumph of mass idols." In *Literature, Popular Culture, and Society.* Englewood Cliffs, N.J.: Spectrum, pp. 109–36.

Lyle, J.
1975 *The People Look at Public Broadcasting, 1974.* Washington, D.C.: Corporation for Public Broadcasting.

———, and H. R. Hoffman
1972 "Children's use of television and other media." In E. A. Rubinstein, G. A. Comstock, and J. P. Murphy (eds.), *Television in Day to Day Life: Patterns of Use.* Television and Social Behavior, vol. 4. Washington, D.C.: U.S. Government Printing Office, pp. 129–256.

Maccoby, E. E. and W. C. Wilson
1957 "Identification and observational learning from films." *Journal of Abnormal and Social Psychology.* 55:76–87.

McCormack, Thelma
1975 "Toward a nonsexist perspective on social and political change." In Marcia Millman and Rosabeth Moss Kanter (eds.), *Another Voice: Feminist Perspectives on Social Life and Social Science*. New York: Doubleday/Anchor, pp. 1–33.

McNeil, Jean C.
1975 "Feminism, femininity, and the television series: A content analysis." *Journal of Broadcasting*. 19:259–69.

Mannes, Marya
1970 "Should women only be seen and not heard?" Reprinted from *TV Guide* in Barry G. Cole (ed.), *Television*. New York: The Free Press, pp. 276–80.

Mendelson, G. and M. Young
1972 "Network children's programming: A content analysis of black and minority treatment on children's television." Prepared for Black Efforts for Soul in Television for Action for Children's Television, Washington, D.C.

Milgram, Stanley
1976 "The image freezing machine." *Society*. 4(1):7–12.

Miller, Hope Ridings
1973 *Scandals in the Highest Office*. New York: Random House.

Miller, M. Mark
1976 "Factors affecting children's choices of TV characters as sex role models." Paper presented at the annual meetings of Association for Education in Journalism, College Park, Maryland, August.

———, and Byron Reeves
1976 "Dramatic TV content and children's sex-role stereotypes." *Journal of Broadcasting*. 20(1):35–50.

Miller, Susan H.
1975 "The content of news photos: Women's and men's roles." *Journalism Quarterly*. 52(Spring):70–75.

Millett, Kate
1974 *Flying*. New York: Ballantine Books.

Mills, C. Wright
1956 *The Power Elite*. New York: Oxford University Press.

Mischel, W.
1970 "Sex-typing and socialization." In P. Mussen (ed.), *Carmichael's Manual of Child Psychology,* vol. 2. New York: Wiley.

Molotch, Harvey and Marilyn Lester
1974 "News as purposive behavior: On the strategic use of routine events, accidents and scandals." *American Sociological Review.* 39(1):101–13.

Morris, Monica B.
1973 "Newspapers and the new feminists: black out as social control?" *Journalism Quarterly.* 50:37–42.

———.
1974 "The public definition of a social movement: Women's liberation." *Sociology and Social Research.* 57:526–43.

———.
1975 "Excuses, justifications and evasions: How newspaper editors account for their coverage of a social movement." Paper delivered at annual meetings of the American Sociological Association, San Francisco, August.

Oakley, A.
1974 *The Sociology of Housework.* London: Martin Robertson.

Oppenheimer, Valerie Kincaid
1970 *The Female Labor Force in the United States: Demographic and Economic Factors Governing Its Growth and Changing Composition.* Population Monograph Series No. 5. Berkeley: University of California, Institute of International Studies.

Ormiston, L. H. and S. Williams
1973 "Saturday children's programming in San Francisco, California: An analysis of the presentation of racial and cultural groups on three network affiliated San Francisco television stations." Prepared by the Committee on Children's Television, Inc., San Francisco, California in cooperation with the Bay Area Association of Black Psychologists, the Chinese Media Committee, and the League of United Latin American Citizens for the Federal Communications Commissions Hearings on Children's Television.

Parsons, Talcott
1949 "Age and sex in the social structure of the United States." *Essays in Sociological Theory.* New York: The Free Press.

Phillips, B. J.
1974 "Recognizing the gentleladies of the Judiciary Committee." *Ms.* 3(November):70–74.

Pifer, Alan
1977 *Women Working: Toward a New Society.* New York: Carnegie Corp. 1977.

Pingree, Suzanne
1976 "The effects of nonsexist television commercials and perceptions of reality on children's attitudes towards women." Paper presented at the annual meetings of the International Communication Association, Portland, Oregon, April.

Pogrebin, Letty Cottin
1975 "Ten cogent reasons why T.V. news fails women." *TV Guide,* October 4, p. 10.

Poulos, R. W., R. M. Liebert, and N. Schwartzberg
1975 "Television's prosocial influence: Designing 'commercials' for cooperative behavior." Paper presented at the 83rd Annual Convention of the American Psychological Association, Chicago, August.

Radcliffe, Donnie
1974 "Pat Nixon: A full partner in the American dream." Chap. VIII in *The Fall of a President.* New York: Dell.

Reeves, Bryon
1976 "The dimensional structure of children's perception of TV characters." Ph.D. dissertation. Michigan State University, East Lansing, Michigan.

Report of the Carnegie Commission on Educational Television
1967 *Public Television: A Program for Action.* New York: Bantam Books.

Roberts, C.
1970–71 "The portrayal of blacks on network television." *Journal of Broadcasting.* 15 (Winter):45–53.

Rosen, Lawrence and Robert R. Bell
1966 "Mate selection in the upper class." *Sociological Quarterly.* 7 (Spring):157–66.

Rubin, Lillian
1976 *Worlds of Pain. Life in the Working-Class Family.* New York: Basic Books.

Ruckelshaus, Jill
1975 Press Conference, discussed *Long Island Press,* September 25.

Schiller, Herbert
1969 *Mass Communications and American Empire,* New York: Augustus M. Kelley.

Schudson, Michael
1976 "Origins of the ideal of objectivity in the professions: Studies in the history of American journalism and American law, 1830–1940." Ph.D. dissertation. Harvard University, Cambridge, Mass.

Schutz, Alfred
1966 *Collected Papers.* Vols. I, II. The Hague: Martinus Nijhoff.

Seegar, J. F. and P. Wheeler
1973 "World of work on TV: Ethnic and sex representation in TV drama." *Journal of Broadcasting.* 17:210–14.

Serbin, L., D. K. O'Leary, R. N. Kent, and I. J. Tonick
1973 "A comparison of teacher response to the pre-academic and problem behavior of boys and girls." *Child Development.* 44(4):796–804.

Sheikh, A. A., V. K. Prasad, and T. R. Rao
1974 "Children's T.V. commercials: A review of research." *Journal of Communication.* 24(2):126–36.

Shrank, H. and D. Gilmore
1973 "Correlates of fashion leadership: Implications of fashion process theory." *Sociological Quarterly.* 14:534–43.

Sigal, Leon V.
1973 *Reporters and Officials: The Organization and Politics of Newsmaking.* Lexington, Mass.: D. C. Heath.

Silver, Sheila
1976 "Then and now—content analysis of *McCall's* magazine."

Paper presented at the annual meetings of Association for Education in Journalism. College Park, Maryland, August.

Silverstein, Arthur Jay and Rebecca Silverstein
1974 "The portrayal of women in television advertising." *FCC Bar Journal.* (1):71–98.

Sloan, Susan Kay
1973 "A critique of the Southern rim power theory." Unpublished paper. University of California, Santa Cruz.

Smith, Dorothy E.
1973 "Women's perspective as a radical critique of sociology." *Sociological Inquiry.* 44(1):7–13.

———.
1975 "An analysis of ideological structures and how women are excluded." *Canadian Review of Sociology and Anthropology.* 12(4):353–69.

Smythe, D. W.
1953 "Three years of New York Television, 1951–1953." Urbana, Ill.: National Association of Educational Broadcasters.

Sommers, Dixie
1974 "Occupational rankings for men and women by earnings." *Monthly Labor Review.* 97(8):34–51.

Sprafkin, Joyce N. and Robert M. Liebert
1976 "Sex and sex-roles as determinants of children's television program selections and attention." Unpublished manuscript. State University of New York at Stony Brook.

———, and R. W. Poulos
1975 "Effects of a prosocial televised example on children's helping." *Journal of Experimental Child Psychology.* 20:119–26.

Stein, A. H. and L. K. Friedrich
1972 "Television content and young children's behavior." In J. P. Murray, E. A. Rubinstein, and G. A. Comstock (eds.), *Television and Social Learning.* Television and Social Behavior, vol. 2. Washington, D.C.: U.S. Government Printing Office, pp. 202–317.

Steiner, F.
1956 *Taboo.* London: Cohen and West.

Sternglanz, S. H. and L. A. Serbin
1974 "Sex-role stereotyping in children's television programs." *Developmental Psychology* 10:710–15.

Steuer, F. B., J. M. Applefield, and R. Smith
1971 "Televised aggression and the interpersonal aggression of preschool children." *Journal of Experimental Child Psychology.* 11:442–47.

Stolz, Gale K. *et al.*
n.d. "The occupational roles of women in magazines and books." Unpublished manuscript. Loyola University, Chicago.

Stone, Vernon
1973–74 "Attitudes toward television newswomen." *Journal of Broadcasting.* 18(1):57–61.

Streicher, H. W.
1974 "The girls in the cartoons." *Journal of Communication.* 24(2):125–29.

Talese, Gay
1966 *The Kingdom and the Power.* New York: World.

Tedesco, Nancy S.
1974 "Patterns in prime time." *Journal of Communication.* 24(2): 119–24.

Thompson, Hunter
1973 *Fear and Loathing on the Campaign Trail.* New York: Popular Library.

Thorne, Barrie
1970 "Resisting the draft: An ethnography of the draft resistance movement." Ph.D. dissertation, Brandeis University, Waltham, Mass.

Tolchin, Susan and Martin Tolchin
1975 *Clout: Womanpower and Politics.* New York: Coward, McCann and Geoghegan.

Tuchman, Gaye
1969 "News, the newsman's reality." Unpublished Ph.D. dissertation. Brandeis University, Waltham, Mass.

———.
1972 "Objectivity as strategic ritual." *American Journal of Sociology.* 77:660–80.

———.
1973a "The technology of objectivity: Doing objective TV news." *Urban Life and Culture.* 2:3–26.

———.
1973b "Making news by doing work: Routinizing the unexpected." *American Journal of Sociology.* 79:110–31.

———.
1974 *The TV Establishment: Programming for Power and Profit.* Englewood Cliffs, N.J.: Prentice-Hall.

———.
1976 "Media values." *Society.* (November/December):51–54.

Turner, Ralph and Lewis Killian
1957 *Collective Behavior.* Englewood Cliffs, N.J.: Prentice-Hall.

Turow, Joseph
1974 "Advising and ordering: Daytime, prime time." *Journal of Communication.* 24(2):138–41.

United States Department of Labor, Women's Bureau
1973 *Why Women Work.* Washington, D.C.: U.S. Government Printing Office, June.

1976 *Handbook on Women Workers.* Washington, D.C.: U.S. Government Printing Office.

Vanek, Joann
Forthcoming. *Married Women and the Work Day: Time Trends.* Baltimore, Md.: Johns Hopkins University Press, chapter 4.

Van Gelder, Lindsay
1974 "Women's pages: You can't make news out of a silk purse." *Ms.* (November):112–16.

Webb, Eugene J., Donald T. Campbell, Richard D. Schwartz, and Lee Sechrest
1966 *Unobtrusive Measures: Nonreactive Research in the Social Sciences.* Skokie, Ill.: Rand McNally & Co.

Weber, Max
1920; rpt. 1956 *The Protestant Ethic and the Spirit of Capitalism.* New York: Scribner's.

Welles, Chris
1972 "Can mass magazines survive?" In Alan Wells (ed.), *Mass Media and Society.* Palo Alto, Calif.: National Press Books, pp. 27–34.

West, J. B.
1973 *Upstairs at the White House.* New York: Coward, McCann & Geoghegan.

White, Orion
1972 "Beyond power politics: Vive la difference as political theory." *Maxwell Review.* 8(2):57–63.

Wise, David
1973 *The Politics of Lying: Government Deception, Secrecy and Power.* New York: Random House/Vintage.

Wolff, K. (ed.)
1959 *Georg Simmel, 1858–1918.* Columbus, Ohio: Ohio State University Press.

Women on Words and Images
1975 *Channeling Children: Sex Stereotyping on Prime Time TV.* Princeton, N.J.: Women on Words and Images.

Worth, Sol and Larry Gross
1974 "Symbolic strategies." *Journal of Communication.* 24:(Autumn), 27–39.

Wright, Charles R.
1975 "Functional analysis and mass communication revisited." In Jay G. Blumler and Elihu Katz (eds.), *The Uses of Mass Communications: Current Perspectives on Gratification Research.* Beverly Hills, Calif.: Sage Publications, pp. 197–212.

Yussen, S. R.
1974 "Determinants of visual attention and recall in observational learning by preschoolers and second graders." *Developmental Psychology.* 10:93–100.

List of Contributors

THE EDITORS

Currently the Education Editor of DQED's "Newsroom," JAMES BENÉT has worked as a reporter and editor at the *San Francisco Chronicle* and the *New Republic.* A contributor to *Change,* he has also published *Guide to San Francisco and the Bay Region* and academic articles on education. He has also served as Associate Professor of Journalism at San Francisco State College.

Professor of Sociology and Head of the Program on Women at Northwestern University, ARLENE KAPLAN DANIELS is editor of the journal *Social Problems.* She has published over two dozen articles on such topics as the sociology of medicine and psychiatry and the sociology of sex roles, has co-edited *Academics on the Line,* and received a Ford Foundation Faculty Fellowship for the study of female power-elites. Active in the Women's movement, she has served as President of Sociologists for Women in Society.

A past Vice-President of Sociologists for Women in Society, GAYE TUCHMAN is presently Associate Professor of Sociology at Queens College and the Graduate Center of the City University of New York. She has also edited *The TV Establishment: Programming for Power and Profit,* published articles on news, culture and women and has been active in professional organizations. Presently, she serves on the editorial board of several journals and is writing a book on news.

THE CONTRIBUTORS

MURIEL G. CANTOR is Professor and Chair of the Department of Sociology of American University and editor of the *Newsletter* of

Sociologists for Women in Society. The author of *The Hollywood TV Producers: His Work and His Audience,* co-editor of *Varieties of Work Experience,* she is presently writing a book on social policy and the federal regulation of television and is engaged in research on acting as an occupation in the United States.

G. William Domhoff is best known for his many books on the power elite, including *Who Rules America?, Fat Cats and Democrats,* and *The Bohemian Grove and Other Retreats.* He is Professor of Psychology and Sociology at the University of California, Santa Cruz.

Cynthia Fuchs Epstein is Professor of Sociology at Queens College and the Graduate Center, City University of New York. She is author of *Woman's Place, The Other Half,* and numerous articles on sex roles and other sociological issues. She has received grants from the Ford Foundation, National Institute of Mental Health, the Department of Labor, and has been awarded a Guggenheim Fellowship. She is currently a fellow of the Center for Advanced Study in the Behavioral Sciences in Stanford, California. Active in professional organizations, she has also served on a Presidential advisory committee on the status of women.

Marjorie Ferguson is a lecturer at the London School of Economics in their Department of Social Science and Administration and is completing her doctorate there. Ms. Ferguson was previously an associate editor of one of the women's magazines of which she writes in this volume.

Helen H. Franzwa is a social science analyst employed by the U.S. Commission on Civil Rights, where she has directed a study of the portrayal and employment of minorities and women in television. Before joining the Commission, Dr. Franzwa was a member of the Department of Communications at Hunter College, City University of New York.

George Gerbner, Dean of the University of Pennsylvania's Annenberg School of Communication, is also editor of the *Journal of Communication* and co-editor of several books on the media. He is author of many professional and popular articles on the mass media and is presently writing a volume on television's violence with Larry Gross.

LARRY GROSS is Associate Professor at the University of Pennsylvania's Annenberg School of Communications, and co-editor with George Gerbner and William Melody of *Communications Technology and Social Policy.* His research interests and writings center on the cultural and psychological determinants of symbolic behavior.

SUZANNE JEFFRIES-FOX is a doctoral student in communications at the University of Pennsylvania. Her co-authored article draws on her dissertation research, a longitudinal study of television's contribution to children's ideas about adult life.

GLADYS ENGEL LANG is Professor of Sociology and Communication at the State University of New York at Stony Brook, and co-author of *Politics and Television* and *Collective Dynamics.* A frequent contributor to professional journals and books, she co-authored a pioneer study on television refraction of reality.

JUDITH LEMON is a graduate student at the Harvard University Graduate School of Education. She has published another professional article on women, blacks and television.

ROBERT M. LIEBERT is Professor of Psychology and Psychiatry at the State University of New York at Stony Brook. His work on television includes *The Early Window: Effects of Television on Children and Youth.*

CAROL LOPATE is a feminist author and anthropologist. Among her writings are a book *Women in Medicine,* articles on women and the media, and published poems and short stories.

HARVEY L. MOLOTCH, Associate Professor of Sociology at the University of California, Santa Barbara, is the author of *Managed Integration* and articles on such topics as the political economy of urban growth, racial integration and news.

E. BARBARA PHILLIPS is Assistant Professor of Sociology at San Francisco State University. Her published articles concern the social organization of news.

STEPHEN SCHUETZ is a graduate student in psychology at the State University of New York at Stony Brook and a participant in the Center for Media Research.

JOYCE N. SPRAFKIN is associated with Long Island Research Institute and the Department of Psychiatry and Behavioral Science, SUNY at Stony Brook. A Clinical Psychologist, she co-authored *Behavioral Personality Assessment* and articles on television's effects.

Index